The publication of the Second Edition of
THE MUNROS
in 1991 marks the Centenary of the
publication of the First Edition of
MUNRO'S TABLES
by the Scottish Mountaineering Club
in 1891

This guidebook is compiled from the most recent information and experience provided by members of the Scottish Mountaineering Club and other contributors. The book is published by the Scottish Mountaineering Trust, which is a charitable trust.

Revenue from the sale of books published by the Trust is used for the continuation of its publishing programme and for charitable purposes associated with Scottish mountains and mountaineering.

The editor acknowledges the help given in the compilation of this new edition by the contributors and the many photographers who have made their pictures available. In particular, the painstaking work of Jim Renny in providing a completely new set of maps is recognised with thanks.

THE
MUNROS

SCOTTISH MOUNTAINEERING CLUB
HILLWALKERS GUIDE
VOLUME ONE

Edited by
Donald Bennet

First published in Great Britain by the Scottish Mountaineering Trust in 1985

Copyright © by the Scottish Mountaineering Trust

Reprinted 1985

Revised and reprinted 1986

Reprinted 1989

Second edition 1991

British Library Cataloguing in Publication Data
The Munros: Scottish Mountaineering Club hillwalkers' guide. -2nd. ed.
    1.   Scotland. Mountains
    I.   Bennet, Donald J. (Donald John) *1928-*
    914.11504859

    ISBN 0-907521-31-2

Illustrations

Front cover:	On the ridge of Beinn Eighe	*D.J. Broadhead*
Rear cover:	The summit of Ben Cruachan from the west	*P. Hodgkiss*
Title page:	The ridges of Glen Coe and the Black Mount	*D.J. Bennet*
Page opposite:	The central Cuillin: Sgurr Dearg, Sgurr na Banachdich	
	and Sgurr a'Ghreadaidh from Sgurr Alasdair	*G. Blyth*

Maps drawn by Jim Renny
Book design by Donald Bennet
Production by Peter Hodgkiss
Typeset by Westec, North Connel
Colour separations and graphic work by Par Graphics, Kirkcaldy and Arneg, Glasgow
Printed by Pillans and Wilson, Edinburgh
Bound by Hunter and Foulis, Edinburgh

Distributed by Cordee, 3a DeMontfort Street, Leicester, LE1 7HD

CONTENTS

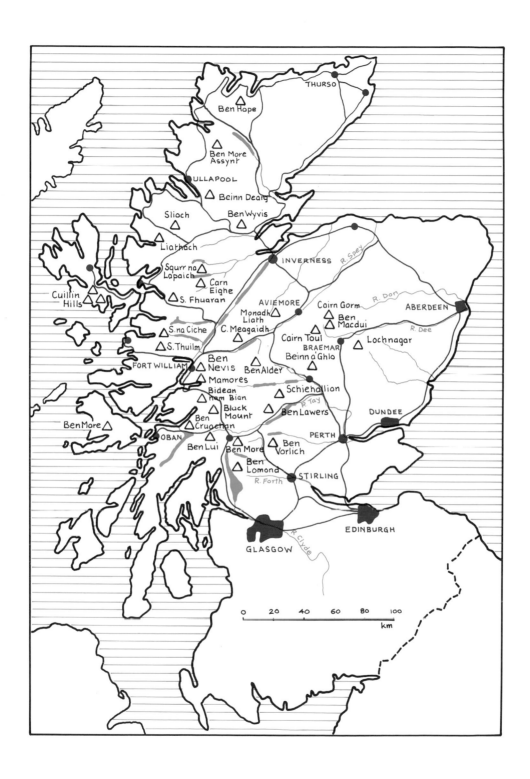

THURSO

Ben Hope △

Ben More
Assynt △

ULLAPOOL ●

Beinn Dearg △

Slioch △   Ben Wyvis △

Liathach △

Sgurr na △   INVERNESS   R. Spey
Lapaich   △ Carn
                     Eighe
Cuillin △   △ S. Fhuaran   R. Don
Hills   AVIEMORE   Cairn Gorm △   ABERDEEN ●
                     Monadh △   △ Ben
                     Liath   △ Macdui
          △ S. na Ciche   C. Meagaidh △   R. Dee
          △ S. Thuilm   Cairn Toul △   △ Lochnagar
                              BRAEMAR
FORT WILLIAM ●   Ben △   Beinn a'Ghlo △
                 Nevis
                 △ Ben Alder
          △ Mamores
          Bidean △   Schiehallion △
          nam Bian
               △ Black   △ Ben Lawers   DUNDEE
               Mount   R. Tay
Ben More △   Ben △   PERTH ●
               Cruachan
OBAN ●   Ben Lui △   Ben More △   △ Ben
                                   Vorlich
               △ Ben   STIRLING ●
               Lomond
                    R. Forth
                                        EDINBURGH
                         R. Clyde
          GLASGOW

0   20   40   60   80   100
                                   km

THE CLIMBER AND THE MOUNTAIN ENVIRONMENT

With increasing numbers of walkers and climbers going to the Scottish hills, it is important that all of us who do so should recognise our responsibilities to those who live and work among the hills and glens, to our fellow climbers and to the mountain environment in which we find our pleasure and recreation.

The Scottish Mountaineering Club and Trust, who jointly produce this and other guidebooks, wish to impress on all who avail themselves of the information in these books that it is essential at all times to consider the sporting and proprietory rights of landowners and farmers. The description of a climbing, walking or skiing route in any of these books does not imply that a right of way exists, and it is the responsibility of all climbers to ascertain the position before setting out. If in doubt it is best to enquire locally.

During the stalking and shooting seasons in particular, much harm can be done in deer forests and on grouse moors by people walking through them. Normally the deer stalking season is from 1st July to 20th October, when stag shooting ends. Hinds may continue to be culled until 15th February. The grouse shooting season is from 12th August until 10th December. These are not merely sporting activities, but are essential for the economy of many Highland estates. During these seasons, therefore, especial care should be taken to consult the local landowner, factor or keeper before taking to the hills.

Climbers and hillwalkers are recommended to consult the book *HEADING FOR THE SCOTTISH HILLS*, published by the Scottish Mountaineering Trust on behalf of the Mountaineering Council of Scotland and the Scottish Landowners Federation, which gives the names and addresses of factors and keepers who may be contacted for information regarding access to the hills.

It is also important to avoid disturbance to sheep, particularly during the lambing season between March and May. Dogs should not be taken onto the hills at this time, and at all times should be kept under close control.

Always try to follow a path or track through cultivated land and forests, and avoid causing damage to fences, dykes and gates by climbing over them carelessly. Do not leave litter anywhere, but take it down from the hill in your rucksack.

The increasing number of walkers and climbers on the hills is leading to increased, and in some cases very unsightly erosion of footpaths and hillsides. Some of the revenue from the sale of this and other SMC guidebooks is used by the Trust to assist financially the work being carried out to repair and maintain hill paths in Scotland. However, it is important for all of us to recognise our responsibility to minimise the erosive effect of our passage over the hills so that the enjoyment of future climbers shall not be spoiled by landscape damage caused by ourselves.

As a general rule, where a path exists walkers should follow it and even where it is wet and muddy should avoid walking along its edges, the effect of which is to extend erosion sideways. Do not take short-cuts at the corners of zigzag paths. Remember that the worst effects of erosion are likely to be caused during or soon after prolonged wet weather when the ground is soft and waterlogged. A route on a stony or rocky hillside is likely to cause less erosion than on a grassy one at such times.

Although the use of bicycles can often be very helpful for reaching remote hills and crags, the erosion damage that can be caused by them when used 'off road' on soft footpaths and open hillsides is such that their use on such terrain must cause concern. It is the editorial policy of the Scottish Mountaineering Club that the use of bicycles in hill country may be recommended on hard roads such as forest roads or private roads following rights of way, but is not recommended on footpaths and open hillsides where the environmental damage that they cause may be considerable. Readers are asked to bear these points in mind, particularly in conditions when the ground is wet and soft after rain.

The proliferation of cairns on the hills detracts from the feeling of wildness, and may be confusing rather than helpful as regards route-finding. The indiscriminate building of cairns on the hills is therefore to be discouraged.

Climbers are reminded that they should not drive along private estate roads without permission, and when parking their cars should avoid blocking access to private roads and land, and should avoid causing any hazard to other road users.

Finally, the Scottish Mountaineering Club and the Scottish Mountaineering Trust can accept no liability for damage to property nor for personal injury resulting from the use of any route described in their publications.

The Scottish Mountaineering Trust will donate £1 from the proceeds of the sale of each copy of this guidebook to grant aid for repair and maintenance of mountain footpaths in Scotland.

The summit ridge of Beinn a'Chlaidheimh   *H.M. Brown*

INTRODUCTION

When Sir Hugh Munro published his first Tables of the 3000-ft mountains of Scotland in 1891 he can have had little idea of the influence that he was to exert on later generations of hillwalkers. He could hardly have expected that his own name would become synonymous with these mountains, nor could he have foreseen the numbers of climbers who, a century later, would be perusing his work and using his Tables as an inspiration for their hill climbing activities.

The publication of the first Tables in 1891 was the outcome of much painstaking research. Prior to that date no one knew exactly how many 3000-ft mountains there were in Scotland. It was thought by some that there were only about thirty. Early in its existence the Scottish Mountaineering Club set out to establish an accurate list, and Sir Hugh Munro, an original member of the Club and an experienced walker in the Scottish hills, was the right man for the task. The publication of his first Tables caused quite a stir. Who would have thought that there were so many distinct mountains in Scotland, and soon the term 'Munro' was coined to denote them.

Munro was working on a revision of his Tables when he died in 1919, so he may not have been entirely satisfied with all the classifications in them. Later members of the Scottish Mountaineering Club, notably J. Gall Inglis, Jim Donaldson, Wilfred Coats and Hamish Brown, have carried on the process of revision, partly in accordance with accurate aneroid measurements by early climbers and revised measurements of heights by the Ordnance Survey, and partly in an attempt to achieve a consistent distinction between Separate Mountains (which have by custom become known as the Munros) and Tops.

However, no definitive criterion exists, and such distinction as does exist is based on the drop in height and the distance between adjacent summits, their character and the character of the intervening ground, and the time that might be taken to go from one to the other. This absence of an objective criterion for classifying Munros has given rise to many a controversy, but it is not the intention of this guide to become involved in this debate. We have taken the 1984 Revision of Munros Tables as the basis for the list of mountains described in this book.

The publication of the Tables in 1891 must have acted as a stimulus to early climbers to ascend as many of the Munros as possible. The first to achieve the complete list, the first Munroist, was the Reverend A.E. Robertson, who in 1901 after what he himself described as 'a desultory campaign of ten years', climbed his last Munro, Meall Dearg on the Aonach Eagach. Recent historical research by Robin Campbell has cast doubt on Robertson's title to be the first Munroist. For some reason Munro's original list defined Sgurr Dearg in the Cuillin as a Munro, with the neighbouring but higher Inaccessible Pinnacle as a Top;

The winter Cuillin: The Inaccessible Pinnacle, Sgurr na Banachdich and Sgurr a'Ghreadaidh from the top of the Great Stone Shoot   *R. Robb*

possibly a case of wishful thinking! Robertson certainly climbed Sgurr Dearg, but there is no record of his having climbed the Inaccessible Pinnacle. He did, however, climb all the Munros as listed in 1901.

Thereafter twenty-two years elapsed before the next climber, Ronald Burn, completed the list, including the Inaccessible Pinnacle. For about sixty years thereafter the number of Munroists increased at the rate of only about one per year. However, nowadays more than fifty new names are added to the list of Munroists each year, and the number of climbers who are afoot in the Scottish mountains steadily ticking off the Munros is numbered in thousands. It is very much with them in mind that this book has been written.

A few words about the purpose and scope of this guide are in order. Each page describes the walking, or in some cases scrambling ascent of one or more Munros that can be climbed in a single day. The lengths of expeditions vary from the few hours needed to climb an easily accessible hill to the many hours required for a remote or distant group. In each case the choice of route has been influenced by the aim of using obvious lines such as footpaths, of avoiding unnecessary difficulties or long routes and of enabling the hillwalker to enjoy the best of the character and scenery of the mountains.

In some cases alternative routes are described that may allow a traverse to be done. There is something more satisfying about doing a traverse rather than going up and down by the same route. However, it is recognised that most climbers, unless they are making an extended journey through the mountains, have

to return to their starting point at the end of the day.

The descriptions in this book refer specifically to summer rather than winter conditions, and no snow or ice routes are described. However, winter routes on the majority of the Munros follow the same lines as summer ones, with the added hazards associated with snow or ice and the fact that footpaths may well be obliterated under snow. All remarks in this book about terrain, paths and routes refer to summer, and it must be remembered that many an easy summer hillwalk can become a serious climb on a snow or ice-clad mountain. Summer scrambles such as the Aonach Eagach, Liathach or the Cuillin are likely to become technically difficult climbs in winter, and the winter hillwalker must have at his or her command skills and equipment far beyond those required in summer. It must also be remembered that the daylight hours in winter are much shorter than in summer; too short for some of the long expeditions described to be completed in a day.

Nevertheless, there can be no doubt that winter snows transform the Scottish mountains, enhancing their appearance as well as their difficulty, and giving them the character of much higher, grander peaks, as many of the winter photographs in this book show. No one can truly claim to know these mountains if he climbs them only in summer, and it behoves every Munroist that he should learn the rudiments of winter hillwalking to enjoy the enhanced pleasures of the winter hills.

It is assumed that users of this guidebook will also use the Ordnance Survey (OS) 1:50,000 maps, as these

Struggle against the elements on An Socach above Glen Affric　　　　　　　　*A. Tibbs*

are ideal for the hillwalker's needs. At the time of publication of this book the most up-to-date versions are the Landranger Series of these maps, and references in the text are to these maps. Heights of Munros and Tops quoted in this guide are taken from the 1984 Edition of Munros Tables. They do not all agree with the heights shown on the OS 1:50,000 maps as in some cases other OS maps, such as the 1:25,000, give more recently surveyed and presumably more accurate figures. Heights of passes, cols and bealachs quoted in the text are either taken from 1:50,000 maps by reference to contour lines, or from surveyed heights shown on 1:25,000 maps. All place names in the text and the specially drawn maps correspond with names and spellings in the OS maps.

The maps in this book are not intended to make the use of the OS map unnecessary, but rather to illustrate the text, and the detail shown on them is intended to be sufficient only to do this. Thus, for example, all footpaths are not shown, only those relevant to the routes being described. Full red lines show the preferred routes described, and dashed lines show alternatives.

In the text, to distinguish between heights and distances, the abbreviation m (e.g. 150m) is used to denote a height, while the use of metre (e.g. 200 metres) denotes distance. Distances and heights are rounded up to the nearest ½km and 10m respectively, and times for ascents are calculated on the basis of 4½km per hour for distance walked, plus 10m per minute for climbing. The time thus calculated is rounded up to the nearest 10 minutes, but no allowance is *made for stops or particularly rough or difficult terrain. (The preceding calculation is similar, but not identical to Naismith's time-honoured formula which is based on 3 miles per hour plus 2000 feet per hour for climbing). The times quoted in the text refer to ascents only, and the total time for the day's expedition must include stops and the descent. Where descriptions relate to the traverse of two or more Munros, times at each summit are cumulative from the day's starting point.*

It should be assumed that most of the Munros lie in privately owned estates in which farming, stalking and shooting are important economic activities. Readers are referred to page vi under the heading **THE CLIMBER AND THE MOUNTAIN ENVIRONMENT** for information and advice concerning approach and access to the Scottish hills.

In areas under the ownership of the National Trust for Scotland the situation as regards access is relatively easy, but it should be remembered that even in these areas culling of deer and hinds may be necessary, and interference in this activity should be avoided.

All the expeditions described in the following pages are one-day trips, although some are very long days. In only a few cases is it positively advantageous to find overnight shelter in the hills. The youth hostels at Loch Ossian and Alltbeithe (Glen Affric) and one or two remote bothies are mentioned in the text as being useful in this respect, but otherwise a complete list of hostels, bothies and other accommodation is not considered necessary.

Retrospect. Looking out across the wilderness of Attadale   *R. Robb*

The Munros - A Personal View *by Hamish Brown*

"Only a hill, but all of life to me,
Up there, between the sunset and the sea."

Munro-bagging is now unashamedly a game climbers play. Gone are the days of clandestine expeditions and surreptitious ticking-off in the Tables. Even members of the Scottish Mountaineering Club do it. There are so many enthusiasts on the job nowadays that the truth has come out: climbing Munros is fun! It brings a drive and a discipline to wandering feet, it widens the appreciation of the Highlands and Islands, it lays up a store of experience and memories, it is open to all, it is freedom, health, awareness and joy - so small wonder that in this erratic, uncertain, nasty world many thousands have found the relaxation they crave in the hills and, within that sphere, Munro-bagging in particular.

A magazine once managed to misprint 'Munro-bagging', or else the editor had a sense of humour, so that it appeared as 'Munro-bogging'. This could be a new synonym, of course. The Munroist, perforce, meets plenty of bog, scree, water, wind, hail, rain, sleet and snow. Much as he may like a warm sleeping bag and a dram, he is quite likely instead to drag off his innocent friends to sample these outdoor delights, such is the magical motivation of the antique figure of three thousand feet.

Not all Munros are equal of course, some are more equal than others and the Ordnance Survey will keep messing about with heights and producing new ones. Nothing is sacred. The term 'Munro' has even been filched by the perfidious Sassenach so that we hear of English Munros and the like.

The quest for the Munros ensures that any climber meets a great variety of experience. He may slither on wet quartzite for one tick on the list, and dance on sunny gabbro for the next. Understandably some Munros are better than others: Beinn Teallach is a poor cousin of An Teallach, and no single Geal Charn (nor all of them) can rival Sgurr nan Gillean. Their diversity of character and geography is a bonus. The critic who decries walking the Munros because it means climbing dozens of boring hills is commenting not on the richness of the hills, but on his own dulled vision. No hill is dull between the sunset and the sea. By the time you have topped a hundred Munros (the incurable stage usually) you will know Scotland - and yourself - in a fuller, richer way, I would claim, despite the odd drawbacks such as Scotland's meteorological instability or the presence of a few million midges with their piranha-like friendliness.

Munro-bagging has now become so popular that it receives the ultimate compliment of being parodied in the outdoor press. Even the national newspapers now use the term without any explanation. It has entered the vocabulary of the sitting-room. Every now and then we have a broadside fired into this ship of state. One magazine not so long ago had a letter demanding: "Why this mania for collecting mountains

Celebration. The Last Munro deserves a good tune on the pipes   D.J. Bennet

like pelts? What is wrong with valleys and passes?", and the writer continued in a very self-righteous way, boasting of not being a Munro-bagger.

Well, I'm not a Munro-bagger either. I climb, ski, canoe, cycle, birdwatch, study hill flora and fauna, geology and history; I draw, paint and take photographs; I walk valleys and passes and enjoy lots more besides, as does every hillgoer in this country of ours, whether above or below the three thousand foot line.

I don't know anyone who is only a Munro-bagger, though some do tend to become a bit single-minded after doing two hundred, nor do Munroists begrudge other hillmen their own particular game. Sir Hugh himself was a man of wide interests: swop his kilt and Balmoral bonnet for a cagoule and woollen balaclava, and he'd be just another bearded lad at home in the Coe. The hills are more than the sum total of all our little games, and we do well to remember our lowly place.

Completing the Munros is apt to be a humbling experience, a poignant time with a layer of sadness below the icing on the celebratory cake. It has meant so much for so long. Only a succession of hills, but so much of life lies suddenly behind. Golden memories instead of brassy expectations, but it was worth every mile and every smile of the way.

There is a peculiar felicitous aptness about Munroing. It is a challenge, a big challenge, but just the right challenge. Were there fewer Munros it would be too easy; many more and it would be impossible for most ordered lives. There is just enough technical difficulty too. You cannot reach every Munro with hands in pockets. Sir Hugh himself never did manage the Inaccessible Pinnacle, largely due to bad luck, and I know quite a few folk who have "done them all except the In Pin". A certain pertinacity is essential in the game.

It is a game, remember. It is a British trait to take politics as a joke and sport seriously, but sometimes we need a reminder that dedication and delight can co-exist. People have gone round the Munros in summer and winter, as teenagers or septuagenarians, alone or in combinations of husband and wife, father and son, even man and dog. They have been done fast and slow, teased out over half a century or tramped in a single journey. They are all things to all men. Thank God for the Munros, however we approach them!

While this is very much a practical guide and has to be brief and to the point, the contributing authors are obviously enthusiasts. They know these mountains as first loves, despite other activities and other hills ranging to the ends of the earth. On their behalf I hope you find the climbing of these hills a joy shared and a fair addition to your "long, golden hills of memory".

Only a hill, or two, or two hundred and seventy seven, it matters not. It's all of life - up there.

The Arrochar Alps from Loch Arklet   *D. J. Bennet*

SECTION 1

Loch Lomond to Loch Tay

Ben Lomond from Beinn Ime   *D.J. Bennet*

Ben Lomond; 974m, (OS Sheet 56; 367029); M179; *beacon hill*

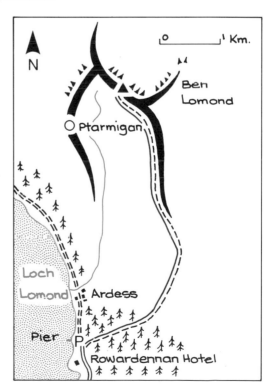

Its isolated position at the southern edge of the Highlands makes Ben Lomond a conspicuous feature from many viewpoints, and from its summit there is an extensive view of both the Highlands and the Lowlands of Scotland. Although Ben Lomond appears from many angles to be quite pointed, the summit is in fact a short level ridge curving round the head of the north-east corrie. Southwards the mountain has a broad grassy ridge extending towards the forest above Rowardennan, and this part, above the forest, is National Trust for Scotland territory. To the north an extensive tract of featureless moorland reaches to Loch Arklet, and to the west, below the outlying spur called Ptarmigan, the Ben drops steeply in wooded crags towards Loch Lomond.

The normal route of ascent starts at the car park at the end of the public road just beyond Rowardennan Hotel. From there a much-trodden path leads NE through the forest to emerge onto the grassy lower slopes of the south ridge. The path continues up towards the middle part of this ridge, and on this hillside much work has been done in recent years to repair the erosion damage on this, one of the most popular mountain footpaths in Scotland.

Higher up the long, nearly level section of the south ridge gives easy walking. In due course the steeper cone of the summit is reached, and the path zigzags up the stony hillside to reach the summit ridge. This is a pleasant narrow crest with a steep drop on its north-east side, where a line of cliffs drops into Ben Lomond's high corrie. Continue NW along this ridge over a few small bumps to reach the top. (5½km; 940m; 2h 50min).

Beinn Bhuidhe from Meall an Fhudair   P. Hodgkiss

Beinn Bhuidhe; 948m; (OS Sheet 50; 204187); M212; *yellow hill*

Beinn Bhuidhe, situated between the upper reaches of Glen Fyne and Glen Shira, is the highest hill in the extensive tract of high undulating moorland between the north end of Loch Lomond and Loch Awe. It is best seen from the north and east, from where its isolated summit shows up well.

The shortest approach is from Glen Fyne where there is a private road up the glen past a small power station. Cars are not permitted along this road, so walk or cycle for 7km up the glen to the house at Inverchorachan. Just beyond the house take to the steep slopes of Beinn Bhuidhe, climbing up beside the small stream which tumbles down the hillside. Just below the point where this stream emerges from a tree-filled gully cross to the north side and continue WNW up steep grass and bracken, climbing steadily to about 600m.

Once the upper corrie is reached at about 550m, it is possible either to continue WNW by a little stream to the lowest point of the ridge between Beinn Bhuidhe and its lower north-east top, or climb this top by its south-east ridge which gives some pleasant scrambling. Once the main ridge of the hill is reached at the col ¾km north-east of the summit, a well-marked path leads to the top which is crowned by an Ordnance Survey pillar. (10km; 950m; 3h 50min).

An alternative approach to Beinn Bhuidhe is by the private road up Glen Shira, but the distance is longer than the Glen Fyne route. The lower reaches of Glen Shira are finely wooded, but higher up the lower slopes of Beinn Bhuidhe have been afforested. Follow the road to the bridge over the Brannie Burn and some distance further up this stream until a break in the forest gives access to the foot of the south-west ridge

of the hill. This long and rather uninteresting ridge leads in 4km over Tom a'Phiobaire and Stac a'Chuirn to the summit. (15km; 950m; 5h).

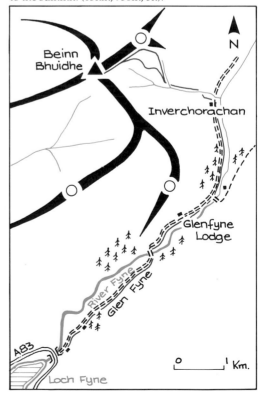

Beinn Narnain from Cruach nam Miseag   *G.S. Johnstone*

Beinn Narnain; 926m; (OS Sheet 56; 272067); M255; *meaning unknown*
Beinn Ime; 1011m; (OS Sheet 56; 255085); M115; *butter hill*

The Arrochar Alps are a fine little group of mountains in the northern part of the Argyll Forest Park north-west of Arrochar, the village at the head of Loch Long. The main cluster of peaks rises opposite the village: The Cobbler, Beinn Narnain and A'Chrois, with Beinn Ime, the highest, hidden behind this trio. These are rocky and rugged peaks with bold outlines.

One much frequented route to Beinn Narnain and Beinn Ime starts at the head of Loch Long where there is a parking place beside the A83 road at the turn-off to Succoth and Glen Loin. A path on the north-west side of the road leads steeply uphill through the forest and onto the open hillside, following a line of concrete blocks which were once part of an old rail-track used at the time of the construction of the Loch Sloy Hydro-Electric scheme. At the top of this track continue NW up the ridge where a path has been worn by many climbers. One or two rocky rises have to be turned before the knoll of Cruach nam Miseag is reached. Beyond it there is a slight dip and the ridge becomes steeper and quite rocky. Follow the path through a few little crags to the base of the Spearhead, the prominent rock prow which crowns the ridge. Finally, climb a short gully on the right (north) of the Spearhead to arrive suddenly on the flat stony plateau of Beinn Narnain about 100 metres east of the trig point which marks its summit. (3km; 950m; 2h 20min).

To continue to Beinn Ime go WNW down a short boulder slope followed by a broad grassy ridge to the Bealach a'Mhaim, a wide flat col crossed by a fence. (Several stiles have been provided for hillwalkers over this fence). From there climb NNW up the long grassy slope to Beinn Ime. Near its top go along a path leftwards (NW) to reach the summit ridge which is followed for a short distance to the top where the large cairn surmounts a crag. (6km; 1320m; 3h 40min).

Return to the Bealach a'Mhaim and follow a path horizontally S for a few hundred metres to the col at the head of the Allt a'Bhalachain (the Buttermilk Burn). Go SE across the boggy col to find the start of the path on the north-east side of the burn which is followed down past the Narnain Boulders to a small dam. From there go NE along a level track for ¾km to reach the uphill route at the top of the concrete staircase, and descend this to Loch Long.

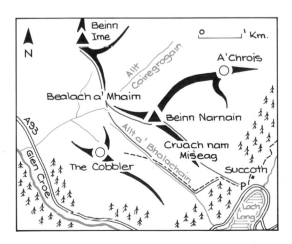

Ben Vane from Coiregrogain; Beinn Ime on the left   *G.S. Johnstone*

Ben Vane; 915m; (OS Sheet 56; 278098); M274; *middle hill*

Among the Arrochar Alps, a group of mountains noted for their steepness and rugged character, Ben Vane is one of the steepest. Its south face rising above Coiregrogain has an angle of almost 45 degrees for a height of 600m. On other sides it is less steep, but it is a very fine little mountain, almost the twin of the slightly lower, but otherwise similar A'Chrois on the opposite side of Coiregrogain.

The ascent is most frequently made from Inveruglas on the A82 road up Loch Lomond, starting on the north side of the bridge over the Inveruglas Water. The approach walk up the private road in Coiregrogain is not particularly attractive as huge electricity transmission pylons march alongside the road, and the Loch Sloy Hydro-Electric scheme, of which these pylons are a part, is visually very obtrusive. Continue up the road for 2km, turn left across the Inveruglas Water and a few hundred metres beyond the bridge leave the road.

The way to Ben Vane goes directly up the southeast ridge, an obvious route with traces of a path. At first the ascent is up easy-angled grass slopes which gradually steepen until many little crags and slabs seem to bar the way. However, it is always possible to thread a route upwards following grassy gullies and ledges between the crags without the need for any scrambling, although for those so inclined there are opportunities for a little mild rock climbing on the many outcrops.

The angle of ascent relents towards the summit, which is a little level plateau. The cairn is near its south edge, and from this edge the long steep drop

to Coiregrogain is revealed. (5km; 880m; 2h 40min).

Note: Car parking at the foot of the private road up Coiregrogain is strongly discouraged, and climbers are asked to leave their cars at the car park about 700 metres north opposite the Loch Sloy power station.

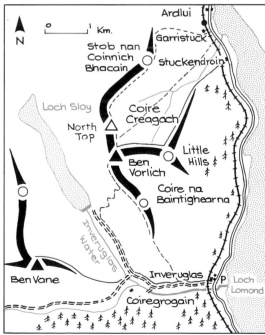

Ben Vorlich from Loch Lomond   *D.J. Bennet*

Ben Vorlich; 943m; (OS Sheets 50 and 56; 295124), M224; *hill of the bay*

Ben Vorlich is the northernmost of the Arrochar Alps, lying north-west of Inveruglas between Loch Lomond and Loch Sloy. The mountain is a long crescent-shaped ridge running roughly from south to north, with an eastward spur, the Little Hills, jutting out above Loch Lomond. To the north and south of this spur are Coire Creagach and Coire na Baintighearna. The west side of Ben Vorlich above Loch Sloy is uniformly steep and craggy.

Surprisingly, considering its accessibility, there is no single route up Ben Vorlich which is most frequented to the exclusion of others. The mountain can be climbed equally well from Inveruglas and Ardlui by routes of similar length and character.

From Inveruglas one can climb the long and undulating south ridge with many ups and downs over several little tops, or one can walk up the private road to the Loch Sloy dam and climb steeply NE from there to reach the south ridge not far from the summit.

From Ardlui one route leaves the A82 road 200 metres south of the station and follows the private road past Garristuck cottage onto the open hillside. From there a path leads WNW towards the main ridge of Ben Vorlich just south of the knoll of Stob an Fhithich. Continue over the not inconsiderable top of Stob nan Coinnich Bhacain and up the north-east ridge past the 931m North Top to the summit, which is on a prominent little crag. The trig point is 200 metres further south.

Coire Creagach gives a fairly quick route, although the ground in the corrie tends to be boggy. Start at the 'cattle-creep' under the railway 400 metres south of Ardlui station and climb directly up the corrie on the north-west side of the burn, aiming for the col between the summit and the North Top.

Possibly the most attractive route up Ben Vorlich is the ridge of the Little Hills, although it does involve more up and downhill work than the other ways. Start at Stuckendroin farm, taking a track under the railway and climbing SW directly up the ridge. High up there are several little knolls, and two quite distinct tops, the Little Hills, are crossed before dropping to a col and climbing the last slope to the summit. The views from this route, particularly south across Loch Lomond to Ben Lomond, are very fine.

Ben Lomond from the Little Hills on Ben Vorlich

Beinn Chabhair from Glen Falloch   *D.J. Bennet*

Beinn Chabhair; 933m; (OS Sheets 50 and 56; 368180); M243; *possibly hill of the hawk*

This mountain is situated at the head of the Ben Glas Burn, 4½km north-east of the north end of Loch Lomond, from which it is not visible. One does, however, get a good view of Beinn Chabhair from Glen Falloch near Derrydarroch from where its principal feature, the long north-west ridge, is well seen rising from the glen over many humps and rocky knolls towards the summit. The upper part of the mountain is quite rugged, there being innumerable rocky outcrops all round the summit, and in misty conditions route-finding may be confusing.

The most direct route to this mountain starts from the A82 road at the foot of Glen Falloch. Cross the bridge over the River Falloch and follow West Highland Way signposts round Beinglas farm. Then climb steeply behind the farm, following a slanting path up the hillside dotted with birch and hawthorn until more level ground is reached above the falls of the Ben Glas Burn. Continue along the north side of the burn following a path which occasionally becomes lost in the boggy ground, but in due course reaches Lochan Beinn Chabhair.

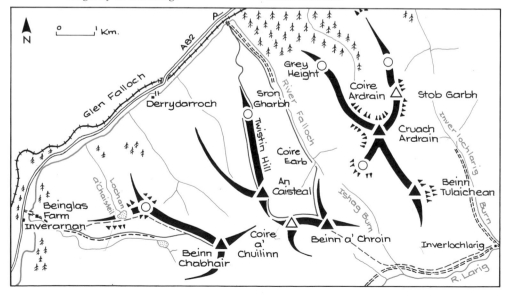

Beinn a'Chroin and An Caisteal from the head of Glen Falloch   *D.J. Bennet*

The upper 400m of the mountain rise above the lochan in grassy slopes with many rock outcrops. There is no single well-defined route up this face, and possibly the best line of ascent climbs diagonally NE from the lochan to reach the north-west ridge of Beinn Chabhair about 1km from the summit. Continue along this ridge following a path. If the crest is adhered to, a small cairn is passed shortly before reaching the summit, where a bigger cairn is perched on top of a small crag. (5½km; 920m; 2h 50min).

The ascent by the north-west ridge past Lochan a'Chaisteil is a fine route, but longer and more strenuous than the one just described. Once fairly level ground is reached above the falls of the Ben Glas Burn bear NE over the first knoll, Meall Mor nan Eag, and drop down to the lochan. Go round its south side and save a little effort by traversing below Stob Creag an Fhithich to reach the ridge and traverse one more top, Meall nan Tarmachan, before the route described above is joined.

An Caisteal; 995m; (OS Sheets 50 and 56; 379193); M144; *the castle*
Beinn a'Chroin; 940m; (OS Sheets 50 and 56; 394186); M227; *hill of harm or danger*

These two mountains stand close together above the headwaters of the River Falloch 6km south of Crianlarich. Typical of the hills in this part of the Southern Highlands, they are grassy on their lower slopes and quite rocky high up near their summits.

An Caisteal has a well-defined summit at the junction of its north-west and north ridges, the latter being known as Twistin Hill. Southwards from the summit the south ridge drops to a col at about 825m below Beinn a'Chroin. This mountain has a 1km long summit ridge, with the highest point at the east end, and two lower cairned points to the west, one of them being the West Top (938m).

To traverse the two mountains, leave the A82 road in Glen Falloch at a car park at (368238) near the obvious bend in the River Falloch. Follow a track under the railway, over the river by a bridge and up its south-west bank. Heading for An Caisteal first, leave this track after about 1km and climb S up the steepening grass slopes of Sron Gharbh. Follow a path along the ridge, Twistin Hill, which is level for some way and then climbs past a curious cleft and over a rocky

knoll to reach the summit of An Caisteal. (4½km; 830m; 2h 30min).

Descend the south ridge which is grassy at first, with a path lower down through rocky outcrops. Cross the level col and climb the rocky north-west end of Beinn a'Chroin, zigzagging left then right to avoid crags. Continue along the undulating crest past two cairned points to the summit. (7½km; 960m; 3h 20min).

Go N from the cairn down a grassy ridge which drops to the stream junction in Coire Earb. Continue down the corrie on the west side of the River Falloch to rejoin the track leading back to the glen.

Beinn a'Chroin can equally well be climbed from the east, approaching from Balquhidder along Loch Voil to the car park ¾km east of Inverlochlarig farm. From there walk W past the farm and continue for a further 3km along a track (which is a right of way) beside the River Larig and across the Ishag Burn. Then climb NW up grassy slopes, passing a little knoll before reaching broken crags just below the summit. (6km; 800m; 2h 40min).

Cruach Ardrain from the Grey Height   *P. Hodgkiss*

Cruach Ardrain; 1046m; (OS Sheets 50,51 and 56; 409212); M84; *stack of the high part*

Cruach Ardrain is one of the most familiar of the mountains that encircle the village of Crianlarich. It has a fine pointed outline, enhanced in winter and spring when snow fills the steep Y Gully on the north face above Coire Ardrain. The plan of the mountain itself is rather like the shape of the letter **Y**, with the summit at the junction of three ridges radiating north-west, north-east and south. The north-east ridge drops steeply from the summit and leads to the rocky Top, Stob Garbh (959m); the south ridge leads to Beinn Tulaichean and the north-west ridge which drops towards Crianlarich provides the usual route of ascent.

This route starts from the A82 road ¾km south of Crianlarich where a bridge over the West Highland Railway gives access to the forest which covers much of the north side of Cruach Ardrain. Once across the railway bear right then back left through a wide clearing in the forest, following a path. After about 200 metres a broken fence is reached; turn right, uphill, along the line of fence posts through a narrow break in the closely planted trees.

At the upper edge of the forest, near a prominent boulder, turn SE up the grassy north-west ridge to reach the Grey Height (685m), the first point on the ridge. For the next few hundred metres the ridge is broad, grassy and featureless

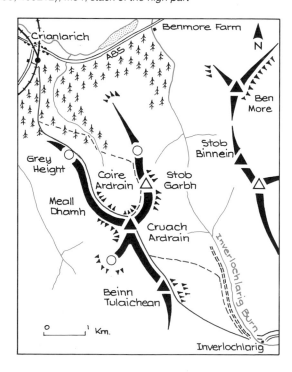

and the next point, Meall Dhamh (806m) is reached. From there a well-defined path leads on, down 50m at first, across a col and then steeply up the shoulder of Cruach Ardrain. The summit of the mountain may be confusing in thick mist; the route just described leads first to a flat top with two cairns about 25 metres apart. To the north-east, across a slight dip in the ridge, is the true summit with a single large cairn. (4½km; 910m; 2h 30min).

The quickest return is by the route of ascent. However, a good traverse can be made over Stob Garbh.

The start goes steeply down NE from the summit cairn. The slope is rocky, and in icy conditions needs care. At its foot a wide col is crossed and the ridge to Stob Garbh climbed; this is perfectly straightforward in good visibility, but confusing in mist as there are many knolls and the ridge itself is not well-defined. From Stob Garbh go N down the broad grassy ridge for about ½km then descend NW into Coire Ardrain. Continue down towards the forest and follow a fire-break through the trees on the west side of the corrie which leads back to join the route of ascent.

Beinn Tulaichean from the south ridge of Cruach Ardrain   D.J. Bennet

Beinn Tulaichean; 946m; (OS Sheet 56; 416196); M217; *hill of the hillocks*

Beinn Tulaichean is at the southern end of the south ridge of Cruach Ardrain, and is in fact not much more than its south peak, the lowest point of the connecting ridge being about 820m. It is rather surprising that Beinn Tulaichean is classified as a separate Munro. On its east, south and west sides it falls in long and in places steep slopes, mostly grassy but with some crags here and there.

The ascent of Beinn Tulaichean is invariably made from the south-east. The public road from Balquhidder along the side of Loch Voil ends at a car park ¾km east of Inverlochlarig, and the start is from there. Walk along the private road (right of way) to Inverlochlarig and climb the south-east flank of Beinn Tulaichean directly above the farm. One can chose one's own route up the wide grassy hillside, and towards the summit a band of crags and huge boulders is reached which can be easily passed by keeping to the west. However, there is no difficulty in finding a more direct way through these crags. The south ridge of

Beinn Tulaichean is reached a short distance from the summit and the climb finishes along a path on this ridge. (4km; 820m; 2h 20min).

The continuation NNW to Cruach Ardrain is straightforward, and gives a perfectly good route to this mountain, no longer than the way from Crian-larich described above. There is a path along the broad grassy connecting ridge, which as noted above drops only 120m from Beinn Tulaichean before rising gently to Cruach Ardrain.

The ridge leads not direct to its summit, but rather to its west, and at a point marked by a small cairn one turns right and goes about 70 metres NE to the two cairns beyond which is the summit of Cruach Ardrain. (5½km; 1030m; 3h).

On the return to Inverlochlarig from Cruach Ardrain the quickest route is back down the south ridge to the col, and then by a descending traverse east towards the Inverlochlarig Burn where a track is reached leading down to the farm.

Ben More and Stob Binnein from Strath Fillan   H.M. Brown

Ben More; 1174m; (OS Sheet 51; 433244); M15; *big hill*
Stob Binnein; 1165m; (OS Sheets 51 and 57; 435227); M17; *either from the Gealic binnein meaning peak,
or from innean meaning anvil*

These two fine mountains, the highest south of Strath Tay, are among the best known and most popular in the Southern Highlands. From many viewpoints they appear as twin peaks, but Stob Binnein is the more elegant, its ridges being better defined and the tip of its summit being cut away to form a little plateau. Ben More, with a few extra metres of height, certainly appears to be more bulky, particularly when seen from Glen Dochart near Crianlarich, for there it shows its full size above Loch Iubhair, and the ascent from that side is a long unrelenting grind.

The traverse of the two mountains from Loch Doine to Glen Dochart, or vice versa, is one of the classic hillwalks of the Southern Highlands, but it needs two cars or a helpful driver. If no such transport arrangements are available, then Benmore farm in Glen Dochart is probably the best place at which to start and finish the traverse.

The normal route to Ben More starts from the A85 road 150 metres east of the farm. Cross a stile to reach a track which is followed uphill for a few hundred metres. Then climb SE up the ever-steepening grass slopes of the north-west shoulder of the mountain. High up a stone dyke is a useful guide, the route being on its north-east side. On the south-west side of the dyke there is a hanging corrie whose headwall is steep and rocky, a potentially dangerous place in bad visibility or in winter. At the top of the dyke there are a few small crags before the angle of the slope eases below the summit, which is on top of a big crag. (3km; 1010m; 2h 30min).

To continue the traverse to Stob Binnein, descend S for a short distance, then SW following an indistinct ridge before going down an open slope S to the wide flat col called the Bealach-eadar-dha Beinn *(the pass between two hills)*. The ascent of Stob Binnein is up its north ridge, a long uniform slope defined on its east side by the steep edge of the north-east corrie. The cairn is at the south edge of the little summit plateau, which is surrounded by steep slopes and crags on all sides except the north. (5km; 1320m; 3h 20min).

Stob Binnein from the south   *D.J. Bennet*

To return to Benmore farm, descend the north ridge to the bealach and from there drop down WNW towards the Benmore Burn to reach the track leading down to Glen Dochart.

The ascent of Ben More described above is steep, unrelenting and not particularly interesting. Its only merit is its directness. A more interesting but longer route is up the north-east ridge, starting from the A85 road 4½km east of Benmore farm. Follow a track which starts just east of the Allt Coire Chaorach bridge, (car park on the west of the bridge) and in about 1km cross this stream (stepping stones may be helpful) and continue up a path S through the forest to reach the open hillside at (458254). Turn right, climbing beside a little stream until above the forest and then bear W to reach the north-east ridge of Ben More and follow this to the summit. At one point the crest of the ridge is quite rocky, but any difficulties can be avoided by traversing to one side or the other. (5½km; 1010m; 3h).

The usual route to Stob Binnein from the south starts from the car park at the end of the public road ¾km east of Inverlochlarig farm. From this point climb directly N up steep grass slopes to Stob Invercarnaig, and continue along a pleasant grassy ridge to Stob Coire an Lochain (1068m). From there descend slightly and climb Stob Binnein by its broad south ridge, which steepens just below the summit. (4½km; 1050m; 2h 50min). The return can be varied by going E from Stob Coire an Lochain to Meall na Dige (966m) and descending its south ridge to the foot of Glen Carnaig.

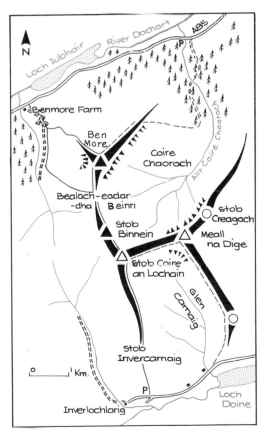

Ben Lui from the River Cononish   *P. Hodgkiss*

Ben Lui (Beinn Laoigh); 1130m; (OS Sheet 50; 266263); M27; *calf hill*
Beinn a'Chleibh; 916m; (OS Sheet 50; 251256); M273; *hill of the creel* or *chest*

Ben Lui is in every respect one of the finest mountains in the Southern Highlands. By virtue of its height it stands high above its neighbours, and its splendid shape is unmistakable. In particular, the great north-east corrie, the Coire Gaothaich, which holds snow most years from mid-winter to early summer, gives the mountain an Alpine character. The finest view of the mountain is from Strath Fillan, looking up the glen of the Cononish River directly at the steep north-east face. Seen from the west, for example from the north-east end of Loch Awe, Ben Lui dominates the upper reaches of Glen Lochy beyond

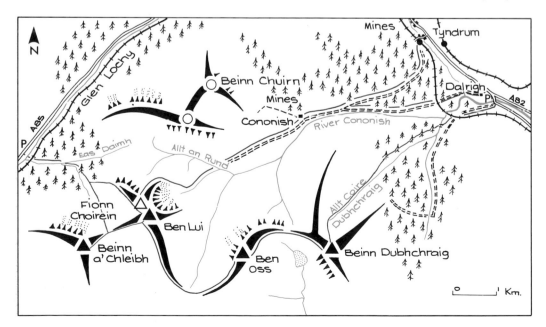

Beinn a'Chleibh from the north-east   H.M. Brown

Dalmally and rises high above its neighbour, Beinn a'Chleibh.

The finest way to Ben Lui, scenically at least, is the walk up the Cononish glen. Other approaches can be made from the north-west in combination with Beinn a'Chleibh, and up the south ridge, traversing from Ben Oss, and these routes are described on this and the following pages.

The Cononish approach to Ben Lui starts either at Tyndrum Lower Station or at Dalrigh just off the A82 road at (344291). The two routes, both following private roads, converge 1½km before Cononish farm. The glen just above the farm is now the scene of Scotland's only gold mine and is not a pretty sight. Continue WSW along a track which ends at the Allt an Rund, cross this stream and climb uphill into Coire Gaothaich by a path on the north-west side of the stream flowing from the corrie.

Once more level ground is reached in the corrie, climb NW up steeper grass slopes to reach the north-east ridge of Ben Lui which forms a prominent spur called Stob Garbh. There is a faint path leading up to the spur and it continues up the crest, which becomes progressively steeper and narrower. There is no difficulty in summer conditions, but in winter this is quite likely to be a serious climb by hillwalkers' standards.

The climb ends suddenly at a cairn a few metres from the North-west Top of Ben Lui (1127m), and there is a short level traverse along the ridge overlooking the steep headwall of Coire Gaothaich to reach the summit. (9km; 930m; 3h 40min).

A much shorter ascent of Ben Lui can be made from Glen Lochy from a point about midway between Tyndrum and Dalmally, and this is also the starting point for Beinn a'Chleibh. The two mountains can readily be climbed together. Start at a car park just off the A85 road at (239278). There is no bridge over the River Lochy at this point. In fair weather it is possible to cross the river dryshod by stepping stones near the outflow of the Eas Daimh, but otherwise wet feet are more likely. (There is a footbridge about 1km down the river which may be essential if there is a spate).

Once across the river, follow a path through the forest on the north side of the Eas Daimh for a few hundred metres, then cross this stream and continue along the path which climbs up into Fionn Choirein on the east side of the stream flowing down this corrie. Above the forest cross a stile over the deer fence to reach the open hillside.

From there the direct route to Ben Lui goes E up the grassy hillside to reach the north ridge well above its lower rocky steps, the Ciochan Beinn Laoigh. Continue up this ridge steeply to the North-west Top and the summit. (4km; 950m; 2h 30min).

The route to Beinn a'Chleibh continues from the stile up the grassy Fionn Choirein to the col at its head, the last part of the climb being quite steep. At the col turn right and climb the broad north-east ridge of Beinn a'Chleibh. (3½km; 740m; 2h). The north-east and north faces of this hill are very steep and craggy, and no attempt should be made to ascend or descend by them.

The traverse from Beinn a'Chleibh to Ben Lui (or vice versa) is very straightforward up or down the south-west side of Ben Lui. This slope forms a very broad ridge, defined on its north-west by the steep headwall of Fionn Choirein.

Ben Oss and Ben Lui from Beinn Dubhchraig   K.M. Andrew

Ben Oss; 1029m; (OS Sheet 50; 288253); M99; *loch-outlet hill*
Beinn Dubhchraig; 978m; (OS Sheet 50; 308255); M171; *black-rock hill*

These two mountains stand together several kilometres west of Crianlarich between Glen Falloch and Strath Fillan. From the south, looking up Loch Lomond, they are well seen with Ben Oss showing a distinctive cone and Beinn Dubhchraig its craggy south face. From Strath Fillan, Ben Oss is almost hidden behind the shoulder of Beinn Dubhchraig which shows the whole of its north flank, the Coire Dubhchraig. This wide grassy corrie forms a great bowl between the north and north-east ridges of Beinn Dubhchraig, and at its foot there is the pine wood of the Coille Coire Chuilc, a beautiful little remnant of the Old Caledonian Forest. Higher up above these old trees the corrie has recently been planted with conifers which will in due course alter its appearance, and possibly also access to the hill. A forest road climbs to about 500m below the north-east ridge, providing an easy but not very aesthetic route to the hill.

The normal route for the traverse of the two hills starts at Dalrigh in Strath Fillan (343291) where it is possible to drive off the A82 road and park near the old bridge over the River Fillan. From there cross the river and follow the rough track on its south side W to a bridge over the railway. Just beyond this bridge leave the track and go W to the footbridge over the Allt Coire Dubhchraig. Follow a path on the north-west side of this stream through the pine wood and near its upper edge cross two deer fences by stiles to reach the open hillside. Continue along a faint path up the north-west side of the Allt Coire Dubhchraig to cross a third fence by a stile at the upper limit of newly planted forest. From there the route goes more or less directly up the grassy corrie, bearing more to the S as the steeper upper slopes are reached, and

leading to the summit of Beinn Dubhchraig. (6½km; 800m; 2h 50min).

Traverse NW along the broad summit ridge, descending first to a lochan on the crest, and then more steeply to the col below Ben Oss. The ascent of a knoll on the ridge to Ben Oss can be avoided by keeping on its south side and then making a rising traverse to a col from which a uniform slope leads SW to Ben Oss itself. (9½km; 1050m; 3h 50min).

On the return to Strath Fillan it is advisable not to descend N from the Oss-Dubhchraig col as the ground is steep and rocky. Instead, climb back up the ridge towards Beinn Dubhchraig as far as the lochan and from there descend easily into Coire Dubhchraig to rejoin the ascent route.

The traverse from Ben Oss to Ben Lui and possibly even on to Beinn a'Chleibh makes a very fine day's hillwalking, although one does finish in Glen Lochy a long way from the starting point at Dalrigh. There is, however, the possibility of catching the Oban to Glasgow bus for the return. From Ben Oss descend SSW, then SW and finally W down a broad and featureless ridge which calls for accurate navigation in mist. The col is a broad grassy expanse and from it the south ridge of Ben Lui leads direct to the summit. (13km; 1460m; 5h 20min).

From there one can either return to Dalrigh by the north-east spur (Stob Garbh) and Cononish, or descend the south-west ridge to the col at the head of the Fionn Choirein. The latter route makes it possible to include Beinn a'Chleibh before descending the corrie to Glen Lochy. Both these routes are described on the previous page.

Map on page 18.

Ben Chonzie and Loch Turret   *A.C.D. Small*

Ben Chonzie (Ben-y-Hone); 931m; OS Sheets 51 and 52; 773309); M246; *probably mossy hill*

This solitary Munro is the highest point of the extensive tract of flat-topped hills and high moorland between Strath Earn and Loch Tay. At the centre of this area, between glens Lednock, Turret and Almond, Ben Chonzie rises just sufficiently above its neighbouring hills to be the most prominent among them, although it does not itself have any outstanding character. The summit is a long broad ridge, and to its east there is a large corrie ringed by grassy crags, but possibly the most noteworthy feature of Ben Chonzie is the large population of mountain hares which inhabits its upper slopes.

The normal approaches are from Crieff by Glen Turret, and from Comrie by Glen Lednock. Of the two, the latter gives probably the easier, though longer climb, as it follows a track most of the way up the hill. Start from the road up Glen Lednock near Coishavachan (743273) and follow the right of way to Ardtalnaig up the Invergeldie Burn. After 1½km cross the burn and follow a track ENE up the hillside past shooting butts almost to the ridge. Then strike NE across heath and blaeberry covered slopes to the broad crest where a fence leads NW then NE to the summit. (6½km; 700m; 2h 40min).

Going by Glen Turret, drive as far as the car park at the Loch Turret dam and walk along the track on the east side of the loch to its head. From there it is possible to make a direct line NW on a rising traverse across the grassy hillside to the summit. Alternatively, continue up the Turret Burn through an area of well-preserved moraines, go round the head of Lochan Uaine and climb W between the grassy crags above the lochan to reach the north-east ridge ½km from the summit. (6km; 570m; 2h 20min).

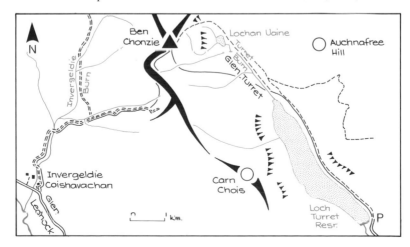

Ben Vorlich and Stuc a'Chroin from Meall an t-Seallaidh   G.S. Johnstone

Ben Vorlich; 985m; (OS Sheets 51 and 57; 629189); M161; *hill of the bay*
Stuc a'Chroin; 975m; (OS Sheets 51 and 57;617175); M176; *peak of harm* or *danger*

Standing on the southern edge of the High-lands and visible from many viewpoints to the south, these two mountains are conspicuous and familiar features of the Highland landscape as seen from the valley of the River Forth. They form two parallel ridges running from south-east to north-west, separated by a col, the Bealach an Dubh Choirein, at a height of about 700m. Ben Vorlich appears from the south as a rather sharp-pointed conical peak, while Stuc a'Chroin has a flatter summit ridge with a steep drop at its east end, the profile of its north-east buttress above the Bealach an Dubh Choirein.

Of several possible starting points for the traverse of the two mountains, Ardvorlich on the south side of Loch Earn is probably the most convenient, particularly if one wants to return to one's starting point. Glen Ample on the west side of the two hills provides a possible route, but recent afforestation in the glen may make access awkward. The route from the south up the Keltie Water from Callander is longer than the other two.

The Ardvorlich approach follows the right of way from there to Callander for 1½km up Glen Vorlich along a good track to a path junction at the foot of Coire Buidhe. The right of way keeps left, but the way to Ben Vorlich goes right, head-ing due S up the grassy hillside on a path marked by a few posts to reach the north ridge. Climb this ridge, which steepens towards the stony summit which is marked by an Ordnance Survey pillar at its north-west end and a large

The summit of Stuc a'Chroin   D.J. Bennet

The approach to Ben Vorlich from Ardvorlich   D.J. Bennet

cairn 100 metres to its south-east . (4½km; 890m; 2h 30min).

The continuation of the route to Stuc a'Chroin is easy to follow, there being a line of fence posts down to the Bealach an Dubh Choirein. From there the first part of the climb is up a short boulder slope to the foot of the prominent buttress which is the true line of the connecting ridge. Its crest gives a good scramble, hard in one or two places if one is not intent on avoiding difficulties, but about 30 metres to the right (NW) a steep zigzag path avoids all difficulties. At the top of the buttress there is a cairn, and the summit of Stuc a'Chroin is about ½km south. (6½km; 1160m; 3h 30min).

To return to Ardvorlich, descend to the Bealach an Dubh Choirein and then traverse horizontally N across the grassy hillside to reach the col at the head of Coire Buidhe. Continue down the south-east side of this corrie to rejoin the right of way in Glen Vorlich.

The approach from Callander follows the southern end of the right of way noted above. One can drive from the town up the minor road on the west side of the Keltie Water to a parking place just before Braeleny farm. From there continue along the track to Arivurichardich and climb N up the path across the grassy hillside to reach a broad col on the long south-east ridge of Stuc a'Chroin. Descend NE across Gleann an Dubh Choirein, where the path has largely disappeared in the eroded peat bog of the corrie, and reach the foot of the south-east ridge of Ben Vorlich which is climbed direct to the summit. (From Braeleny: 9km; 900m; 3h 30min). Traverse to Stuc a'Chroin and from its summit descend the long easy-angled south-east ridge to rejoin the uphill route.

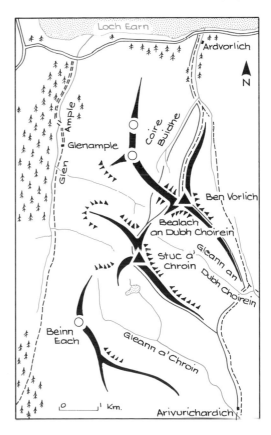

Looking south-west from Ben Lawers over Beinn Ghlas to Stob Binnein and D. Green
Ben More (left) and the Ben Lui group (right)

SECTION 2

The River Tay to Rannoch Moor

Schiehallion from the north-west   *D.J. Bennet*

Schiehallion; 1083m; (OS Sheet 51; 714548); M57; *the fairy hill of the Caledonians (acc. to W.J.Watson)*

Schiehallion is one of the best known of Scottish mountains by virtue of its striking appearance and isolated position in the centre of the Highlands. It is a conspicuous feature from many viewpoints; from the east and west it appears as a steep conical peak, but from the north or south its true shape is more apparent: a long whale-backed ridge dropping quite steeply to the west, but much more gradually to the east.

A narrow road leaves the A846 between Coshieville and Tummel Bridge and goes round the north side of Schiehallion to Kinloch Rannoch. Just east of Braes of Foss farm on this road there is a Forestry Commission car park. At it a plaque commemorates the experiment carried out on the slopes of Schiehallion by Maskelyne, once the Astronomer-Royal, to determine the earth's mass by observing the deflection of a pendulum caused by the mass of Schiehallion itself.

Starting at the car park, follow the route marked 'Schiehallion Path', and go WSW across the grassy moorland past a prominent cairn to meet a track coming up from Braes of Foss. Cross this track and keep heading WSW across the grassy lower hillside along a path towards the mountain. Higher up, as the slope steepens, the route goes up peaty ground which has been badly eroded by the passage of many boots. In places along the east ridge the path has become deeply gouged in the soft ground. Further on the terrain changes again, becoming very stony, and the upper part of Schiehallion is covered with angular quartzite boulders, giving rough walking. The last 1½km of the route along the broad ridge is marked by many small cairns. (4½km; 760m; 2h 20min).

The alternative route up the east side of the Tempar Burn mentioned in the previous edition of this book is now discouraged by the landowner who has erected a notice at the bridge over the Tempar Burn asking climbers to use the route described above.

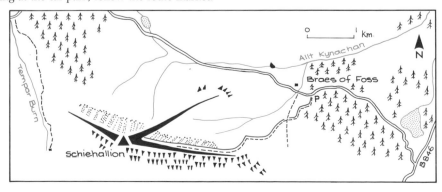

Carn Mairg and Creag Mhor from Glen Lyon   D.J. Bennet

Carn Gorm; 1028m; (OS Sheet 51; 635501); M100; *blue hill*
Meall Garbh; 968m; (OS Sheet 51; 646517); M182; *rough hill*
Carn Mairg; 1041m; (OS Sheet 51; 684513); M88; *may be hill of sorrow, pity or folly, or hill of the boundary, or perhaps from Gaelic marag, meaning pudding*
Creag Mhor; 981m; (OS Sheet 51; 695496); M167; *big rock*

This group of hills is on the north side of Glen Lyon, and forms a great arc of broad high ridges above Invervar. The nature of the terrain along the tops is more characteristic of the Grampians or Cairngorms than of the neighbouring Breadalbane mountains such as Ben Lawers; the ridges are wide and level and the corries easy-angled and devoid of crags. Although of no interest for climbing, these corries are of prime importance for stag shooting, and the whole range should be avoided in the stalking season.

The south side of the range above Glen Lyon is quite steep, and the southern shoulder of Creag Mhor is craggy. The north side is much less impressive and drops gradually across wide tracts of moorland and forest towards Loch Rannoch. Between the four Munros the drops along the ridge are fairly small, although the distances are considerable, so that the traverse of all four is a good high-level expedition. It can, however, be shortened at almost any point by descending one of the easy corries or shoulders towards the Invervar Burn.

The best starting point for the traverse of these hills is at Invervar in Glen Lyon. There is a parking place a short distance down the narrow road which crosses the River Lyon opposite Invervar. Take the track which starts a few metres west of this narrow road and leads north through the forest. In ½km the open hillside is reached and the track is followed for 1km further at which point there is a footbridge across the Invervar Burn on one's left. Cross this and follow a narrow path N for a short distance beside the forest to its northern edge. From that point the ascent of Carn Gorm is very straightforward, bearing W across the rising moorland to the steeper slopes which lead NW to the level summit ridge. The trig point is about a hundred metres beyond the highest point. (4½km; 830m; 2h 30min).

Descend quite steeply N and bear round NE along a broad ridge towards the little pointed Top, An Sgorr (924m), which can be easily avoided if one does not want to climb it by a traverse across its north-west side. This leads to a broad col (830m) where there is a cairn. Climb NE and reach a line of fence posts leading E to the summit of Meall Garbh. The flat summit of this hill has two tops of almost equal height; the north-west one (which is on the line of posts) seems to be considered the higher. The other one is about 70 metres south of the fence. (6½km; 1020m; 3h 10min).

Continue E, following the line of fence posts down past a lochan to another wide col, and from there go ESE to Meall a'Bharr (1004m) whose summit is a long level ridge with the highest point marked by a cairn on a little rocky outcrop. There is only a very slight drop at the east end of this level ridge to the next col, and the route bears SE towards Carn Mairg, still following the line of rusty fence posts. For a short distance the crest of the ridge is quite narrow and bouldery, and beyond it the summit of Carn Mairg, with its large cairn, is soon reached. (10km; 1240m; 4h 20min).

Carn Mairg from the east   *J. Renny*

Some care is needed on the descent south-east from Carn Mairg in thick weather for the slope is quite steep and there is a small crag. Once below this the ground is very easy and a descent south down grassy slopes leads to the next col at the watershed between Gleann Muilinn and the Allt Coire a'Chearcaill.

From there climb S to the level summit ridge of Creag Mhor. The ascent leads towards the SW top, and the true summit, reached across ½km of flat featureless plateau, is a little rocky tor. (12½km; 1380m; 5h 10min).

Descend due W to get onto the long easy-angled ridge on the south side of the Allt Coire a'Chearcaill. Continue very easily down this ridge, gradually bearing WSW along its crest.

Towards the foot it is possible to follow a stalker's path on the south side of the ridge, or continue down the crest. In either case the track on the east side of the Invervar Burn is reached a short distance above the forest.

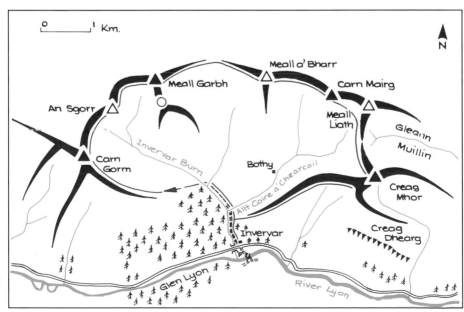

Ben Lawers, Beinn Ghlas and An Stuc from Meall Garbh   *D. Green*

For much of its length, Loch Tay is dominated on its north-west side by the great sweeping slopes and high summits of the Ben Lawers group. The name refers not only to the highest point, but to the whole range of seven distinct peaks, six of them Munros, linked by a twisting ridge 12km long which at only one point drops below 800m. It is the highest and most extensive mountain massif in the Southern Highlands. The range gives the impression of being very grassy, and this is certainly true of most of the peaks. Only in the north-east corrie of Ben Lawers itself, above Lochan nan Cat, are there crags of any size, and they too are vegetatious, of more interest to the botanist than the climber, for the whole area has a reputation for the wealth of its alpine flora.

Meall Corranaich, Ben Lawers and Beinn Ghlas from the south-west   *D.J. Bennet*

Most of the south-eastern side of Ben Lawers, from the summit ridges well down towards Loch Tay, is owned by the National Trust for Scotland, so there are no restrictions on climbing on that side of the mountain at any time of the year. The Trust's Visitor Centre is high up on the narrow road which crosses the west end of the range from Loch Tay to Glen Lyon, and it is a focal point for walkers, climbers and botanists on the mountain. It is worth noting that this road is not normally kept open by snow ploughs in winter, and may be blocked when there is much snow on the ground.

It is quite possible for any reasonably fit hillwalker, particularly if he or she has a co-operative car driver, to traverse all the peaks of Ben Lawers in a single day. The easiest way to do this is to start near the summit of the Loch Tay to Glen Lyon road, climb Meall a'Choire Leith first and continue over the tops to Meall Greigh, finally descending to Lawers village. Alternatively, if one has to start and finish at the same

point, the traverse is best undertaken from the Glen Lyon side, starting at Camusvrachan. It is in effect a circuit of the peaks surrounding the Allt a'Chobhair from Meall a'Choire Leith to Meall Garbh, with a final excursion 3km east to Meall Greigh, followed by a long return to Camusvrachan.

However, attractive as the complete traverse may be to those who are fit, most hillwalkers may find it a bit too strenuous. In the following descriptions the ascent of the six Ben Lawers Munros will be taken in three separate days, all of them quite short and easy and allowing time for diversions to explore the range and its features of interest. Although these descriptions tend to concentrate on the southern side of the mountain, for it is the most accessible, the northern side overlooking Glen Lyon should not be forgotten. Scenically it is just as attractive, if not more so, and one is much less likely to meet other climbers on that side of the mountain.

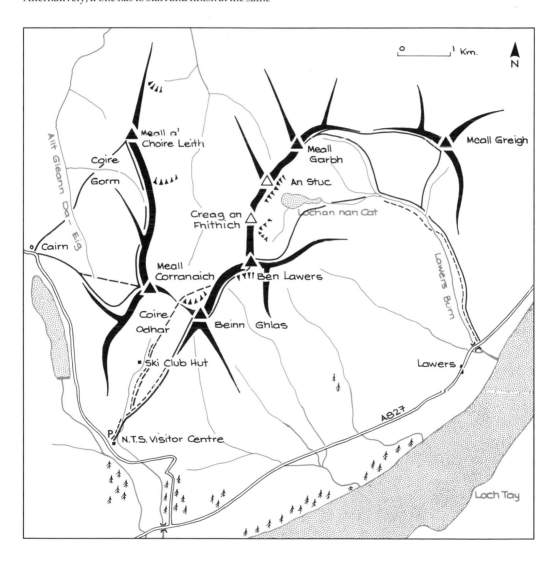

Meall Corranaich; 1069m; (OS Sheet 51; 616410); M65; *perhaps notched, prickly, hooked or crooked hill, or possibly hill of lamenting*
Meall a'Choire Leith; 926m; (OS Sheet 51; 612439); M257; *hill of the grey corrie*

These two hills are at the western end of the Ben Lawers range, Meall Corranaich overlooking Lochan na Lairige on the watershed between Loch Tay and Glen Lyon, and Meall a'Choire Leith lying 3km to the north, halfway along a long ridge extending towards Glen Lyon.

The nearest point of access for both hills is the summit of the road which crosses the western end of the Ben Lawers range. Just north of the north end of Lochan na Lairige there is a prominent cairn above the road, and a short distance to the west there is a rather restricted space where two or three cars can be parked.

Going to Meall Corranaich first, cross rough moorland SE over peat hags to reach the Allt Gleann Da-Eig. Follow this stream uphill and gradually trend E to reach the south-west ridge of Meall Corranaich. Continue up this ridge to the summit. (A shorter and steeper route goes directly up the west face of the hill). The small summit cairn stands close to the edge of the steep north-east face. (3km; 520m; 1h 40min).

The traverse to Meall a'Choire Leith goes N down a broad easy-angled ridge which in 1km divides into two, enclosing the Coire Gorm. Go down the north ridge, which is on the east side of Coire Gorm, to the crags at the head of the little Coire Liath, and bear NW round the edge of these crags to reach a col about 780m. To the north of this col the ridge merges into the flat- topped dome of Meall a'Choire Leith. (6km; 670m; 2h 30min).

To return to the day's starting point, descend SW from Meall a'Choire Leith, cross the stream in Coire Gorm and continue in the same direction to the Allt Gleann Da-Eig. Finally, climb gradually across rough peaty terrain to the col at (596419) and follow a track down to the road near the prominent cairn.

The route described is almost entirely outwith National Trust for Scotland territory, and may be subject to restrictions in the stalking season.

Map on page 29.

Meall Corranaich from the Tarmachans   D.J. Bennet

Beinn Ghlas   *D.J. Bennet*

Beinn Ghlas; 1103m; (OS Sheet 51; 626404); M45; *greenish-grey hill*
Ben Lawers; 1214m; (OS Sheet 51; 636414); M9; *from Gaelic labhar, meaning loud (describing the noise of a stream)*

These two Munros form the central and highest part of the range. They are most easily climbed from the National Trust for Scotland's Visitor Centre, which, being at a height of 450m, gives a good start for the climb. As noted earlier, the road from Loch Tay to Glen Lyon is not kept open in winter, and in bad snow conditions the Visitor Centre may not be accessible by car. In that case the climb will have to start some distance further from the mountain and lower down the road.

From the car park at the Visitor Centre take the path (which for the first hundred metres or so is a timber walkway across boggy ground) NE up the west side of the Burn of Edramucky. In about ½km a signpost indicates the way to Ben Lawers across the burn to its east side. The path, which cannot possibly be missed in summer, goes NE up the grassy hillside onto the south ridge of Beinn Ghlas, and along this ridge, marked by many cairns. The summit of Beinn Ghlas has no cairn, but is unmistakable for the drop on the north side is precipitous. (3½km; 660m; 2h).

Continue NE down the broad easy-angled ridge, following an obvious and much eroded path to the wide col at about 950m. For the first few metres on the Ben Lawers side the ridge is rocky, but thereafter the path continues up a wide grassy slope at a uniform angle to reach the summit where little now remains of the huge cairn that was once built to raise Lawers to the select company of Scotland's 4000ft mountains. (5km; 920m; 2h 40min).

The quickest return is probably by the same route. It is possible, but not particularly recommended, to avoid the reascent of Beinn Ghlas by going WSW from the Lawers-Ghlas col, descending slightly across the grassy hollow of the north corrie of Beinn Ghlas to reach the col at the head of Coire Odhar. There the old track down the east side of the corrie can still be discerned, and followed back to the Visitor Centre.

An attractive alternative route to Ben Lawers, which avoids the usual crowds and eroded footpath of the way just described, is to start at Lawers village, as the group of cottages and farms on the A827 road near the foot of the Lawers Burn is known. Car parking is a problem at the start of this climb; there is parking available (for a price) at the foot of the private road up to Machuim farm, and room for two or three cars a short distance up this road. Follow the road to Machuim farm and continue past it by a path along the edge of the fields above the Lawers Burn. The path leads up the east side of the burn to a small dam, from where one continues W along the stream to Lochan nan Cat. This lochan is at the heart of the range, lying in a beautiful remote corrie above which Ben Lawers and its neighbouring rocky peak of An Stuc rise in steep craggy slopes. Climb S from the lochan to reach the east ridge of Ben Lawers and follow this to the summit. (7½km; 1000m; 3h 20min). No restrictions on either of these routes in the stalking season.

Map on page 29.

Ben Lawers and An Stuc from Meall Greigh   *J.Renny*

Meall Greigh; 1001m; (OS Sheet 51; 674438); M134; *hill of horse studs*
Meall Garbh; 1118m; (OS Sheet 51; 644437); M35; *rough hill*

These two mountains form the north-eastern end of the great Ben Lawers range. Meall Greigh is the endmost point, well seen from the road near Lawers Hotel; it is a rounded hill, grassy on all sides with a few small crags just east of the summit. Meall Garbh is not well seen from the road, being almost hidden behind the lower rising hillside. Its craggy south face overlooks Lochan nan Cat, and with An Stuc and Ben Lawers it forms a grand semi-circle of steep mountains enclosing this beautiful lochan. To the north it throws down two long grassy ridges, north-north-west and north-east, to Glen Lyon.

The ascent of these two mountains can equally well be made from Glen Lyon or along the Lawers Burn above Loch Tay. The Glen Lyon approach starts from the bridge across the River Lyon at Invervar, but should probably be avoided during the stalking season. The route by the Lawers Burn, being almost entirely within National Trust for Scotland territory, can be followed at any time of the year, and has the further advantage of giving very fine views of Ben Lawers rising above Lochan nan Cat.

The start is from the A827 road just north-east of the bridge over the Lawers Burn where a private road leads uphill to Machuim farm. (Car parking is a problem at this point. There is a little space for two or three cars a short distance up the private farm road, and parking is possible at the foot of this road, at the cottage just north-east of the Lawers Burn bridge, but at a price). Continue past the farm by a track along the

edge of the fields above the Lawers Burn and reach National Trust for Scotland territory a short distance further on. Once beyond the highest wall it is possible to leave the path and climb due N up the grassy hillside to a small knoll (805m) and then NNE to the summit of Meall Greigh. Alternatively the path may be followed up the east side of the Lawers Burn for a further 1½km until a stream coming down from Meall Greigh is reached. In thick weather this stream may provide a useful landmark on an otherwise featureless hillside, and it can be followed up its west side towards the summit. This is a smooth rounded dome, and there is a lower top with a small cairn 200 metres north-west of the summit. (4½km; 820m; 2h 30min).

The west ridge of Meall Greigh leading towards Meall Garbh is broad, grassy and featureless. In thick weather an accurate compass bearing is essential to reach the col (830m) between the two hills. Beyond this col the route continues more steeply up the grassy shoulder of Meall Garbh until the north-east ridge is reached, and a fairly well-defined path leads SW to the top where a small cairn is perched on the crest of the ridge. (8km; 1110m; 3h 40min).

On the descent it is best to follow, in part at least, the uphill route back towards the 830m col, and then descend SE to the little dam on the Lawers Burn. In this way the rather steep east face of Meall Garbh is avoided.

Map on page 29.

On the ridge from Meall nan Tarmachan towards Meall Garbh   *D.J. Bennet*

Meall nan Tarmachan; 1043m, (OS Sheet 51; 585390); M87; *hill of the ptarmigan*

The Tarmachan Hills, as they are commonly called, are among the best-known peaks of the Southern Highlands, and the knobbly outline of their four summits seen from the River Dochart at Killin is one of the most familiar of our mountain landscapes. They lie about 5km north of Killin and only the highest one, Meall nan Tarmachan, is a Munro, the others being Tops. The southern front of the group overlooking Loch Tay has a discontinuous line of crags just below the summit ridge along its entire length.

The nearest approach to Meall nan Tarmachan by road is ½km north-west of the National Trust for Scotland Visitor Centre on the road from Loch Tay to Glen Lyon. A rough private road branches off SW and contours round the south side of the Tarmachans, but it is possible to drive for only a short distance along it to a locked gate. Walk along the road beyond this gate for a few hundred metres, then climb W up easy grassy slopes to reach the broad south ridge of Meall nan Tarmachan. Follow this ridge over a small knoll (c.920m) and descend a short distance to the col below the craggy south-east face. Continue straight ahead up a steepening slope to reach a rake below the upper rocks, turn right (north) along this rising rake for about 150 metres and finally climb up steep grass on the left (west) to the summit cairn. (3½km; 600m; 1h 50min).

The return can be made by the same route, but this short outing hardly does justice to the Tarmachans. It is much better to continue the traverse over the three lower Tops. A broad grassy ridge leads SW from Meall nan Tarmachan to a col marked by two tiny lochans. From there a well-defined path leads up the ridge to the sharp rocky summit of Meall Garbh (1026m), which may well be considered to be the finest peak of the Tarmachans.

Continue W along a narrow level ridge for a short distance and then drop steeply to the next col. From there the ascent to Beinn nan Eachan (c.1000m) might be confusing in mist were it not for the path which twists and turns along the knolly ridge. From that Top go SW down a grassy slope to the level continuation of the ridge across the next col, and up to Creag na Caillich (916m).

The east face of this Top is the biggest mass of crags in the Tarmachans, and it is necessary to return NE towards the col to outflank them before descending SE into Coire Fionn Lairige. Continue down this grassy corrie to reach a disused quarry and the road which leads in 4km back to the day's starting point.

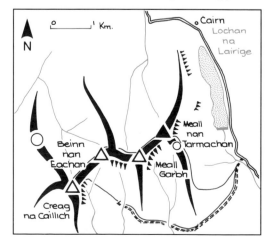

Meall Ghaordaidh from Glen Lyon   *D.J. Bennet*

Meall Ghaordaidh; 1039m; (OS Sheet 51; 514397); M90; *possibly from Gaelic gairdean, meaning a shoulder, arm, hand*

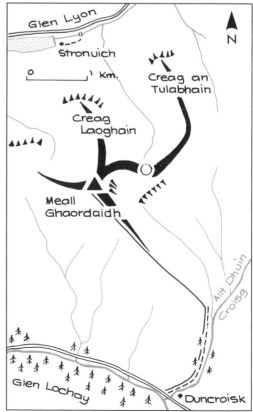

Meall Ghaordaidh rises between Glen Lochay and Glen Lyon, about 10km north-west of Killin. It is rather an isolated hill, being far enough away from its neighbours, the Tarmachans to the east and Beinn Heasgarnich to the west, to be usually climbed by itself, and it gives quite a short day.

On its south side overlooking Glen Lochay, Meall Ghaordaidh has uniform featureless grassy slopes rising from glen to summit in a single sweep. On the north side above Glen Lyon there are two prominent spurs, Creag an Tulabhain and Creag Laoghain, which rise steeply above the glen. Although the Glen Lyon side of the hill is the more interesting, and it is quite possible to climb Meall Ghaordaidh from the bridge over the River Lyon near Stronuich and up the corrie between the two spurs, the Glen Lochay approach is more usually followed.

There is a right of way from Duncroisk in Glen Lochay through the Lairig Breisleich to Glen Lyon, but its line on the east side of the Allt Dhuin Chroisg is rather overgrown. A better route exists on the west side of this stream, starting about 300 metres west of Duncroisk. A track leads through some fields onto the higher open hillside and in about 1½km reaches a sheepfank at some old shielings.

From there climb NW directly towards the summit of Meall Ghaordaidh up a broad shoulder of grass and heather. An iron post marks the way and beyond it for several hundred metres the gradient is easy until some small outcrops of rock are reached, and just above them the summit appears. The Ordnance Survey trig point stands inside a fine circular cairn. (4½km; 890m; 2h 30min).

Stuchd an Lochain above Lochan nan Cat   *D.J. Bennet*

Stuchd an Lochain; 960m; (OS Sheet 51; 483449); M194; *peak of the little loch*
Meall Buidhe; 932m; (OS Sheet 51; 498499); M244; *yellow hill*

Far up Glen Lyon, just beyond Meggernie Castle, the Allt Conait (a tributary of the River Lyon) flows down from Loch an Daimh. Between this loch and Glen Lyon itself, Stuchd an Lochain occupies a commanding position, its great bulk filling the westward view up the glen. On the north side of Loch an Daimh, Meall Buidhe is rather an undistinguished hill, the highest point of the vast tract of high undulating moorland between upper Glen Lyon and Loch Rannoch. Loch an Daimh itself is the enlarged loch formed by raising the level of Loch Giorra and Loch Daimh, which are now one.

Four kilometres west of Bridge of Balgie in Glen Lyon a branch road leads up to the dam at the east end of Loch an Daimh, and both hills are accessible from there. The loch is at a height of about 430m, so the amount of climbing on each is not great. In fact, the ascent of both in one day is no more strenuous than many a Munro by itself.

Climbing Stuchd an Lochain first, walk past the south end of the dam for 150 metres and climb a faint path S up the steep grassy hillside to reach the ridge above Coire Ban at a line of fence posts. These are followed W to Creag an Fheadain (887m), then SSW across a dip in the broad ridge to Sron Chona Choirein (c.920m), and finally W and WNW to Stuchd an Lochain. (4½km; 600m; 2h). A very attractive feature of this hill is its northern corrie which holds in its depths the dark circular Lochan nan Cat. The return to the Loch an Daimh dam takes a little more than an hour.

Starting again at the dam, this time at its north end, climb due N up easy slopes to Meall a'Phuill (878m), marked by two cairns. Continue W then NNW along the broad crest past some small cairns to reach the big

cairn which marks the summit of Meall Buidhe at the north end of a level ridge 1km long. (4½km; 520m; 2h). Return to the dam by the same route.

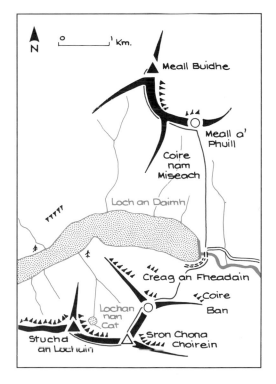

The upper part of the Sron nan Eun ridge leading to Creag Mhor   G.S. Johnstone

Creag Mhor; 1048m; (OS Sheets 50 and 51; 391361); M80; *big rock*
Beinn Heasgarnich; 1076m; (OS Sheet 51; 413383); M61; *perhaps sheltering or peaceful hill*

These two mountains in the Forest of Mamlorn are on the north side of Glen Lochay near its head, some 17km west of Killin. In common with many of their neighbouring hills in Breadalbane, they are for the most part grassy, with no notable crags or rocky corries. Creag Mhor has two well-defined ridges enclosing Coire-cheathaich at the head of Glen Lochay, and its north face immediately below the summit is fairly steep and rocky. Beinn Heasgarnich is a massive mountain of broad grassy ridges and wide corries, lacking any outstanding features. There is a considerable area of peat moor at a height of about 650m to the east of its summit.

The public road up Glen Lochay ends just beyond Kenknock farm. A private road climbs NW out of the glen at this point and crosses the east side of Beinn Heasgarnich at about 530m before dropping to Glen Lyon near the dam at the east end of Loch Lyon. If, as is sometimes the case, the gates on this road are not locked, there seems to be no objection to driving up it and across from one glen to the other. There is also a rough private road up Glen Lochay from Kenknock, but access along it by car is not permitted.

To traverse these two mountains, climbing Creag Mhor first,
walk along this private road for 5km to Batavaime. From there climb the steep grassy hillside NW to reach the east ridge of Creag Mhor at Sron nan Eun, and continue up this ridge following traces of a path to the summit. (9km; 830m; 3h 30min).

Avoid the steep rocky descent of the north-east face of Creag Mhor by going NW for ½km then N for about the same distance down the broad ridge leading to Meall Tionail. Then turn E down a grassy corrie which leads to the wide flat col at Lochan na Baintig-

Looking to Creag Mhor from Beinn Achaladair   D.J. Bennet

Beinn Heasgarnich from Coire Ban Mor   *K.M. Andrew*

hearna at about 660m. From there the route to Beinn Heasgarnich climbs steeply at first up grassy slopes and then continues along a broad undulating ridge to the flat summit. (13km; 1260m; 5h).

Descend E down Coire Ban Mor, following the Allt Tarsuinn until it reaches flat ground north of Lochan Achlarich. From there one can either continue NE down the stream to reach the road between Glen Lochay and Glen Lyon and walk down it, or one can take a line SE across the level peaty corrie and the west shoulder of Creag nam Bodach to the lower grassy hillside above the day's starting point.

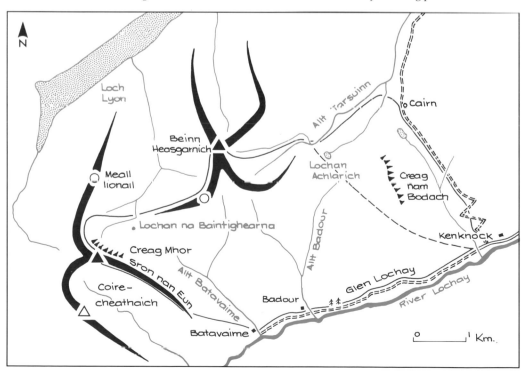

Sgiath Chuil from Glen Dochart   *D.J. Bennet*

Meall Glas; 960m; (OS Sheet 51; 431322); M193; *greenish-grey hill*
Sgiath Chuil; 935m; (OS Sheet 51; 463318); M238; *back wing*

Between Glen Dochart and Glen Lochay there is a range of low hills. Meall Glas and Sgiath Chuil are the only two Munros in this area, and they can easily be climbed together from Auchessan in Glen Dochart. From this glen both hills rise gradually from the wide strath over rough moorland to their steeper upper slopes. Meall Glas shows a fairly continuous escarpment of steep grass and broken rocks around its southern flank, and Sgiath Chuil is characterised by its prominent summit rocks which resemble the prow of a ship.

Car parking is not possible on the roadside at the point where the private road to Auchessan leaves the A85. The nearest available place is a few hundred metres west along the main road. Walk down the private road across the River Dochart to Auchessan and take the track on the east side of the stream which flows down from Creag nan Uan. This track ends once high ground is reached, and a course slightly west of north should be taken over rough featureless moorland to aim for the col just east of Meall Glas, where an easy grass slope leads up to the ridge. From there the summit of Meall Glas is a short distance west. (6km; 800m; 2h 40min).

Return E along the broad ridge, passing a prominent cairn at Pt.908m to reach Beinn Cheathaich (937m). The direct descent ESE from this Top is very steep for a short distance; however, a short diversion N before turning ESE avoids this minor difficulty. Lower down easy grassy slopes lead to the wide peaty col at the head of the Allt Riobain.

The west face of Meall a'Churain (918m) rises directly above the col in uniformly steep grass slopes 300m high, and the ridge from this Top to Sgiath Chuil

is almost level. The cairn of this peak is right on the edge of the crag which is so prominent from below. (10½km; 1180m; 4h 20min).

Descend SW towards the Allt Riobain, and follow it for about 1km before bearing away SW below Creag nan Uan to rejoin the uphill route.

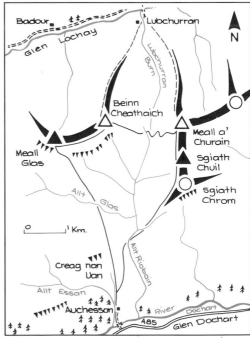

Ben Challum from the west; Ben More and Stob Binnein beyond   K.M. Andrew

Ben Challum; 1025m; (OS Sheet 50; 387322); M103; *Malcolm's hill*

The north-east side of Strath Fillan between Crianlarich and Tyndrum is dominated by the slopes of Ben
Challum, the largest and highest of the hills on that
side of the strath. Seen from the south, from Crianlarich or the head of Glen Falloch, the main impression
of the mountain is of the wide expanse of grassy hillside above the River Fillan, rising at an easy angle to
the dome of the South Top (997m), behind which the
true summit is hidden. The remoter side of the mountain above the head of Glen Lochay is very different,
for the north face is steep and craggy and the summit
appears to be quite pointed.

The most convenient starting point in Strath Fillan
is at Kirkton farm. (Cars should be left at the roadside
before crossing the bridge over the River Fillan). Near
Kirkton farm are the remains of St Fillan's Priory, and
nearby there are two old graveyards. From the priory
take the track uphill past the higher graveyard and
cross the West Highland Railway by an unofficial
level crossing. Leave the track and strike NE directly
uphill. There is no path and none is needed; the only
hazard may be an electric fence across the hillside, so
it is worth looking for the gates in the fence. On a clear
day this climb, which is otherwise rather dull, gives
fine views of the great mountains Ben More, Stob Binnein and Ben Lui on the far side of the strath.

The ascent goes over flatter ground and a slight
knoll, and a fence on the right shows the way up the
next rise. Beyond the fence, continue N up the broad
ridge to reach the South Top, whose summit is a large
rock with a cairn nearby.

In clear weather the continuation to the summit of
Ben Challum is obvious, but in a 'white-out' the ter-
rain may be confusing as a descent due N from the
South Top would lead one astray. Drop down quite

steeply W for a few metres from the South Top to cross
a little narrow hollow and climb onto the ridge on its
far side. Once on this ridge there are no route-finding
problems; a gradual descent N followed by a steeper
ascent leads to the large summit cairn overlooking the
steep north face. (5½km; 900m; 2h 50min).

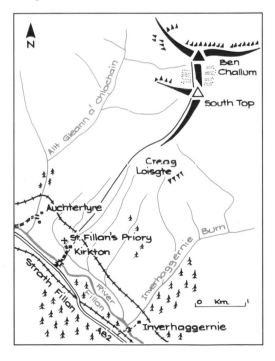

Beinn Dorain; 1076m; (OS Sheet 50; 326378); M62; *from Gaelic dobhran, hill of the streamlet*
Beinn an Dothaidh; 1002m; (OS Sheet 50; 332408); M130; *hill of the scorching or singeing*

These two peaks are the southern half of the semi-circular range of mountains which overlook Loch Tulla and the headwaters of the River Orchy. Beinn Dorain in particular, with its great upsweep above the West Highland Railway and its conical shape, is one of the most familiar mountains in Scotland, in full view from the A82 road between Tyndrum and Bridge of Orchy. Beinn an Dothaidh may not be so spectacular in appearance, but it too presents an un-interrupted bastion above Loch Tulla, and has a fine corrie on its north-east face. The two mountains are easily accessible from Bridge of Orchy.

From the station car park go through the underpass below the railway and emerge onto the rising moorland. Bear left (NE) for about 100 metres past a little fenced enclosure along a well-worn path which continues up the south bank of the Allt Coire an Dothaidh. Higher up the corrie the path becomes less obvious, and to avoid some discontinuous crags

straight ahead bear left (NE) beside the stream which flows down from a steep Y-shaped gully on Beinn an Dothaidh. Once a line of rusty fence posts is reached climb more directly E and then make a rising traverse rightwards below a line of crags to reach the col between the two mountains, marked by a large cairn.

Going to Beinn Dorain first, there is a path to follow for most of the way. Climb due S up an easy-angled slabby rib which is the edge of a rocky escarpment. In a few hundred metres the rocks end and the ascent continues up a broad grassy slope, bouldery higher up, to a large cairn. This is not the summit, as might be thought on a misty day, and one must continue 200 metres further south beyond a slight drop in the ridge to reach the topmost point of Beinn Dorain. (4½km; 890m; 2h 30min).

After returning to the col, climb NNE up the grassy south flank of Beinn an Dothaidh. This leads to the summit ridge of the mountain where there are three

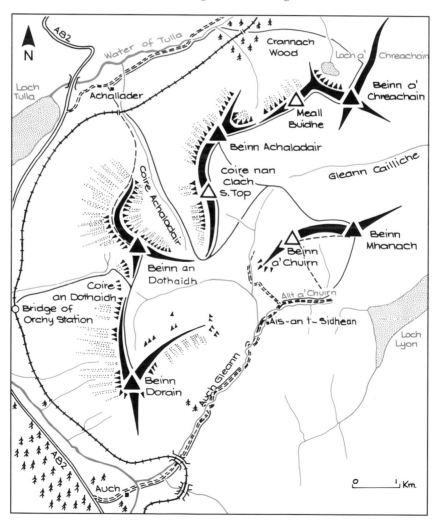

Beinn Dorain from the south   D.J. Bennet

tops, the central one being the highest. (7½km; 1140m; 3h 40min). A few hundred metres away is the West Top (1000m) which is a good viewpoint, and from there a course south leads back to the col and the return to Bridge of Orchy.

An alternative descent route from the West Top, which gives a good traverse if one's transport arrangements permit, is to go W then NNE round the edge of the north-east corrie of Beinn an Dothaidh and follow the ridge towards Achallader farm. After descending quite steep broken slopes for a short distance, continue down easy ground to reach the path on the west side of the Allt Coire Achaladair leading to a bridge over the railway just above the farm.

Beinn Achaladair and Beinn an Dothaidh from Loch Tulla   H.M. Brown

Beinn Achaladair from Crannach Wood   *G.F. Brunton*

Beinn Achaladair; 1039m (OS Sheet 50; 346433); M91; *from the name of the settlement, which is from early Celtic meaning the field of hard water*
Beinn a'Chreachain; 1081m; (OS Sheet 50; 373441); M59; *hill of the rock, or hill of the clamshell*

These two splendid mountains form the northern perimeter of the Bridge of Orchy group of peaks, presenting a great curving rampart above the Water of Tulla and the south-western corner of Rannoch Moor. Beinn Achaladair in particular has a continuously steep hillside above Achallader farm, and it extends along the flank of Meall Buidhe to Coire an Lochain below the summit of Beinn a'Chreachain. The south-east side of these mountains is less impressive, forming a series of shallow grassy corries above Gleann Cailliche.

The traverse of these two mountains is best done from Achallader farm, which is 1½km off the A82 road at the north- east end of Loch Tulla. Cars can be driven along the rough private road to the farm and parked there.

It is probably better to climb Beinn a'Chreachain first as the subsequent traverse to Beinn Achaladair has splendid views ahead. From the farm go NE along a track which is the line of the old right of way to Loch Rannoch. The crossing of the Allt Coire Achaladair may present a problem if it is in spate. Follow the track to the bridge over the Water of Tulla and continue along a path which leads to the lower edge of Crannach Wood, a beautiful remnant of the Old Caledonian forest. Climb uphill along a track through the ancient pines to cross the West Highland Railway by a footbridge and continue E, climbing gradually through the old forest and the higher fringe of birches

to reach the open hillside below Coire an Lochain. Keep on SE up grassy slopes to reach the north-east ridge of Beinn a'Chreachain just south-west of Pt.959m and climb the ridge, with one pleasantly narrow section, to the dome of the summit. (7½km; 900m; 3h 10min).

Descend stony slopes WNW to the col above Coire an Lochain and climb a short distance W to the north-east end of the level summit ridge of Meall Buidhe (977m). Continue SW along this ridge past a cairn and down to the col at 820m below the steep north-east face of Beinn Achaladair. The ascent goes steeply up the broad rocky ridge whose north edge is defined by this face, and one gradually bears round NW up an easier slope leading to the summit of Beinn Achaladair. This is perched right on the edge of the steep north-west face at the top of the north ridge, and commands a superb view towards the Black Mount and Rannoch Moor. (10½km; 1070m; 4h 10min).

Traverse SW then S along the broad high ridge of Beinn Achaladair over the South Top (1002m) and on down the long easy south ridge to the col at the head of Coire Daingean. Descend N down this corrie and its lower extension, Coire Achaladair. Cross to the west side of the stream halfway down the corrie and follow the path which leads directly to the footbridge over the West Highland Railway a short distance above Achallader farm.

Map on page 40.

Looking up the Auch Gleann to Beinn Mhanach   K.M. Andrew

Beinn Mhanach; 954m; (OS Sheet 50; 373412); M205; *monk hill*

The twin rounded summits of Beinn Mhanach and its slightly lower Top, Beinn a'Chuirn (923m) are well seen looking up the Auch Gleann from the A82 road midway between Tyndrum and Bridge of Orchy. They fill the distant head of the glen 8km to the north-east, and occupy a remote setting between the main chain of the Bridge of Orchy mountains and the head of Loch Lyon.

Beinn Mhanach is for the most part a grassy hill, steep on its south side, but craggier on its remote and seldom visited north face. Beinn a'Chuirn is also steep, particularly at its western end.

The most direct approach to these hills seems to be up the Auch Gleann, but another less obvious route which is slightly shorter is from Achallader farm by Coire Achaladair, and this way enables the ascent of Beinn Mhanach to be combined with Beinn Achaladair and Beinn a'Chreachain.

For the Auch Gleann route, cars must be left at the A82 road as the side road down to Auch is private. There is only very limited space for parking at this point at the side of the A82. Walk down the private road past Auch and on up the right of way along the Auch Gleann under the viaduct of the West Highland Railway. The track up the glen crosses and recrosses the Allt Kinglass several times. In wet weather, if the stream is in spate, the walker will be forced to stay on the south-east side of the stream as far as the ruined cottage at Ais-an t-Sidhean. The celebrated Gaelic poet Duncan Ban MacIntyre lived in this cottage for several years.

Continue across the Allt a'Chuirn and go E along the track on the north side to its end at the watershed. From there climb N up a steep grassy slope of almost 600m to the flat mossy summit dome of Beinn Mhanach. (9½km; 760m; 3h 30min).

The descent may be made by the same route, or a traverse can be made to Beinn a'Chuirn along a broad mossy ridge. The descent from this Top in a west or south-west direction should be undertaken with great caution, for the slope is steep and rocky in places. It is safer, though longer, to descend south-east towards the end of the track.

The alternative route from Achallader farm goes up Coire Achaladair by the path on the west side of the Allt Coire Achaladair to the col at the head of Coire Daingean between Beinn Achaladair and Beinn an Dothaidh. From there traverse horizontally NE along a good sheep track (possibly an old stalker's path). This path crosses the grassy flank of Beinn Achaladair and drops gradually to the 630m col at (354417). From there follow a fence ESE to reach the flat col 1km west of Beinn Mhanach, and continue E along the broad mossy ridge to the summit. (8½km; 920m; 3h 30min).

This route can very conveniently be extended to include Beinn Achaladair and even Beinn a'Chreachain. Return to the col at (354417) and from there climb NW up grassy slopes into Coire nan Clach and continue more steeply onto the ridge of Beinn Achaladair where the route described on the preceding page is joined.

Map on page 40.

Looking east from Bidean nam Bian to the peaks of the Buachaille Etive Mor and Beag   C. Simpson

SECTION 3

Strath Orchy to Loch Leven

Beinn a'Chochuill from Beinn Eunaich   *D.J. Bennet*

Beinn a'Chochuill; 980m; (OS Sheet 50; 110328); M168; *hill of the hood or shell*
Beinn Eunaich; 989m; (OS Sheet 50; 136328); M152; *fowling hill*

These two hills are the highest points on a long ridge of 12km between Loch Etive and Glen Strae which is separated from Ben Cruachan by Glen Noe. Beinn a'Chochuill has a long, fairly level spine running from east to west, joined to the Ben Cruachan massif to the south by a bealach at 550m. Beinn Eunaich has a more pyramidal shape and is well seen from the main A85 road west of Dalmally. With the exception of Beinn Eunaich's west ridge, both hills give easy going on short grass, and both provide magnificent views of Ben Cruachan's majestic peaks and ridges.

Start from the B8077 road 2½km WNW of Dalmally at (137288) where a rough road leads off NW across a cattle-grid and through a stand of Scots pine. Follow this road N skirting Castles Farm to the left to reach the Hydro-Electric Board road which traverses NW across the lower slopes of Beinn Eunaich. Follow this track for 3km, climbing gradually, until less than ½km beyond a bridge the track divides. Take to the hillside of Beinn a' Chochuill and climb steeply N. The open grassy slopes gradually steepen and form an ill-defined ridge which leads NW to the east fore-top (896m). Beyond it the main ridge climbs very gradually W for 1km to the summit of Beinn a'Chochuill. (5½km; 930m; 2h 50min).

To continue the traverse to Beinn Eunaich, retrace the route back to the 896m fore-top, and continue down the ridge ENE to the bealach at 728m. Above, the west ridge of Beinn Eunaich has a rightward turn at 800m and beyond that point grows rockier and steepens steadily almost to the cairn, set at the north end of a short plateau. (8½km; 1200m; 4h).

Descend S down the broad grassy ridge leading to Stob Maol. The crags at the foot of this ridge can be avoided by keeping to the west side of the crest to reach the hydro-electric road about ½km north-west of Castles Farm. On this descent there are fine views of Loch Awe and the long parallel ridges of the Dalmally Horseshoe.

No access problems by the route described in the stalking season.

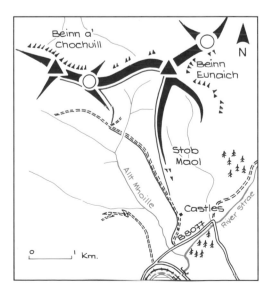

Ben Cruachan from Beinn a'Chochuill   *D.J. Bennet*

Ben Cruachan; 1126m; (OS Sheet 50; 069304); M31; *stacky hill*

This sharp peak is the culminating point of a huge and complex massif, one of the finest and best known of Scottish mountains. It rises grandly above Loch Awe and its outlet through the Pass of Brander. The main spine of the mountain with its several peaks runs from east to west, and from it two arms go south enclosing an open corrie now dammed to hold the Cruachan Reservoir. Ben Cruachan itself lies at the junction of the westerly arm with the main spine, a peak with the classical form of four ridges rising from the four points of the compass to merge at the small top. Its northern slopes fall very steeply into wild corries. With its high ridge of seven satellite peaks, Ben Cruachan is a very distinctive mountain as seen from other hills, and it is also prominent in views from the main A85 road between Tyndrum and Oban.

The most direct ascent starts from this road several kilometres west of Dalmally in the Pass of Brander at the Cruachan Power Station. There are one or two roadside parking places nearby, but parking in the power station's Visitor Centre is discouraged.

Opposite the power station scramble under the left-hand arch of the railway bridge over the Falls of Cruachan burn, and immediately start climbing steeply up the path which goes along the west bank of the burn through open woodland. The path leads up to more boggy ground above 300m and from there the best route strikes NW to the broad and grassy south ridge of Cruachan's southern Top, Meall Cuanail (918m). An alternative route to this point uses the hydro-electric road from Lochawe village to the Cruachan Reservoir; although 3½km longer, it is possible to cycle up this road to the dam.

The south ridge of Meall Cuanail leads easily to that Top; it provides good views of lochs and islands, and there is a mere 70m of descent beyond the summit before starting up the south ridge of Ben Cruachan. This ridge is littered with granite boulders through which a faint path leads intermittently to the sharp summit. (5km; 1200m; 3h 10min).

The quickest descent is by the route of ascent, but a fine traverse of the horseshoe surrounding the reservoir continues with a descent of Cruachan's east ridge, which involves a little very easy scrambling. The next Top, Drochaid Ghlas (1009m), lies a short distance along a northward spur just off the main ridge. Further east, at Stob Diamh, the main ridge turns S over Stob Garbh and down 250m to a bealach from which easy grassy slopes lead down SW to the reservoir.

Stob Diamh; 998m; (OS Sheet 50; 095308); M141; *peak of the stag*

This hill, one of Ben Cruachan's many peaks, lies near the east end of the main spine of the great massif, at the apex of an east-facing arc of peaks and ridges known as the Dalmally Horseshoe. To its north-east and south are two slightly lower satellites, Sron an Isean (966m) and Stob Garbh (980m). The circuit of these three peaks is over smooth terrain set at a generally easy angle.

Start 2½km WNW of Dalmally on the B8077 road where a gate at (133284) marks the beginning of an

The Dalmally Horseshoe from Strath Orchy   *J. Renny*

old railway track to a disused lead mine. Follow the track NW for 1 km and continue in the same direction on a faint path to a bridge across the Allt Coire Ghlais at (120296). Due west there is some wet, humpy ground before the angle increases to lead onto the south arm of the Horseshoe. Above 450m the ridge levels out and there are fine views southwards to the crags of Beinn a' Bhuiridh. At 900m the ridge merges with that running S from Stob Garbh, and a faint path is joined leading N to this Top. The ground drops steeply for 60m north of Stob Garbh and then rises gradually to Stob Diamh along a broad ridge. (5km; 1000m; 2h 50min).

There is another steep descent of 100m ENE beyond Stob Diamh before the ridge rises to Sron an Isean. From this last Top an easy-angled descent follows its east ridge, eventually curving SE and descending steep grass slopes to the same wet humpy ground of the start and to another bridge at (122297) just below the confluence of the Allt Coire Ghlais and the Allt Coire Chreachainn. From there the disused lead mine is several hundred metres SE.

The routes described above are all accessible during the stalking season.

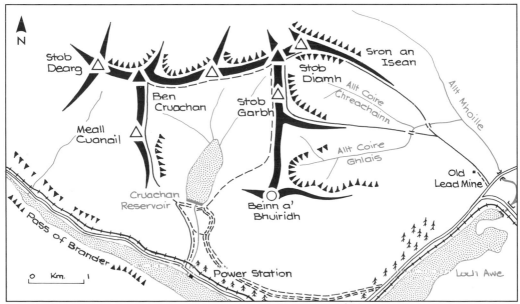

Ben Starav from Glen Etive   A. Thrippleton

Ben Starav; 1078m; (OS Sheet 50; 126427); M60; *origin unknown*
Glas Bheinn Mhor; 997m; (OS Sheet 50; 153429); M142; *big greenish-grey hill*

Both these hills rise prominently at the foot of Glen Etive, and are well seen from the road near the foot of this glen. Ben Starav looks its full height and is clearly of great bulk, having a distinctive north ridge rising in one sweep from sea-level to summit. Glas Bheinn Mhor presents a classical pyramidal form with a very steep north face, but it is really a subsidiary peak on the high ridge which extends east from Ben Starav.

From the Glen Etive road at (137468), where there is limited space for car parking, follow a private track (not readily seen from the road) which drops E to cross the River Etive and reach the cottage of Coileitir. Continue SW along a path to the Allt Mheuran and SE to a bridge 200 metres upstream. Cross the bridge and continue along the path on the west bank for ½km before bearing right to gain the broad lower slopes of the north ridge of Ben Starav. The great length and height of this ridge are very apparent, and its angle eases only at two shoulders, at 500m and 800m. Steep slopes fall away on both sides until a parallel ridge merges with it at the 800m shoulder. The uppermost 200m steepens and is littered with granite boulders. There is a splendid view from the top, looking down Loch Etive to Ben Cruachan, and on a clear day further to the Paps of Jura. (5km; 1060m; 3h).

Going SSE along the nearly level summit ridge, the Top of Stob Coire Dheirg (1068m) is soon reached. Turn NE and descend a rocky ridge to a small peak where the ridge turns ESE and drops to a bealach at 760m. Continue E, climbing over a minor grassy top (892m), dropping 70m and finishing up a broad rockier ridge to the summit of Glas Bheinn Mhor. (8½km; 1370m; 4h 10min).

Do not descend NNW from the summit of Glas Bheinn Mhor for the ridge in that direction is very steep, possibly dangerously so if the grass is wet or there is snow. Instead, descend the east ridge until after ½km it is easy to drop down N into the corrie at the head of the Allt Mheuran and follow this stream back to Glen Etive by the path on its north-east side.

Map on page 50.

Beinn nan Aighenan; 960m; (OS Sheet 50; 148405); M192; *hill of the hinds*

This is a truly remote hill, lying 6km south-east of the head of Loch Etive and hidden behind other hills at the head of Glen Kinglass. It is bulky, with steep lower slopes and one distinctive high-level ridge running east from the summit over extensive pavements of granite.

Beinn nan Aighenan can be combined with Ben Starav and Glas Bheinn Mhor, adding 4km and 500m of climbing to the traverse of those two mountains, or it may be climbed by itself. In the latter case the start is the same as for Ben Starav as far as the foot of the north ridge of that mountain. Proceeding to Beinn nan Aighenan, continue S up the west bank of the Allt nam Meirleach. There is a good path for a long way up this stream, and where it ends a faint path continues steeply to the bealach at 760m on the ridge above.

In poor visibility very careful navigation is needed for the next section of the route, taking a slanting descent SSE across featureless slopes and past a sprinkling of tiny lochans to the next bealach at 610m, 1½km NNW of Beinn nan Aighenan. Above the bealach a craggy ridge leads steeply SSE to the summit

Glas Bheinn Mhor from the north ridge of Ben Starav   *D.J. Bennet*

of the hill. (8km; 1100m; 3h 40min). Return by the same route, with another 150m of ascent to reach the ridge between Ben Starav and Glas Bheinn Mhor.

A much longer route to Beinn nan Aighenan starts at Forest Lodge at the west end of Loch Tulla. Follow the right of way west past Loch Dochard and over the pass into the head of Glen Kinglass. From the bridge over the River Kinglass climb the long east ridge over several knolls and pavements of cream-coloured granite. (13km; 1000m; 4h 40min).

Map on page 50.

Beinn nan Aighenan from the Starav-Glas Bheinn Mhor col   *D.J. Bennet*

Looking west from Stob Ghabhar to Ben Starav, Stob Coir'an Albannaich and Meall nan Eun   D.J. Bennet

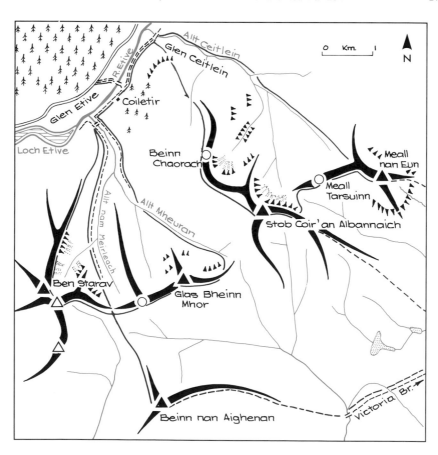

Approaching Stob Coir'an Albannaich along the south-east ridge   P. Hodgkiss

Stob Coir'an Albannaich; 1044m; (OS Sheet 50; 169442); M86; *peak of the corrie of the Scotsmen*
Meall nan Eun; 928m; (OS Sheet 50; 192449); M250; *hill of the birds*

These two hills lie near the foot of Glen Etive and to its east. Stob Coir'an Albannaich rises so steeply from the glen that its summit cannot be seen above the lower slopes, while Meall nan Eun can be glimpsed at the head of the Allt Ceitlein. From the opposite viewpoint, however, near the west end of Loch Tulla, Stob Coir'an Albannaich shows its sharp pointed summit and Meall nan Eun appears as a great dome with a distinctive concave corrie on its south-east flank. These hills form the north-eastward extension of the great undulating ridge which starts at Ben Starav and separates Glen Etive from the streams flowing towards Glen Kinglass and Loch Tulla.

The starting point for the traverse is the same as for Ben Starav, but after crossing the River Etive turn N and follow the track to the bridge across the Allt Ceitlin. From there climb the north-west ridge of Stob Coir'an Albannaich. Above about 550m the angle becomes less steep as one reaches the broad north-west shoulder of the mountain, and the going is much easier up the broad ridge over extensive pavements of bare granite. At 850m a minor bump, Beinn Chaorach, is passed and after a short descent S round the edge of Coire Glas the route bears ESE up an open slope which converges to a narrow ridge where the large summit cairn of Stob Coir'an Albannaich stands above the granite cliffs of the north-east face. (5km; 1040m; 3h).

The continuation to Meall nan Eun involves a series of 'dog-legs' that require accurate compass work in bad visibility, although the route is obvious in clear weather. From the summit of Stob Coir'an Albannaich descend E for less than ½km to a levelling in the ridge at 880m. At this point the cliffs on the north

side of the ridge disappear and it is possible to go NNW steeply down mixed rock and grass to a 750m bealach sprinkled with tiny lochans. At that point turn ENE and climb over the top of Meall Tarsuinn (875m), descend to 790m and climb again to the summit plateau of Meall nan Eun, whose cairn lies some distance away to the south-east. (8km; 1310m; 4h).

To return to Glen Etive go NW across the plateau and descend in the same direction down a broad ridge to the headwaters of the Allt Ceitlein. Cross to the north bank to reach a path and easy going down to the foot of Glen Ceitlein where the track leads back to the day's starting point.

These two mountains can also be climbed from the east, starting at Forest Lodge at the west end of Loch Tulla. Follow the right of way westwards up the Abhainn Shira to the west end of Loch Dochard. Go NW across very boggy ground to the foot of Stob Coir'an Albannaich and climb the broad south-east flank of the mountain. There is a choice of routes, but the best-defined one is up the right-hand edge along the ridge overlooking the Allt Coire Chaorach. (11½km; 870m; 4h 10min). The traverse to Meall nan Eun follows the route described above. (14½km; 1140m; 5h 10min).

Meall nan Eun, despite its flat-topped, lumpy shape, is very well defended on its north, east and south flanks by steep slabby slopes which make any descent route difficult, if not dangerous, unless great care is exercised. An ill-defined shoulder going E then ESE from the summit provides a possible way down to the Allt Dochard. From there it may be preferable to climb 240m to cross the Mam nan Sac and follow the path down to Clashgour rather than negotiate the rough ground along the north shore of Loch Dochard.

Stob a'Choire Odhair and Stob Ghabhar from Rannoch Moor   *D.J. Bennet*

Stob Ghabhar; 1087m; (OS Sheet 50; 230455); M54; *goat peak*
Stob a' Choire Odhair; 943m; (OS Sheet 50; 258461); M223; *peak of the dun-coloured corrie*

These two hills lie a few kilometres north-west of the west end of Loch Tulla, from where Stob Ghabhar in particular makes a fine sight through the fringe of mature Scots pine along the lochside. The approach to these hills is along the A8005 road from Bridge of Orchy past Inveroran Hotel to the end of the public road at Victoria Bridge. Stob Ghabhar is a well-formed peak with deeply scalloped corries and its

On the ridge from Stob a'Choire Odhair to Stob Ghabhar   *D.J. Bennet*

summit is at the apex of three ridges. Stob a'Choire Odhair, with its south-east shoulder Beinn Toaig, though lower, is more prominent in views from the A82 road north of Bridge of Orchy.

From Victoria Bridge follow the track west along the north side of the Abhainn Shira for 1½km to a small corrugated iron hut. Turn N and continue along a good, but sometimes very wet path on the east side of the Allt Toaig for a further 2km. At (252446) the path crosses a burn on whose west side a broad heathery ridge rises towards the summit of Stob a'Choire Odhair. Though not at first apparent, there is a well-engineered stalker's path zigzagging for 300m up this ridge, and this is followed. The path ends on bouldery ground, and more open slopes lead to the stony summit of Stob a'Choire Odhair. (6km; 760m; 2h 40min).

Descend W along a broad ridge to the wide knolly bealach between Stob a'Choire Odhair and Stob Ghabhar at about 680m. Continue W gradually uphill for ½km, then turn SW and climb more steeply up rough slopes with some scree to reach the crest of a narrow ridge called the Aonach Eagach (991m). Turn W and follow a faint path on the crest which at one point is quite narrow and exposed for a few metres across a little gap. Two minor bumps on the ridge are passed before it merges with the south-east ridge and this is climbed along the edge of the steep north-east face of Stob Ghabhar to the top. (9km, 1220m; 4h 10min).

On the descent go down the south-east ridge of Stob Ghabhar for about 1½km and continue ESE across open grassy slopes to cross the Allt Toaig and regain the path on its east side.

The traverse of the entire Black Mount range from Inveroran to Kingshouse over Stob Ghabhar, Clach Leathad, Creise and Meall a'Bhuiridh is one of the classic hillwalking expeditions in Scotland, linking two old and famous hostelries. It is quite a long and strenuous day involving about 20km and 1600m of ascent. (The shorter traverse of the last three of these mountains is described on the next page).

From the summit of Stob Ghabhar (which is most quickly reached by reversing the descent route described above) continue down the broad ridge initially NW then N over bouldery ground. After 1½km the ridge flattens and starts to veer NNW over a series of rocky knolls. At the fourth knoll (224475) turn NE and descend steep ground which develops into a ridge leading to the Bealach Fuar-chathaidh. From there climb steeply NE for 300m up grass and broken rocks to easier-angled bouldery ground leading to Clach Leathad (1098m).

Continue NNW then N across a slight dip in the broad bouldery ridge to reach the cairn (1068m) which is at the top of the spur dropping east towards Meall a'Bhuiridh. Creise is ½km north along the level ridge. The traverse ends by descending the spur, climbing Meall a'Bhuiridh by its west ridge and continuing down to the car park at the foot of the White Corries chair lift, as

described on the next page. (Victoria Bridge to the White Corries car park: 17km; 1600m; 6h 30min).

If returning to Victoria Bridge, descend E from the summit of Meall a'Bhuiridh to the top of the ski tow and continue along the level stony ridge for a further 300 metres. Then go ESE, at first on the crest of the ridge, then down the shallow corrie of the Allt Creagan nam Meann to reach the ruins of Ba Cottage. From there walk back along the West Highland Way to the day's starting point.

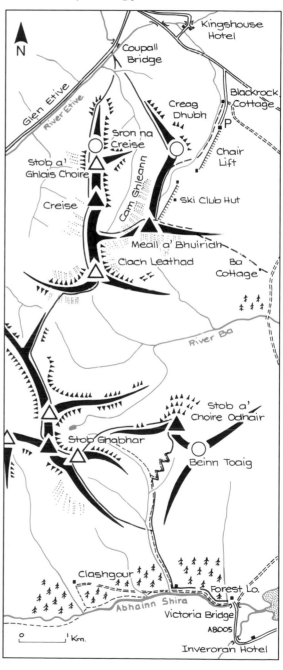

Clach Leathad and Meall a'Bhuiridh from Rannoch Moor   D.Scott

Creise; 1100m; (OS Sheets 33 and 41; 238507); M48; *origin unknown*
Meall a'Bhuiridh; 1108m; (OS Sheets 33 and 41; 251503); M43; *hill of the bellowing (of stags)*

These two mountains are the highest points at the northern end of that great range on the west edge of Rannoch Moor, the Black Mount. They form a horseshoe ridge overlooking the head of Glen Etive, and it is from there, near the point where the narrow road down Glen Etive leaves the A82, that the finest view of the group is had. All the peaks are visible, and the finest feature is the steep north-east face of Stob a'Ghlais Choire (996m), the north Top of Creise. Meall a'Bhuiridh is a particularly prominent mountain, fronting onto Rannoch Moor and having on the long-lasting snowfields of its north-east corrie the chair lifts and tows of one of Scotland's principal ski mountains. Behind it, Creise (which is not named on the Ordnance Survey 1:50,000 map) is the highest point of the 3km long ridge which extends from Sron na Creise to Clach Leathad.

The traverse of this group is a fine mountaineering expedition, with river crossings and some steep scrambling to give it character and interest. These difficulties can be avoided, and in bad weather probably should be avoided, by an alternative route.

For the longer traverse, assuming fair conditions, start from the Glen Etive road just north of the bridge over the River Coupall and cross the River Etive. Bear S across the rough moor, crossing two burns, to reach the foot of the north ridge of Sron na Creise. Careful route finding will enable a way to be found up this fine steep ridge, and high up there is some good scrambling (avoidable on the left) before the top is reached. Now follow the broad rocky ridge S over Stob a'Ghlais Choire to Creise. (4km; 900m; 2h 30min).

Continue S along the ridge for 600 metres to an almost imperceptible top (1068m), a little beyond which a spur falls steeply E. Descend this spur over granite boulders (faint path) to a well-defined col, and climb the ridge leading ENE to Meall a'Bhuiridh. (6km; 1100m; 3h 10min).

Descend N along the broad shoulder above Cam Ghleann, thus avoiding the machinery (and possibly crowds) of the ski slopes, and at Pt.749m turn NW down the Creag Dhubh ridge to the moor and the re-crossing of the River Etive.

In bad weather, particularly if the River Etive is in spate, the preceding route may well not be possible. In that case start at the car park at the foot of the White Corries chair lift and climb the path under the lift to the more level slopes of Coire Pollach. Bear SW to reach the descent route described in the preceding paragraph and follow this in reverse to Meall a'Bhuiridh and Creise. Return by the same way.

Map on page 53.

Beinn Sgulaird; 937m; (OS Sheet 50; 053461); M233; *meaning unknown*

Beinn Sgulaird stands at the head of Loch Creran, and forms a distinctive undulating ridge of granite running from south-west to north-east. Three kilometres of this ridge lie above 800m, and although there are extensive grasslands on the lower western slopes, much granite is exposed elsewhere, particularly on the summit ridge and in the corrie on its north-west side, where smooth pink slabs drop steeply below the summit. There is a fine view of the mountain from the road on the north shore of Loch Creran.

In order to walk round the policies of Druimavuic, start from the A828 road about ⅓km north of the house at (009451) where there is a gate giving access to a path. After skirting a stone wall this path soon reaches a second gate in open ground and continues E up the north bank of the Allt Buidhe. Leave the path 200 metres beyond the second gate and strike uphill ENE to a minor top at 488m. A short steep descent is followed by the continuation of the ridge, broad and grassy, until the first of the granite tops is reached (863m) where there is a tiny lochan on the ridge between the two cairns.

Bear NE and descend a steep bouldery slope for 70m, then climb the rough, rocky ridge to the next top (848m). Descend again quite steeply for 60m, and finally go up the narrowing ridge of granite slabs and boulders to the large summit cairn. (5½km; 1110m; 3h 10min). Views to the west down Loch Creran include the island of Lismore and the hills of Mull and Morvern.

The return by the same route involves more ups and downs along the ridge, but the effort is repaid in good weather by superb views.

A quicker return to Druimavuic can be made by descending NW from the summit for a short distance down a steep rocky spur, then W on a long descending traverse down easy grass slopes and through scattered birch woods to a hill track leading to Taraphocain farm. From there a private road leads to the A828 ½km from the day's starting point.

Beinn Sgulaird from the north-east   D.N. Williams

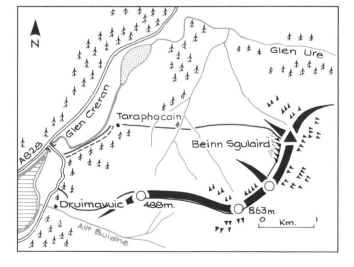

Beinn Fhionnlaidh from the head of Loch Creran   *D.J. Bennet*

Beinn Fhionnlaidh; 959m; (OS Sheets 41 and 50; 095498); M196; *Finlay's hill*

Beinn Fhionnlaidh is a shy hill lying to the west of Glen Etive, and only well seen from Sgor na h-Ulaidh or from Glen Creran to the south-west. It forms an east-west spine about 6km long with steep and craggy slopes to the south and north, and the east end of the spine ends abruptly in a rocky bluff whose precipitous nature is only hinted at on the OS 1:50,000 map. It is mainly composed of schistose rock, with bands of limestone providing the fertile basis for some rare alpines on the Glen Creran side. The summit ridge is bare and boulder strewn.

The shortest ascent route is from Glen Etive. From the A82 road drive almost 16km down the glen to within the second large afforestation where, 150 metres beyond the bridge over the Allt Charnan, there is a turn-off right to Invercharnan. Behind the house a Forestry Commission road leads SSW then WNW,

parallel to the Allt nan Gaoirean, and it is followed for 3km to a sharp right turn. There on the left a path (marked by a small cairn) leads NW through a fire-break for 200 metres to a stile and the open hillside. Bear W, descending slightly to cross the Allt nan Gaoirean and climb the grassy hillside opposite towards the little shoulder of Meall nan Gobhar, ½km south of Pt.821m.

From the shoulder climb N up stony slopes, but before reaching Pt.821m bear NW to reach the ridge of Beinn Fhionnlaidh, marked by a line of fence posts. Follow these W to a slight dip, at which point the fence-line turns S. Continue W then WSW up the narrowing ridge with an abrupt drop on its north side at the final steepening where, if the crest is followed, there are two short easy rocky steps to climb. (7½km; 960m; 3h 20min).

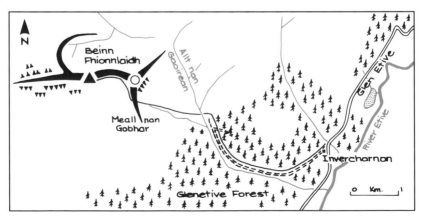

Sgor na h-Ulaidh and Stob an Fhuarain from the east   *J. Renny*

Sgor na h-Ulaidh; 994m; (OS Sheet 41; 111518); M146; *peak of the treasure*

Among the Glen Coe mountains, Sgor na h-Ulaidh is very much the forgotten and neglected one, hidden from the main road by the prominent projecting ridge of Aonach Dubh a'Ghlinne and lacking the bold features of Bidean nam Bian, in whose shadow it lies. However, it can be clearly seen from Beinn a'Bheithir, and from the hills on the south-east side of Glen Etive. Despite its retiring nature, Sgor na h-Ulaidh does have a distinctively mountainous character which is evident as one walks up the Allt na Muidhe into the wild glen which leads up to its steep northern face, and it is this glen which provides the usual approach.

Start from the A82 road in Glen Coe 2km west of Loch Achtriochtan along a track that follows the west bank of the Allt na Muidhe for 1km before crossing to the east bank and continuing to the farmhouse of Gleann-leac-na-muidhe. The track continues for a further 1km, ending near a junction of streams where the glen turns south and Sgor na h-Ulaidh comes into view.

Keep to the east bank of the burn and head S up the glen which is steeply enclosed by Creag Bhan and Aonach Dubh a'Ghlinne. After 1½ km turn E and climb steeply up grass slopes riven by drainage channels of many little streams, and reach the ridge just north of the outlying Top of Stob an Fhuarain (968m). Traverse this peak and descend SW to the col at 860m. This col can be reached directly from the head of the Allt na Muidhe, but the final slope is very steep and craggy. Continue SW up increasingly rocky ground to the cairn of Sgor na h-Ulaidh, which is on the brink of the steep north face. (6½km; 1040m; 3h 20min).

An easier alternative route to Sgor na h-Ulaidh which avoids any very steep ground is from Glen Etive. Start as for Beinn Fhionnlaidh (see page 56) and once above the forest bear due N to reach the col between Meall a'Bhuiridh and Sgor na h-Ulaidh. From there climb the south-east ridge direct to the summit. (7km; 950m; 3h 10min).

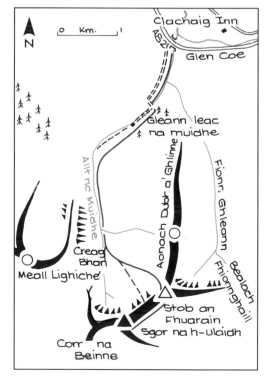

Buachaille Etive Mor   *J.E.S. Bennet*

Buachaille Etive Mor, Stob Dearg; 1022m; (OS Sheet 41; 223543); M106; *big herdsman of Etive, red peak*

The Buachaille Etive Mor, and in particular its highest peak Stob Dearg, is one of the grandest and best-known mountains in Scotland, standing as it does in isolation and rising abruptly above the north-west corner of Rannoch Moor. The great walls, gullies and buttresses of Stob Dearg give that peak a decided air of impregnability, at least as far as the hillwalker is concerned. However, the great cliffs which encircle the peak are breached on the north-west by Coire na Tulaich which gives a fairly easy walking route to the summit. The Buachaille Etive Mor is not just a single peak, but a 7km long ridge rising steeply above Glen Etive with three other peaks, Stob na Doire (1011m), Stob Coire Altruim (941m) and Stob na Broige (956m) along its length. The whole mountain is in National Trust for Scotland territory.

Start at Altnafeadh on the A82 road and follow the track down to the bridge across the River Coupall. Behind the white cottage of Lagangarbh take the right fork in the path and continue SSW into Coire na Tulaich, crossing a burn and climbing up the path on its west bank. A few short rocky steps call for a little easy scrambling, and the path ends at the foot of a scree slope at about 700m. Continue up the scree towards a narrowing gully which is probably best avoided by scrambling up rocky ledges on its east bank to emerge onto the broad ridge of the mountain at a flat bealach.

Turn E and follow the path worn over pink rock and boulders, with many cairns, finally trending NE along the narrowing ridge to the summit. The view is extensive, most notable being the vast expanse of Rannoch Moor with the prominent peak of Schiehallion at its far edge. (3km; 750m; 2h).

The complete traverse from Stob Dearg to Stob na Broige is a fine ridge-walk, and the return to Altnafeadh is best made by returning over Stob Coire Altruim to the col at (203531) between that peak and Stob na Doire. From there descend NNW to the Lairig Gartain and return along the path to reach the A82 road a short distance west of Altnafeadh. Alternatively the descent from Stob na Broige can be made to Glen Etive, descending the south-west ridge to a little knoll at 550m. From there the final descent must be undertaken with care as the lower slopes are steep and rocky; the best way down is SE from the knoll.

No restrictions on climbing at any time.

Buachaille Etive Beag, Stob Dubh; 958m; (OS Sheet 41; 179535); M197; *small herdsman of Etive, black peak*

The Buachaille Etive Beag is in size and character the small brother of the Buachaille Etive Mor, and it has many similarities, both when seen from Rannoch Moor and from the lower reaches of Glen Etive. However, it lacks the grandeur of its big brother, and its highest point, Stob Dubh, is at the south-west end of its 4km ridge, the far end as seen from the A82 road.

Only when seen from Glen Etive does the Buachaille Etive Beag match its big brother in height and appearance. It lies entirely in National Trust for Scotland territory.

From the north one ascent route starts on the A82 road at (188563) where a signpost indicates the right of way 'Lairig Eilde to Glen Etive'. Follow the path

Buachaille Etive Beag from Glen Etive   *D.J. Bennet*

SW for ¼km, then start a rising traverse S for 1km, keeping below the higher craggy slopes, and then climb directly uphill to a col at 750m. This col can also be reached from its opposite side by taking the right of way from the A82 road at (213560) through the Lairig Gartain for 2½km and climbing its south-west side. A short diversion NE from the col leads to the Top of Stob Coire Raineach (925m).

Continue the climb SW up steepening stony slopes to a little top beyond which the ridge is level for ¾km to the final short climb to Stob Dubh. (4km; 740m; 2h 10min). There is a fine view down Glen Etive from the cairn just beyond the summit.

A shorter route which might appeal to those staying in Glen Etive is the direct ascent of Stob Dubh from Dalness by its south-west ridge. This grassy ridge rises at a steady steep angle from the glen, and gives the climber no respite until the summit is reached. (2½ km; 870m; 2h).

No restrictions on climbing at any time.

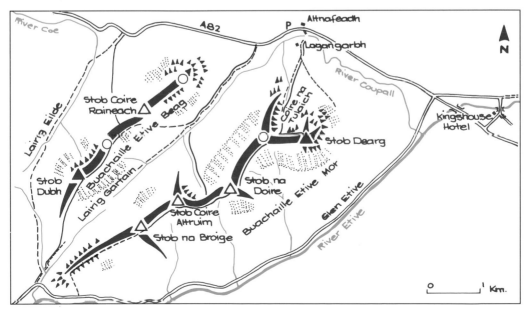

Looking west along the Aonach Eagach towards Sgorr nam Fiannaidh   P. Hodgkiss

Meall Dearg; 953m; (OS Sheet 41; 161584); M208; *red hill*
Sgorr nam Fiannaidh; 967m; (OS Sheet 41; 141583); M183; *peak of the Fian warriors*

The north side of Glen Coe is hemmed in by the steep flanks of the Aonach Eagach, *the notched ridge.* From the roadside in the glen it is difficult to appreciate its true character, the narrow crest and sharp pinnacles, and it is not easy to identify the individual summits along it. Meall Dearg is the lower of the two Munros on the ridge, and is near its east end. Sgorr nam Fiannaidh is more easily identified at the west end rising directly above Loch Achtriochtan in a single steep and uninterrupted hillside 900m high.

The traverse of the Aonach Eagach is one of the best ridge traverses on the mainland, continuously narrow and in places exposed, and there is a lot of excellent scrambling. The best way to climb these two Munros is to traverse the ridge, but for those who prefer easier routes, alternatives are suggested. However, it is for the traverse that the Aonach Eagach is renowned.

The best direction for the traverse is from east to west. Start from the A82 road in Glen Coe a few hundred metres west of Allt-na-reigh and take the signposted path which climbs steeply NE from the roadside. The path soon reaches the crest of the southeast ridge of Am Bodach. Continue up this ridge which in places is quite steep and rocky, almost a scramble, although there is a path all the way. Higher up the angle eases and the ridge leads directly to Am Bodach (943m), the easternmost peak of the Aonach Eagach.

Descend WNW along the narrowing crest of the ridge and soon reach a sudden drop of about 20m. Scramble down on the north side of the ridge and traverse left to the crest where there is a steep descent of two or three metres on good holds. It may be prudent to use a rope at this point. The traverse continues along a path on the narrow but perfectly easy crest, gradually climbing to a little top beyond which a rocky slope leads to Meall Dearg. (3km; 870m; 3h).

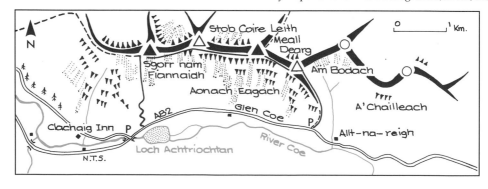

The next section along the ridge to the col below Stob Coire Leith is the hardest part of the traverse. It involves a lot of excellent and in places exposed scrambling, up and down little gullies, slabs and chimneys and round and over some little pinnacles. The route is obvious (in summer at least) and the rock is sound. From the col, where all difficulties end, there is a steep pull up to Stob Coire Leith (940m) followed by an easy and fairly level walk to Sgorr nam Fiannaidh. (5½km; 1000m; 4h).

The most direct descent from this peak to Glen Coe is due S down a continuously steep slope of boulders and stones near the top, and grass lower down. Care is needed not to dislodge stones which might roll a long way down, but otherwise the route is not difficult. In winter it, and the whole traverse of the Aonach Eagach is very different; a serious mountaineering expedition that may be difficult and time-consuming.

For those who seek a less continuously steep descent, the best alternative is to go ¾km WSW then 1km NNW from Sgorr nam Fiannaidh to the col below the Pap of Glencoe. From there descend SW to the road between Glencoe village and Clachaig Hotel. Do not descend S from this col as that leads one down across the grazing land above Leacantuim farm, which should be avoided.

There is an obvious path on the west side of Clachaig Gully immediately north of Clachaig Hotel, but it should be avoided as a route of descent or ascent as it is badly eroded with a lot of loose stones and rock which, if dislodged, can be a hazard to climbers in the gully. This route is not recommended.

Looking across Glen Coe from the Aonach Eagach   G. Morice to Bidean nam Bian

Easy ascent routes to Sgorr nam Fiannaidh which avoid any scrambling are provided by either of the two recommended descent routes described above. The direct ascent from Loch Achtriochtan is a long continuous slog. (1½km; 900m; 1h 50min). The route by the Pap of Glencoe col, though longer in distance, is probably more enjoyable. (4km; 950m; 2h 30min).

The only easy route to Meall Dearg is from the north. Start from the A863 road on the south side of Loch Leven just east of Caolasnacon and climb up the north side of the Allt Gleann a'Chaolais to the col at the foot of the north-east ridge of Meall Dearg. This ridge leads easily to the summit. (4½km; 910m; 2h 40min).

The southern flank of the Aonach Eagach is in National Trust for Scotland territory, and there are no restrictions on climbing on that side of the ridge in the stalking season.

Looking east from Sgorr nam Fiannaidh to Stob Coire Leith, Meall Dearg and Am Bodach   D.J. Bennet

Bidean nam Bian from Beinn a'Bheithir   G.S. Johnstone

Bidean nam Bian; 1150m; (OS Sheet 41; 143542); M 23; *peak of the mountains*

The highest mountain in Argyll, Bidean nam Bian is a compact and complex massif, the name applying to the highest point as well as to the mountain as a whole. The main ridge is a north-facing arc with a subsidiary **Y**-shaped ridge projecting northwards to enclose three fine corries above Glen Coe. So high and steep are the peaks above the glen, the Three Sisters, that it is difficult to get a view of the summit of Bidean, which is hidden behind them, but from Loch Achtriochtan there is an impressive glimpse of the two huge buttresses beneath the summit. The two slightly lower Tops Stob Coire nan Lochan (1115m) and Stob Coire nam Beith (1107m) are more prominent when seen from the glen, both appearing as great rock peaks. The whole massif is rocky and steep-sided, and even the easiest walking routes to the summit of Bidean involve some mild scrambling.

Start just west of Loch Achtriochtan where the road to Clachaig Hotel leaves the A82. Climb over the wall at the west end of the bridge over the River Coe and follow the path on the west side of the burn coming down from Coire nam Beith. This path leads high up into the corrie, passing some fine waterfalls and at one point traversing across a steep rocky hillside where some easy scrambling is needed. At about 520m there is a confluence of streams on the east side of the path, and at this point, with the great rock cone of Stob Coire nam Beith directly ahead, there is a choice of routes.

One way goes SE, across a stream and up the corrie towards Bidean, still following a path with the great buttresses of Stob Coire nam Beith on one's right. Higher up, with the path fading, aim for the bealach at 1000m between Bidean nam Bian and Stob Coire nan Lochan, and climb steep boulder and scree slopes to reach that point. There turn SW and climb steeply and directly, passing the level shoulder at the top of the Diamond Buttress, to the summit of Bidean. (3½km; 1040m; 2h 30min).

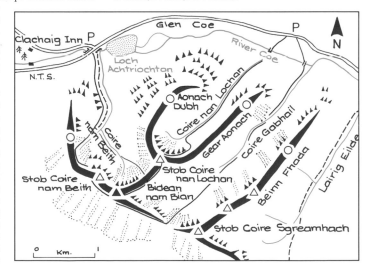

Looking along the ridge from Stob Coire Sgreamhach to Bidean nam Bian   K.M. Andrew

The alternative route continues SSW from the confluence of streams in Coire nam Beith up a steepening slope of grass, boulders and scree to reach the main ridge of the mountain ½km WNW of Stob Coire nam Beith. Follow the path up the ridge to this peak, then SE to the west peak of Bidean, and finally a few hundred metres E to the summit. (3½ km; 1080m; 2h 40min).

Two other routes may be mentioned which are as fine as the ones described above, and taken in conjunction with them can give a variety of excellent traverses of Bidean. Both can be started at the large car park beside the A82 road in Glen Coe at (172568). For the Coire nan Lochan route, cross the River Coe by the bridge at (167566) and take the narrow path up the corrie high on the south-east side of the stream. Once the level upper corrie is reached, bear SE and climb the steep east ridge of Stob Coire nan Lochan. From there traverse SW to reach the summit of Bidean.

The route up Coire Gabhail (The Lost Valley) starts at the same place and crosses the River Coe by a footbridge at (173564), thereafter following a good path up towards the corrie. At the mouth of the corrie the path disappears under a maze of huge fallen boulders, but it reappears higher up and is followed on the north-west side of the deep gorge through

which flows the Allt Coire Gabhail. Continue SW up a scree and boulder slope to the col at the head of the corrie (950m) and finally climb the south-west ridge of Bidean for 1km to the summit.

The N side of the mountain is in National Trust for Scotland territory, and there are no restrictions on climbing on that side at any time.

Bidean nam Bian from Stob Coire nan Lochan   P. Hodgkiss

Sgorr Dhearg from Sgorr Dhonuill   *I. Brown*

Sgorr Dhearg; 1024m; (OS Sheet 41; 056558); M104; *red peak*
Sgorr Dhonuill; 1001m; (OS Sheet 41; 040555); M132; *Donald's peak*

Beinn a'Bheithir, meaning *hill of the thunderbolt,* is a fine mountain rising above the narrows at the entrance to Loch Leven at South Ballachulish. Its two peaks lie on a long curving ridge which encloses north-facing corries, and except on their steepest and highest slopes these corries are clothed with vast areas of conifers which cover the lower hillsides and extend high up into the heart of the mountain. Thus access to the north side of the mountain is effectively restricted to one or two routes following roads through the forest. Above the tree-line most of the ground is bouldery, that on Sgorr Dhearg being a pink quartzite, and that on Sgorr Dhonuill granite. There is a splendid view of the whole mountain from the A82 road near North Ballachulish, and there are superb views on a clear day from the summits, views which combine the mountains of Glen Coe and Lochaber with the seascapes to the west.

Leave the A828 road at (044595) about 1km west of the Ballachulish bridge and follow the minor road SSE for ½km to the group of houses at the foot of Gleann a'Chaolais where cars can be left. Continue S up the Forestry Commission road on the west side of the main stream, ignoring branch roads to the right. After 2km the road zig-zags up steeper ground, trending left past an old quarry and reaching a cross-road. Continue straight across and round another zig-zag until the road (which is now heading NE) levels out at a concrete bridge and crosses a burn at (047569).

Just east of this burn a cairn by the roadside marks the start of a path, cairned in places, which climbs SE through the trees onto the open hillside. Above the tree-line continue S up rough grassland and boulders to the bealach (757m) between the two peaks of Beinn a'Bheithir.

From the bealach both peaks are easily reached along the main ridge of the mountain. There is a faint path up the stony ridge to Sgorr Dhearg. (5½km; 1000m; 3h). Return to the bealach and climb the ridge due W to a level section at 930m, followed by a steep and narrow scramble to Sgorr Dhonuill. (7½ km; 1250m; 3h 50min). Return to the bealach and descend by the route of ascent.

An alternative ascent of Beinn a'Bheithir, which can be combined with the above route to give a fine traverse, starts from Ballachulish. Go S from the school for 1km along a path (which is the start of the right of way leading to Glen Creran) then climb SW up a steep and well-defined ridge which leads to the main spine of the mountain a few hundred metres north-east of Sgorr Bhan (947m), the north-east Top of Sgorr Dhearg. The ridge connecting these two summits forms a beautiful curving arc leading to Sgorr Dhearg (4km; 1040m; 2h 40min), and from there the traverse to Sgorr Dhonuill may be continued as described above.

No access problems in the stalking season.

Sgorr Dhonuill from Sgorr Dhearg   *I. Brown*

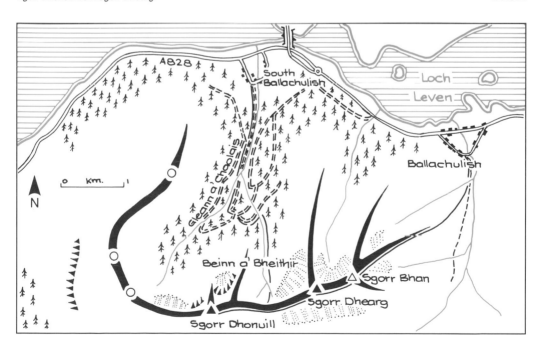

The Mamores, with Binnein Beag and Binnein Mor prominent, seen from the north   *D.N. Williams*

SECTION 4

Loch Linnhe to Loch Ericht

The Mamores

Between Loch Leven and Glen Nevis there stretches for 15 kilometres one of the finest mountain ranges in Scotland, the Mamores. Eleven Munros are linked by narrow curving ridges, their flanks scalloped by many corries, while through the mountains there is a remarkable network of stalker's paths, climbing up the corries and along the ridges, some of them taking spectacular lines across steep hillsides thus giving easy routes to many of the peaks.

There are three points of access to the Mamores that are particularly useful. On the south side one can either start at sea-level from Kinlochleven, or drive up a rough road to Mamore Lodge at a height of 200m and park a car there for a charge. From the lodge a Land Rover track traverses across the hillside, both to the east and west, at a height of about 250m, and gives access to the southern corries.

If starting from Kinlochleven and heading for the eastern peaks, the following directions will be useful: Leave the the A82 at the northern end of Kinlochleven, turning ESE along a street to reach a very simple white church in 250 metres (188623). From the east of the church a path starts north, soon turning east for 200 metres before descending to a bridge across a burn. Beyond, the path climbs through trees and, at their upper limit, forks. Take the right fork and follow it for 750 metres through humpy and undulating ground to a ford, beyond which is another fork.

The left path goes north to the foot of Coire na Ba, the right path goes east towards Loch Eilde Mor, both paths joining the Land Rover track in a further few hundred metres.

If heading towards the western peaks from Kinlochleven, follow the West Highland Way from the village school and climb diagonally north-west up the wooded hillside, crossing the Mamore Lodge access road and reaching the Land Rover track higher up.

On the north side of the Mamores access is gained along the public road up Glen Nevis. Achriabhach is the starting point for the western peaks. Beyond there the road becomes very narrow and liable to congestion in summer, and it continues for a few kilometres to the car park at its end. From there the walk through the magnificent gorge of the River Nevis leads to the upper glen and the eastern peaks of the range.

This approach also serves for the Aonachs and Sgurr Choinnich Mor at the western end of the Grey Corries.

Many different combinations of the Mamore peaks can be climbed in a single day, from one alone to all eleven. The latter is a magnificent traverse, but only for the very fit. It is not unduly difficult to do them all in two or three days. However, in the following descriptions a more leisurely approach is taken, none of the expeditions described being at all long or strenuous.

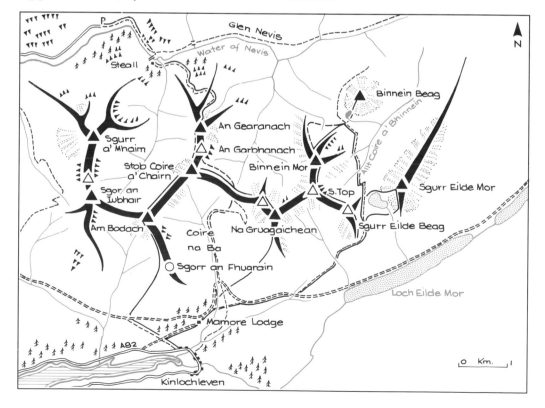

Sgurr Eilde Mor above Coire an Lochain   D.J. Bennet

Sgurr Eilde Mor; 1008m; (OS Sheet 41; 231658); M120; *big peak of the hind*

This is the remotest of the Mamores, lying 6km north-east of Kinlochleven, and separated from the other peaks at the east end of the range by a low col at 740m. In appearance, particularly when seen on the approach from Kinlochleven, it is a steep conical peak of scree and quartzite boulders rising splendidly above Coire an Lochain. North-eastwards from the summit the spine of the hill goes for 3½km towards the head of Glen Nevis, its crest paved with distinctive platelets of schist broken by outcrops of quartz.

Start the ascent from Kinlochleven or Mamore Lodge, and follow the Land Rover track E from the lodge to within 1km of Loch Eilde Mor (208635). There take the good stalker's path which climbs NE,

quite gradually at first, then more steeply to reach Coire an Lochain where a high loch is set in a fine position among spectacular surroundings. Above the loch Sgurr Eilde Mor rises for 270m in uniformly steep scree slopes of rather uninviting appearance. Two routes are possible. Either cross the level corrie on the south side of the loch and climb the south ridge, or go round the north side of the loch and climb the easiest line up the fairly well-defined west ridge. The two routes are very similar, both being on steep and bouldery quartzite with a few small crags. (From Kinlochleven: 7km; 1010m; 3h 20min).

Map on page 67.

Binnein Mor; 1128m; (OS Sheet 41; 212663); M30; *big peak*
Binnein Beag; 940m; (OS Sheet 41; 222677); M228; *small peak*

These two mountains lie north-east of Kinlochleven at the eastern end of the Mamore ridge. Binnein Mor is not only the highest, but also the finest of the range, having the classic mountain form of ridges and corries sweeping upwards to a narrow summit crest. From the north or south it appears as a single sharp peak, while from the east or west its level summit ridge gives it the appearance of a great tent. By comparison, Binnein Beag is small and quite different in shape, being a little conical peak. The two are separated by a high bealach at 750m.

The approach from Kinlochleven or Mamore Lodge follows the same route by track and stalker's path as that described above for Sgurr Eilde Mor as far as Coire an Lochain. From there keep N along the path, dropping slightly, going left at a fork and descending NW for a further 100m. A rising traverse

follows across the east face of Binnein Mor, crossing the headwaters of the Allt Coire a'Bhinnein to reach the wide bealach between the two peaks. Leave the stalker's path which has been followed to this point, and climb NE over scree and schistose boulders to the sharp summit of Binnein Beag. (9km; 1080m; 3h 50min). There is a splendid view, very open to the east towards the distant mass of Ben Alder, while the great bulk of Binnein Mor towers above in the south-west.

Return to the bealach and climb SSE to the toe of the ridge bounding the little north-east corrie of Binnein Mor on its north side. This ridge is narrow and steep and gives an excellent scramble on sound schist. It emerges on the sharp summit ridge 200 metres north of the cairn. (11½ km; 1460m; 5h). An easier alternative for the ascent of Binnein Mor is to traverse ¾km SW from the bealach to reach the NNW ridge

Binnein Beag   *A. O'Brien*

and climb the fine, but perfectly easy crest which curves up to the summit.

Continue S along the summit ridge to the South Top (1059m), then turn SE down a broad ridge for 1km to another Top, Sgurr Eilde Beag (956m). From there descend SSE until at 840m a stalker's path is reached which leads in well-engineered zigzags down to join the path of the uphill route, and so back to Kinlochleven.

Map on page 67.

Binnein Mor and Na Gruagaichean from the west   *D.J. Bennet*

Na Gruagaichean; 1055m; (OS
Sheet 41; 203652); M71; *the
maidens*
Stob Coire a'Chairn; 981m;
(OS Sheet 41; 185661); M165;
peak of the corrie of the cairn
Am Bodach; 1032m; (OS
Sheet 41; 176651); M96; *the old
man*

These three peaks form an arc
of ridges immediately north of
Kinlochleven, and they make a
natural traverse of not too great a
length. Na Gruagaichean is particularly prominent when seen
from the A82 road on the south
side of Loch Leven, from where it
has a huge tent-like appearance,
and it is often mistaken for the
hidden Binnein Mor. It has two
tops separated by a rocky ridge
which drops to a narrow gap
between them. Am Bodach is
another fine mountain with a particularly steep and rocky east face
above the head of Coire na Ba. Between these two Stob Coire
a'Chairn is a more modest peak
situated at the point where the An
Gearanach ridge runs out to the
north. With the exception of the
summits of Am Bodach and Na
Gruagaichean, this part of the
Mamore ridge is fairly grassy and
gives easy walking.

Start from Kinlochleven or Mamore Lodge and reach the Land
Rover track between Coire na Ba
and Loch Eilde Mor as described
for Sgurr Eilde Mor. From this
track climb NE up steep grassy
slopes for 500m to gain a stony
ridge which leads NNW and narrows towards the summit of Na
Gruagaichean. (4km; 1060m;

The North-west Top of Na Gruagaichean   D.J. Bennet

2h 40min). Descend very steeply NNW down a rocky
slope to a narrow col and climb an equally steep ridge,
very exposed on its north-east side, to the North-west
Top (1036m). Cross the short level summit and continue down the grassy ridge to the open bealach
(783m) at the head of Coire na Ba.

Three stalker's paths converge at this point. Continue NW along the one which leads up the broad
easy ridge to Stob Coire a'Chairn. (6km; 1300m;
3h 30min). Descend equally easily, crossing a small
bump, to the next bealach from where the north- east
ridge of Am Bodach rises abruptly. This ridge is steep

and rocky enough to make a pleasant scramble, and
the angle is maintained almost to the summit cairn.
(8km; 1550m; 4h 30min).

In descent follow the south-east ridge of Am
Bodach towards Sgorr an Fhuarain. Do not climb this
minor top, but descend to its west and bear SW to
avoid its steep and craggy south face. Grassy slopes
lead easily down to the Land Rover track 1½km west
of Mamore Lodge at the point where the path forming
part of the West Highland Way leads down to Kinlochleven through open woodland.

Map on page 67.

An Gearanach; 982m; (OS Sheet 41; 188670); M162; *the complainer*

An Gearanach is the northerly and highest point of
the short narrow ridge which projects north from Stob
Coire a'Chairn on the main spine of the Mamores.
This latter peak is not named on the OS 1:50000 map;

it is at (185661). The ridge passes over the rocky Top
of An Garbhanach (975m) and for about a hundred
metres at that point the crest is very narrow, rocky
and exposed, falling steeply on both sides. The An

An Gearanach and the Steall Waterfall from Glen Nevis   *W.D. Brooker*

Gearanach end is broader, grassy and perfectly easy, and north of this peak the ridge drops steeply towards Glen Nevis.

An Gearanach can be climbed equally well from Glen Nevis or, with rather more effort, from Kinlochleven. The Glen Nevis route starts at the car park at the road end and goes through the gorge, from where there is a magnificent view of the peak with its pendant waterfall. The path clings to the steep hillside, with crags above and the torrent of the River Nevis rushing below. Shortly after emerging onto the grassy flats of the upper glen, cross the river by a three-strand wire bridge and go E past the white climbers' cottage at Steall. Continue for ½km below the waterfall and past a wooded buttress until the path turns S up a little glen and becomes better defined. Climb the path in wide zigzags until the last long traverse leads onto the north ridge of An Gearanach, and follow this to the summit with fine views on either hand. (4½km; 850m; 2h 30min). The traverse along the narrow ridge to An Garbhanach is a pleasant airy walk, with some scrambling at its far end.

The alternative route from Kinlochleven involves first the ascent to the bridge where the Land Rover track crosses the Allt Coire na Ba, and then the ascent of the stalker's path up this corrie to the col at its head. From there either climb Stob Coire a'Chairn and descend steeply NNE to the bealach below An Garbhanach, or traverse below its north-east face to reach the bealach more directly.

The ascent of An Garbhanach and its traverse are rocky, and some scrambling is involved before the ridge widens and leads easily to An Gearanach. (7km; 1130m; 3h 30min). This route can readily be combined with that described on the previous page to enable An Gearanach to be traversed with its three neighbouring peaks. Map on page 67.

An Garbhanach with Ben Nevis beyond   *D.J. Bennet*

Sgurr a'Mhaim, with Stob Choire a'Mhail to its left, from Sgor an Iubhair   A. O'Brien

Sgurr a'Mhaim; 1099m; (OS Sheet 41; 165667); M49; *peak of the large rounded hill*
Sgor an Iubhair; 1001m; (OS Sheet 41; 165655); M133; *peak of the yew*

The dominating mountain in the western half of the Mamore range is Sgurr a'Mhaim, standing at the end of the longest of the arms projecting northward from the main ridge. There is a clear view of the peak from lower Glen Nevis, its great bulk fills the valley and the quartzite capping of its summit is very evident in certain lights. On its north and north-east sides there are two finely sculptured corries, below which the lower slopes of the mountain end abruptly in cliffs dropping into the Nevis gorge.

Southwards from the summit of Sgurr a'Mhaim the ridge leading to the main spine of the Mamores is one of the finest sections of the range; it forms a sharp arête, the Devil's Ridge, which near its mid-point rises to the Top of Stob Choire a'Mhail (980m), and continues to Sgor an Iubhair, a flat-topped summit on the main ridge. (Neither of these peaks is named on the Ordnance Survey 1:50,000 map). The traverse of the Devil's Ridge is one of the highlights of hillwalking in the Mamores. Everyone will find it an exhilarating scramble, some may consider it to be a bit too exposed for their liking, but there are no real difficulties.

Start in Glen Nevis 300 metres east of Achriabhach and take the path up the east bank of the Allt Coire a'Mhusgain. After ½km leave the path and climb SE up the steep shoulder between the north and west faces of Sgurr a'Mhaim. Half way up, the zigzags of

a stalker's path on the west side of the shoulder give some respite from the steady steep climb, and at 800m the angle eases and the grassy slopes of the lower hillside give way to quartzite boulders and scree. Higher up the route follows the rim of the north corrie to the cairn of Sgurr a'Mhaim. (3km; 1050m; 2h 30min).

To continue the traverse, descend S down open slopes which soon converge to the narrow arête of the Devil's Ridge. Near the lowest point there are two short, exposed and slightly awkward sections where some might welcome the security of a rope, particularly in winter. Continuing up the ridge, there is an airy climb up the very exposed crest to the Top of Stob Choire a'Mhail. From there the route is much easier, descending to a broad col and climbing steeply up boulders to the flat top of Sgor an Iubhair. (4½km; 1190m; 3h).

Descend SW then W for 1km along a stalker's path to the col at the head of Coire a'Mhusgain, then turn N down the path in this corrie to return to Achriabhach.

Alternatively, from the col it is very straightforward to continue the traverse over Stob Ban and Mullach nan Coirean by following in reverse the route described on the following pages.

Map on page 75.

Stob Choire a'Mhail from the north   *D.J. Bennet*

The north ridge of Stob Choire a'Mhail   *D.J. Bennet*

Stob Ban from the east   A. O'Brien

Mullach nan Coirean; 939m; (OS Sheet 41; 122662); M231; *summit of the corries*
Stob Ban; 999m; (OS Sheet 41; 148654); M138; *white peak*

These two peaks lie at the western end of the Mamore ridge, and are most easily accessible from Glen Nevis. Mullach nan Coirean is a sprawling mass of grassy ridges enclosing several corries, as befits its name. Stob Ban makes a contrast with its shapely summit cone and fine line of buttresses and gullies on the north-east side of the peak. It makes a fine sight from the road near Glen Nevis youth hostel with its cap of quartzite looking curiously like snow in some lights. Though the Mullach is itself relatively shapeless, it does present an attractive profile when seen from the path through the Nevis gorge, and its summit is an unexpectedly rewarding viewpoint.

Start the traverse at Achriabhach in Glen Nevis from where access to the north-east ridge of Mullach nan Coirean can be gained through the forest. Go through the gate opposite the cottages and about 150 metres along the forest road take a path left (SW) through the trees to reach in about 300 metres the same road higher up. Turn left, round the next bend and then straight on NW to the road end at a stream. Climb up a path on the east bank of the stream out of the forest and then follow the fence SE to reach the north-east ridge of Mullach nan Coirean. This leads at an easy angle for 2½ km to the summit. (4km; 890m; 2h 30min). There are fine views from this ridge of the great hump of Ben Nevis, and from the summit there is an equally fine view down Loch Linnhe.

The north-east face of Stob Ban   D.J. Bennet

Mullach nan Coirean from the west ridge of Stob Ban   D.N. Williams

To continue to Stob Ban, descend SE down easy slopes along the rim of one of the northerly corries and follow an undulating ridge that goes SE and then S over a minor bump to the Mullach's South-east Top (917m). Beyond, the ridge becomes better defined and rockier, bearing NE over a minor top, then dropping E to the col (846m) between the two mountains. At this point the red granite rocks of Mullach nan Coirean suddenly change to the pale grey quartzite that gives Stob Ban its name. Finally, climb E then S

more steeply up angular quartzite boulders along the rim of the north-east cliffs to the summit of Stob Ban. (7½km; 1130m; 3h 40min).

In descent, follow the narrow shattered east ridge steeply down to grassier slopes, reaching a stalker's path near the col at the head of the Coire a'Mhusgain. Follow the branch of this path that goes N down the corrie on the east side of the stream, leading directly back to Achriabhach.

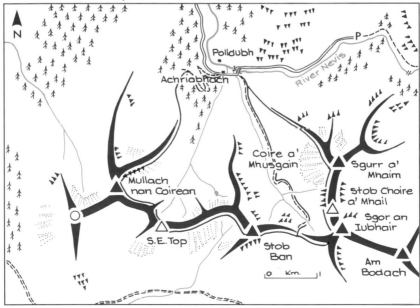

Ben Nevis from the Carn Mor Dearg Arête   *D. Scott*

Ben Nevis; 1344m; (OS Sheet 41; 166713); M1; *possibly from an old Gaelic word meaning venomous*
Carn Mor Dearg; 1223m; (OS Sheet 41; 177722); M7; *big red hill*

For the average hill-goer, Ben Nevis is not just the highest mountain in the British Isles, its traverse combined with that of Carn Mor Dearg provides a taste of mountaineering amongst scenery of a magnificence not to be found elsewhere on the mainland of Britain. The two peaks form a vast horseshoe facing north-west, with the simple shape of Carn Mor Dearg's slender ridge contrasting starkly with the huge and complex mass of Ben Nevis, whose north-east face presents the grandest array of cliffs of any Scottish mountain. Another contrast appears between the pink granite of Carn Mor Dearg and the grey andesite of the Ben, a contrast made more obvious by the great exposure of rock, boulders and scree on both mountains.

Unfortunately, the hillwalker on the 'tourist route' up Ben Nevis gets little impression of its great mountain architecture, and one has to go round to the north-east side of the mountain, into the glen of the Allt a' Mhuillin, to appreciate its scale and grandeur. For this reason the traverse from Carn Mor Dearg to Ben Nevis is recommended as the finest way for a fit and competent hillwalker to reach the summit of Scotland's highest mountain. The best roadside view is from the A82 a few kilometres north-east of Fort William, and even from a distance of several kilometres the scale of the cliffs in the great northern cirque can be appreciated.

The route to Ben Nevis starts at Achintee on the east side of the River Nevis and follows the excellent path which climbs across the flanks of Meall an t-Suidhe. The same path can be reached from the Glen Nevis youth hostel by a bridge across the river. After 2½ km

and 500m of ascent the path emerges onto the broad bealach holding Lochan Meall an t-Suidhe, and starts a series of uphill zigzags. It is worthwhile following the path as any short-cuts involve rough going. Above, the path crosses a deep gully, the Red Burn, and continues its zigzags up increasingly bouldery ground to the extensive summit plateau. At the top there are the remains of the observatory, a small shelter, several cairns and a trig point, and a few metres to the north the cliffs drop vertically. In spring and early summer the cornices at the cliff-edge are likely to be dangerously unstable, so beware of approaching the edge too closely. (7km; 1340m; 3h 50min).

To reach Carn Mor Dearg, follow the Ben Nevis path as far as Lochan Meall an t-Suidhe. Continue NNE along a level path for about 1km and there, where the path turns ESE, descend NE across rough heathery ground to cross the Allt a' Mhuilinn near (154739). Now climb E up rough bouldery slopes for 600m to reach Carn Beag Dearg (1010m), and from there traverse the high ridge which stretches for 2km over Carn Dearg Meadhonach (1179m) to Carn Mor Dearg. (8km; 1450m; 4h 10min). The crest of this ridge provides easy walking and splendid views of the great cliffs of Ben Nevis's northern cirque.

To continue the traverse to Ben Nevis, follow the well-defined ridge S. After 200m of descent it sharpens to a narrow arête composed of huge granite blocks. Keeping to the crest makes for a fine scramble, but a faint path just below the crest on its south-east side avoids the tricky sections and much of the exposure. Throughout its length the Carn Mor Dearg Arête gives a superb view of the Ben's great ridges and

Looking up the Arête to Carn Mor Dearg   *P. Hodgkiss*

corries, with the outline of the North-East Buttress growing more and more impressive.

About 300 metres beyond the lowest point of the arête, at a level place below the final steep climb towards Ben Nevis, a post on the right-hand (N) edge of the ridge marks the start of a moderately easy descent into Coire Leis which might be used as an escape route in bad weather or failing light. However, if there is snow on the headwall of Coire Leis this descent is not advised unless the party has ice-axes or crampons. Above that point the arête merges into the bulk of Ben Nevis and it is worthwhile hunting for the faint path that climbs for 250m through the litter of giant boulders to the top. (10km; 1750m; 5h 10min).

No restriction on climbing during the stalking season.

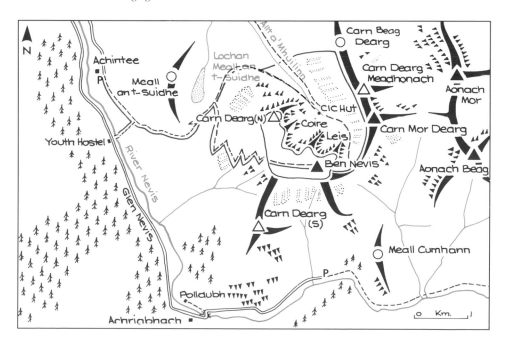

Aonach Mor from Glen Spean   D. Scott

Aonach Beag; 1234m; (OS Sheet 41; 196715); M6; *little hill*
Aonach Mor; 1221m; (OS Sheet 41; 193730); M8; *big hill*

The Aonachs (as these two mountains are often called) form a great high ridge, several kilometres long from south to north, lying to the east of Ben Nevis and Carn Mor Dearg, and connected to the latter by a high bealach at 830m. Although the crest of the ridge, particularly on Aonach Mor, is fairly flat and broad, the slopes to east and west are very steep, forming wild and remote corries, so these two mountains call for respect, especially in bad weather. They make a fine natural traverse, best approached from Glen Nevis, although an ascent from the north is also possible.

Aonach Mor is a long flat-topped mountain whose finest feature is its steep and scalloped east face which holds snow well into summer. Aonach Beag has a more rounded summit guarded by crags and corries on all sides. The best impression of this pair is gained from the Grey Corries from where their east-facing corries are well seen, with Ben Nevis appearing over the connecting ridge.

Start from the car park at the end of the road in Glen Nevis and take the path through the Nevis gorge and along the north side of the Water of Nevis to the bridge across the Allt Coire Giubhsachan at the ruined Steall cottage. Above, to the NE, Aonach Beag forms a wide corrie, enclosed by its south-west ridge on one side and the pointed Top of Sgurr a'Bhuic (965m) on the other. Bear NNE over hummocky ground and climb steeply towards the corrie for 1½ km, trending N to reach the south-west ridge of Aonach Beag. This ridge leads easily to the top. (6½ km; 1100m; 3h 20min).

A longer and more scenic route bears NE from the Steall ruin to reach the south-west ridge of Sgurr a'Bhuic. Traverse this Top and descend steeply NE along a rocky ridge with crags on the right to a col at 898m. Climb again to a small unnamed point (1049m), turn W over the Top of Stob Coire Bhealaich (1101m) and finally NW up stony ground to the summit of Aonach Beag. (8km; 1200m; 3h 50min).

To continue the traverse descend NW down rocky slopes that fall away to the right in steep crags, and reach the well-defined bealach at 1080m. Beyond, an easy rise up a broad grassy ridge leads in just over 1km to the cairn of Aonach Mor which, in poor visibility, may not be easy to find on the featureless expanse of the summit plateau. (9½km; 1330m; 4h 20min).

To return to Glen Nevis, retrace the route south, keeping near the western cliffs of Aonach Mor for about ¾km to (192722). At this point turn W down a steep, ill-defined spur to the bealach at 830m under Carn Mor Dearg. In bad visibility careful navigation is required to find the correct point of descent, as the ground on either side is very steep. Finally go S down Coire Giubhsachan to reach the path in Glen Nevis.

The northern approach to Aonach Mor has been made easier, and at the same time much less attractive, by the ski developments in the corrie of the Allt an t-Sneachda. It is possible to take a gondola up to about 650m and walk up the upper half of the mountain. However, if one's transport arrangements permit, the descent by this route after traversing Aonach Beag from Glen Nevis is a fine expedition, with meals and refreshments available at the Snow Goose restaurant at the top of the gondola before riding down to the Leanachan Forest.

Sgurr Choinnich Mor from the north-east   D.J. Bennet

Sgurr Choinnich Mor; 1095m; (OS Sheet 41; 227714); M50, *big peak of the moss*

This sharp and shapely peak lies directly north of the watershed at the head of Glen Nevis, and with its smaller companion Sgurr Choinnich Beag (966m) it marks the south-western end of the Grey Corries ridge. Sgurr Choinnich Mor has a narrow rocky summit ridge, dropping steeply on both sides, and it is the finest of the Grey Corries, comparable with Binnein Mor on the opposite side of Glen Nevis, and having the vast and steep corries of Aonach Beag close to the west to add to its mountainous setting.

Although Sgurr Choinnich Mor can be climbed from the north in combination with other peaks of the Grey Corries, that approach is quite long. A rather shorter route is from the car park at the road end in Glen Nevis. Follow the path through the Nevis gorge, and stay on the path along the north side of the Water of Nevis to the bridge over the Allt Coire Giublisachan and the ruined cottage at Steall. Continue along the path for a further 2km until it leaves the main river to cross a minor side stream.

From that point climb NNE up grassy slopes beside this stream to reach the bealach at the foot of the south-west ridge of Sgurr Choinnich Beag. Climb this ridge which steepens and becomes quite narrow as it nears the distinctive Top. Descend E for 70m to a high col, and continue ENE up increasingly rocky ground to the summit of Sgurr Choinnich Mor. (8½km; 1030m; 3h 40min).

The north-east ridge of Sgurr Choinnich Mor, which connects it to the rest of the Grey Corries, has a rocky section at about its mid-

point where the path goes on the east side of the crest. Below that point the ridge drops to a broad col from which rises the rocky south-west ridge of Stob Coire Easain.

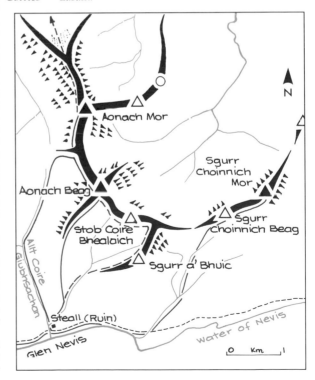

On the ridge of the Grey Corries looking north-east to Stob Choire Claurigh   J. Renny

Stob Choire Claurigh; 1177m; (OS Sheet 41; 262739); M14; *claurigh is probably from Gaelic clamhras, brawling or clamouring*
Stob Coire an Laoigh; 1115m; (OS Sheet 41; 240725); M37; *peak of the corrie of the calf*

These two peaks are 3km apart at the ends of a high ridge to the south of Spean Bridge and the extensive Leanachan Forest. They are part of the long chain of mountains extending eastwards from Ben Nevis over Aonach Beag and Sgurr Choinnich Mor. The pale grey quartzite screes which cover their higher slopes earn for them the name The Grey Corries, and when viewed in good lighting from the north-west, e.g. from the Commando Memorial above Spean Bridge, the aptness of this name is very obvious. The roll-call of two Munros and six Tops flatters to deceive, for the crest of the ridge undulates gently, its lowest point being 980m, and it gives an excellent high-level ridge walk.

The best approach is on the north side, from Corriechoille farm in Glen Spean which is reached from Spean Bridge by the narrow public road on the south side of the River Spean. The road which goes 2km S past the farm to the disused tramway is private, but at the time of writing no objection is made to driving up to the remains of the narrow gauge track that was laid to facilitate cutting the tunnel from Loch Treig to the Fort William Aluminium Works.

Continue SE through the forest up the road which leads to the Lairig Leacach. In 1½km leave the forest and turn SSW up steep grassy slopes which continue unrelentingly for 600m to the first Top, Stob Coire na Gaibhre (955m). Beyond, the ridge becomes narrower with steep slopes on the left dropping into Coire na Ceannain with its almost perfectly circular lochan,

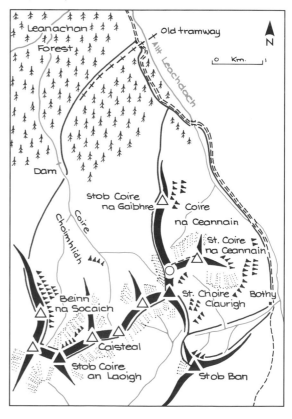

and higher up past a minor bump it forms a narrow rocky crest for a few hundred metres before the summit of Stob Choire Claurigh is reached, (6km; 1020m; 3h 10min).

Turning WSW, the ridge undulates gently and a faint path eases the rough going over sharp and angular quartzite scree. From east to west the traverse includes the Tops of Stob a' Choire Leith (1105m), Stob Coire Cath na Sine (1080m), and Caisteal (1104m) before reaching the second Munro, Stob Coire an Laoigh, not named on the Ordnance Survey 1:50,000 map, but notable for its dark northern cliff. (9km; 1220m; 4h 10min).

The crest continues WNW to the Top of Stob Coire Easain (1080m) at which point a ridge running N to the last Top, Beinn na Socaich (1007m) marks the line of descent. Continue along the broad ridge for 1½km past this Top, then turn NE down into Coire Choimhlidh by grassy slopes. Cross to the east side of the Allt Coire Choimhlidh above the forest, and descend past a small dam to reach the end of the road. Go along this road for ½km and then turn NE along the clearing of the tramway back to the day's starting point.

Stob Ban from the Lairig Leacach   D.J. Bennet

Stob Ban; 977m; (OS Sheet 41; 266724); M173; *white peak*

Stob Ban is a remote peak, far distant from any main road and hidden behind its higher neighbours. It lies at the east end of the Grey Corries ridge, separated from it by a bealach of 800m, and it is from viewpoints near the head of Glen Nevis or in the Lairig Leacach that one gets the best views of this solitary conical peak.

The shortest approach is from Corriechoille farm in Glen Spean, as described above for Stob Coire Claurigh, by the track to the Lairig Leacach. Cross this pass and descend on its south side for 1½km to a small bothy from where there is a good view of Stob Ban. Beyond, the track fords a burn and forks; take the right fork and after 100 metres bear SW up the grassy hillside. At 650m the slope narrows to a ridge which at 750m levels to a flat shoulder before the final steep rocky rise to the summit. (9km; 790m; 3h 20min).

The return can be pleasantly varied by descending

NW down a short slope of quartzite screes, then N to the 800m bealach where there is a small lochan. From there turn ENE and go down a giant's staircase of quartzite slabs which spills downwards for over 150m and gives an easy scramble when dry. Below, the burn leads back to the bothy and the short climb over the Lairig Leacach on the return to Glen Spean.

Stob Ban can be combined with some of the other peaks of The Grey Corries. From the 800m bealach, a broad ridge leads N and levels out to turn NW to the summit of Stob Choire Claurigh. If descending N from there back to Glen Spean, it is worth making the short diversion to Stob Coire na Ceannain. This is a very fine looking peak, rather detached from the main ridge of the Grey Corries. The short connecting ridge is narrow and rocky, and gives a pleasant easy scramble.

Stob Coire Easain from Stob a'Choire Mheadhoin   W.D. Brooker

Stob Coire Easain; 1116m; (OS Sheet 41; 308730); M36; *peak of the corrie of the little waterfall*
Stob a'Choire Mheadhoin; 1106m; (OS Sheet 41; 316736); M44; *peak of the middle corrie*

These two mountains form a high ridge 10km long to the east of the Grey Corries. The two summits are near the middle of this ridge, and are separated by a col at 960m. To the east and west there are steep slopes, those to the east being particularly so and giving Loch Treig a fiord-like character. The two mountains are prominent in views from the south, appearing like twins, while from the north in Glen Spean there is a fine view of Stob a'Choire Mheadhoin, with Stob Coire Easain just appearing behind it. It is from Glen Spean that the two are most usually climbed.

Leave the A86 road in Glen Spean 7½km east of Roy Bridge and drive along the narrow public road to Fersit almost to the outflow of An Dubh Lochan (349790). Start the ascent from there and go SW across level ground for a short distance, cross the line of the old tramway and continue SSW along the crest of the ridge. In 3km there is a steep climb to Meall Cian Dearg, the best way being on the east side of the nose, and above it the ridge continues with level sections and short rises to the summit of Stob a'Choire Mheadhoin. (7km; 870m; 3h). Descend SW to the col and climb quite steeply to the summit of Stob Coire Easain (8km; 1030m; 3h 30min).

The descent may be made by retracing the ascent, with the additional climb over Stob a'Choire Mheadhoin. Alternatively, from the col between the two peaks descend NW into a fine corrie and continue downhill, gradually bearing N then NE down Coire Laire. In due course a path is joined on the south-east side of the Allt Laire, and further down the line of the old tramway leads back to the starting point.

A fine traverse of these two peaks can be made from Corrour Halt on the West Highland Railway to Fersit. From Corrour follow the track to Creaguaineach Lodge at the head of Loch Treig. Cross the Allt na Lairige and from a point 1km along the path to the Lairig Leacach climb the long south ridge of Stob Coire Easain. Continue the traverse as described above.

Looking south across the flat summit of Chno Dearg to Meall Garbh; Beinn na Lap on the left   *K.M. Andrew*

Stob Coire Sgriodain; 976m, (OS Sheet 41; 356744); M174; *peak of the corrie of the scree*
Chno Dearg; 1047m; (OS Sheet 41; 377741); M82; *on early maps the name appears as cnoc dearg, red hill*

Together with Chno Dearg's southern Top, Meall Garbh (977m), these hills make an easy hillwalking circuit from Fersit, the small group of cottages at the north end of Loch Treig reached by a minor road leaving the A86 7½km east of Roy Bridge. Stob Coire Sgriodain is a rugged hill on the east side of Loch Treig, dropping very steeply into the loch at an average angle of over 30 degrees. Above 500m it forms a north-south ridge that is rough and craggy and has three distinct tops. This ridge curls round to the south-east and merges with Chno Dearg, a rounded and featureless hill with open and easy-angled northern slopes. Both hills are well seen from the main road in Glen Spean.

Starting at Fersit, follow the forestry road E for almost ½km and then turn S across rough ground, usually wet and boggy for the first 1½km. Beyond a minor craggy top at 450m, the open slopes steepen to form a ridge with small crags which can easily be turned on one side or the other, and the next top, Sron na Garbh-bheinne is reached. A short level shoulder is passed, and the ridge narrows and rises to the summit of Stob Coire Sgriodain, from where there is a splendid view of the fiord-like Loch Treig. (4½km; 730m; 2h 20min).

A combination of knolly tops and two intervening drops makes the next section of the traverse confusing in bad visibility. Descend S for 60m to a pronounced col and turn SE up the South Top of Stob Coire Sgriodain (960m). Continue ESE over knolly ground and reach another distinct double-headed top (925m) in ½km. A short descent, still ESE, leads to an open col with a scatter of tiny lochans. Continue in the same direction, climbing easily to the ridge of Meall Garbh,

and turn S to reach the cairn on its south top. Return N then NNE across another open col above which easy slopes covered by dwarf vegetation lead to the flat, boulder-strewn summit of Chno Dearg. (8½km; 1020m; 3h 40min). Descend NNW down a wide grassy corrie in a direct line back to Fersit.

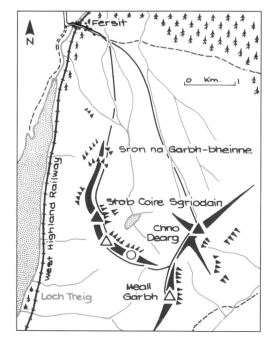

Creag Pitridh from Moy in Glen Spean   *H.M. Brown*

Beinn a'Chlachair; 1088m; (OS Sheet 42; 471781); M53; *stonemason's hill*
Geal Charn; 1049m; (OS Sheet 42; 504812); M78; *white hill*
Creag Pitridh; 924m; (OS Sheet 42; 488814); M260; *meaning uncertain, perhaps from the surname Petrie*

This group of mountains lies south of Loch Laggan and is most readily approached from the A86 road. Beinn a'Chlachair is prominent in the roadside view from Moy, looking like a great whaleback with a prominent corrie scooped out of its north flank just below the summit. To its north-east Creag Pitridh is a much smaller peak with a pointed summit and broken crags on its west face overlooking Lochan na h'Earba. Between these two Geal Charn appears as rather a featureless flat-topped hill, but the best view of it is from the north-east, looking up the glen of the River Pattack from the vicinity of Laggan Bridge. The group is penetrated by an extensive system of estate roads and stalker's paths which makes access to the tops fairly easy, even though they are some distance from the road.

Leave the A86 road at the concrete bridge over the River Spean 1km south-west of the outflow of Loch Laggan near Moy, and follow the rough road up the east side of the Amhainn Ghuilbinn for about 1 km. Then take a left turn (still on a dirt road) and go E for ½km, then go right along another track which leads horizontally round the base of Binnein Shuas to the south-west end of Lochan na h-Earba. Leave the track (which continues along the loch) and follow a stalker's path SE up the Allt Coire Pitridh for about 1½km, then bear S up the very open slopes on the north-east flank of Beinn a'Chlachair. Above 900m the ground levels out at a shoulder and the route bears round the rim of Coire Mor a'Chlachair over a waste

of boulders, many of them of surprisingly regular shape. The large summit cairn is set a short distance back from the edge of the corrie. (9km; 840m; 3h 30min).

Go ENE along the broad summit ridge for almost 2½ km, at which point the level shoulder ends abruptly above a large crag. Descend N to avoid this crag and soon reach a stalker's path which forks a short distance lower. Take the right path and go N, climbing slightly to its highest point on the west flank of Geal Charn. Turn E and climb easy slopes of heath and boulders to the flat summit. (14km; 1150m; 5h 10min).

Retrace the route to the col west of Geal Charn and make the short, easy ascent of Creag Pitridh, keeping to the left of craggy ground. (16km; 1300m; 5h 50min). Descend SW to regain the stalker's path along the Allt Coire Pitridh, and return by the outward route.

Beinn a'Chlachair and Geal Charn can also be climbed from the east, although Creag Pitridh is not so accessible from that direction. It is necessary to reach Loch Pattack first, possibly by bicycle from Dalwhinnie along the private road beside Loch Ericht. From Loch Pattack follow the track west to the ford across the Allt Cam and continue up the path towards Loch a'Bhealaich Leamhain. From a point 1km along the path from the ford it is straightforward either to bear W to reach the outer end of Beinn a'Chlachair's north-east ridge, or bear NNW up open slopes to Geal Charn.

Beinn a'Chlachair from Loch Pattack   H.M. Brown

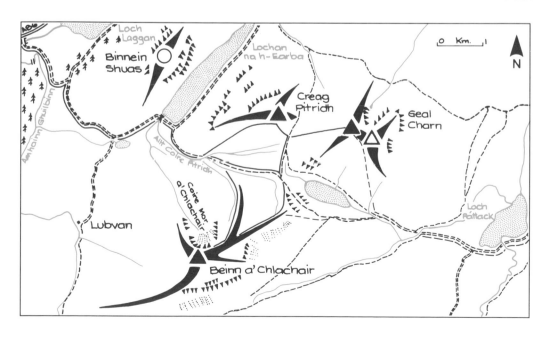

Beinn na Lap from Loch Ossian   P. Hodgkiss

Beinn na Lap; 937m; (OS Sheet 41; 376696); M232; *mottled hill? (lap means a defective spot in a colour)*

Beinn na Lap may be classed as one of the easiest ascents among the Munros, although it does require a train journey to reach its foot. It lies 4km north-east of Corrour Halt, altitude 400m, on the West Highland Railway and looms quite steeply above the northern shore of Loch Ossian. There is a clear view of the hill from Corrour, but from elsewhere its featureless whaleback is not readily identified.

Reach Corrour by either the south or north-bound train and follow the track E towards Loch Ossian. After 1¼ km take the left fork in the track along the north side of the loch, and soon leave it to climb N on easy-angled slopes of dwarf vegetation. At 700m a broad ridge is reached and followed ENE to the summit of Beinn na Lap, which provides a remarkable contrast in views, with the wide expanse of Rannoch Moor to the south-west and a complicated tangle of peaks around the northern arc. (5km; 540m; 2h).

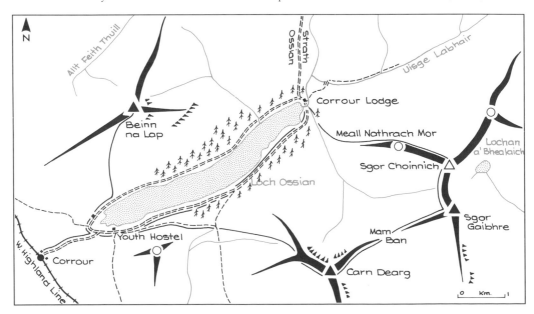

The north-east face of Sgor Gaibhre above Lochan a'Bhealaich   *P. Hodgkiss*

Sgor Gaibhre; 955m; (OS Sheets 41 and 42; 444674); M203; *goat's peak*
Carn Dearg; 941 m; (OS Sheets 41 and 42; 418661); M225; *red hill*

These hills, together with the Top, Sgor Choinnich (927m), make a fine round from Corrour Halt on the West Highland Railway. It is quite a long circuit, and one may have to move fast to complete it between the morning and evening trains. Sgor Gaibhre and Carn Dearg lie between Loch Ossian and Loch Ericht and enclose in their open corries the gathering grounds for some of the largest herds of red deer in Scotland. In general they are rounded hills without distinctive features, and from Corrour there is not a clear view of them, but the two Sgors rise steeply above Lochan a'Bhealaich and present a bold profile when seen from the east. The total distance of 22km for this round is lightened by an excellent track for the first 7km and the smooth terrain of the hills themselves.

Follow the track ENE from Corrour Halt along the south shore of Loch Ossian to reach the cottages at the foot of the loch. Cross the bridge over the outflow, then immediately turn NE along a path to recross the river by a wooden footbridge and continue along the path west round a copse to reach open ground. (This avoids having to find a way through the forest at the east end of the loch). Bear SE and climb at an easy angle to a fore-top Meall Nathrach Mor, and beyond a short drop continue at an even easier angle to Sgor Choinnich. Descend S for 120m to a well-defined bealach and climb a broad steepening ridge to the summit of Sgor Gaibhre which provides a splendid view of Ben Alder and Loch Ericht. (12km; 720m; 4h).

Turn WSW and descend easy slopes of moss and heath to the broad bealach, the Mam Ban, riven by peat-hags. Continue in the same direction up Carn Dearg, climbing 220m to the cairn which overlooks the whole expanse of Rannoch Moor, while to the north the glacial trench of Strath Ossian is very prominent. (15km; 940m; 5h).

For the return to Corrour, descend the north-west ridge, soon reaching the head of an open corrie. Go down this corrie and in 2½km reach the path, known as The Road to the Isles, which can be followed W to the station.

Aonach Beag and Geal-Charn from Beinn Eibhinn   *J. Renny*

Beinn Eibhinn; 1100m; (OS Sheets 41 and 42; 449733); M47; *delightful hill*
Aonach Beag; 1114m; (OS Sheets 41 and 42; 458742); M38; *little hill*

These two remote mountains lie in the hinterland between Loch Laggan and Loch Ericht, part of the range which forms the northern wall of the long glen cutting through the hills in a straight line from Loch Ossian to Loch Pattack over the Bealach Dubh. The only view of these hills from any public road is from the north, on the A86 near the west end of Loch Laggan, from where they can be seen rising beyond the forests of Glen Spean. Aonach Beag is a fine peak, with three well-defined ridges converging at its top.

Beinn Eibhinn is a more extensive mountain, with a level summit ridge curving round Coire a'Charra Mhoir and its south-west side forming a series of rounded ridges and open corries well seen from Loch Ossian.

The ascent of these two mountains can be made from Corrour Halt on the West Highland Railway. Given clear visibility and good conditions underfoot, it should be possible to do the round trip comfortably between the morning and evening trains at Corrour, but attention must be paid to the clock and the railway timetable. Fortunately half the distance to and from the peaks is along the excellent track beside Loch Ossian which makes for quick progress.

From Corrour Halt follow the route described for Sgor Gaibhre to the outflow of Loch Ossian. Take the path NE across the River Ossian, round the west side of the copse and continue along this path to the footbridge across the Uisge Labhair. A fair path continues up the north side of this stream past a fine rocky linn. After crossing the Allt Feith a'Mheallain head NNE up the grassy slopes of the rounded ridge Creagan na Craoibhe. Higher up the going becomes very easy on short heath and grass, past a huge rounded boulder on the crest to the Top of Meall Glas Choire (922m). Beyond a short drop into a square-cut col, easy slopes soon lead onto the stony summit ridge of Beinn Eibhinn, whose

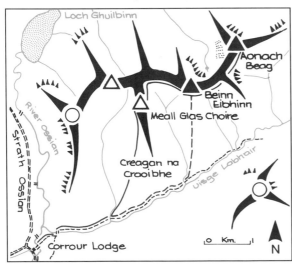

north-east face drops steeply to Lochan a'Charra Mhoir. The summit cairn is at the east end of this ridge. (13½ km; 730m; 4h 20min).

The narrow ridge continues NE in splendid surroundings, dropping 120m in a graceful curve before climbing again to Aonach Beag, whose summit is a small flat plateau. (15km; 860m; 4h 50min).

The best return is probably by the outward route over Beinn Eibhinn as described above. It may be shorter in distance (though less pleasant) to descend fairly directly S from the summit of Beinn Eibhinn down steep, rough ground to reach the faint path beside the Uisge Labhair near the foot of the Allt Glaschoire.

Geal-Charn; 1132m; (OS Sheet 42; 470746); M25; *white hill*
Carn Dearg; 1034m; (OS Sheet 42; 504764); M95; *red hill*

These hills lie in that great tract of mountainous country between Loch Laggan and Loch Ericht which is penetrated by no public roads. Geal-Charn is the highest point on the elevated ridge stretching from Strath Ossian to Loch Pattack, the north-easterly extension of Beinn Eibhinn and Aonach Beag just described, and Carn Dearg continues the range to its end above Loch Pattack. Geal-Charn has a large summit plateau surrounded by corries and steep hillsides, and it throws out two easterly spurs enclosing Loch an Sgoir. The southern one forms a well-defined Top, Sgor Iutharn (1021m), whose terminal ridge is the steep and narrow Lancet Edge. The ascent of this ridge and descent of the more northerly spur is a fine mountaineering expedition which can be continued over Carn Dearg.

The shortest approach, from Dalwhinnie, involves a distance of 40km for the round trip and may entail a night out, possibly at Culra Bothy which is well situated bothy at the base of these hills. Alternatively, a bicycle can be used for 11km along the private estate road from Dalwhinnie to Loch Pattack as described for Ben Alder. (See page 90).

From the shed on this road ½km east of Loch Pattack take the path for 3½km SW across the level moor and along the south-east bank of the Allt a'Chaoil-reidhe. Cross the stream by a footbridge near Culra Bothy and continue SW on a parallel path for a further 3km to the crossing of the stream from Loch an Sgoir.

Above and to the west steep rough ground leads to the Lancet Edge, a ridge sharp enough to require careful scrambling, and providing magnificent views, right to the waterfalls feeding Loch an Sgoir and left to the mass of Ben Alder. The ridge ends at Sgor Iutharn, beyond which the ground broadens to form a wide col. Continue W across this col then NW up the final slope to the rim of the plateau which has to be crossed for 1km W to reach Geal-Charn's summit. (From Loch Pattack: l0km; 800m; 3h 30min).

Sgor Iutharn from the north-east   *D.J. Broadhead*

To continue the traverse, cross the green fertile plateau ENE for 1km to reach the spur dropping steeply between the north and east corries of Geal-Charn. In poor visibility an exact compass bearing is needed to find the correct route. Descend to a narrow level ridge and climb a short way to an intervening Top, Diollaid a'Chairn (922m). Finally, a long, broad and stony ridge leads to Carn Dearg. (14km; 1000m; 4h 50min).

For the return descend due E to Culra Bothy and retrace the outward route.

Map on page 91.

Ben Alder from Culra Bothy   R. Aitken

Ben Alder; 1148m; (OS Sheet 42; 496718); M24; *from the Alder Burn, which may be from the Gaelic alldhobhar meaning rock water*
Beinn Bheoil; 1019m; (OS Sheet 42; 517717); M110; *hill of the mouth*

Ben Alder is one of the great remote mountains of Scotland, a vast high plateau surrounded by corries in the heart of the Central Highlands between Lochaber and the Cairngorms. For such a remote hill, however, there is a remarkable roadside view of it from Dalwhinnie, the eye being drawn 20km along the length of Loch Ericht to its great north-eastern corries, which hold snow into early summer. Other views from the west tell more of the plateau-like form of Ben Alder, but only a traverse can reveal its enormous bulk and fascinating complexity of ridge and corrie. By contrast, Beinn Bheoil has a simple north-south ridge, dropping steeply on both sides, but its position between Ben Alder and Loch Ericht gives it a very mountainous setting.

There is a strong mountaineering flavour to the traverse of these two peaks, and their remoteness may make necessary an overnight stop in the hills, possibly at Benalder Cottage or Culra bothy. Alternatively, the use of a bicycle along the private road from Dalwhinnie to Loch Pattack brings them within easier reach on a long summer day. Ben Alder can also be climbed from Corrour Halt on the West Highland Railway, but one would have to move very fast to do this between the morning and evening trains. For anyone staying at Loch Ossian youth hostel this constraint would not matter.

The Dalwhinnie approach starts just south of the station. Cross the railway and follow the estate road along the north-west shore of Loch Ericht. There are locked gates, but a bicycle can be used as far as Loch Pattack, 3km west of Ben Alder Lodge and 11km from Dalwhinnie. Just before reaching this loch, at a large shed, take to a path which leads SW across wet level moorland to the east bank of the Allt a'Chaoil-reidhe. Follow this path, passing Culra bothy on the opposite side of the stream, for about 7km until it reaches the burn flowing from the Loch a'Bhealaich Bheithe. Cross the burn and choose which of the prominent ridges above to climb: the Short Leachas lies SW and directly above, while the Long Leachas is reached by a traverse further west. The Short Leachas is steeper and involves frequent scrambling, while the Long Leachas is easier and has better situations. Both emerge onto the summit plateau near a minor top, beyond which 1km of stony and near-level ground leads SSW to the summit cairn. (From Loch Pattack: 10km; 750m; 3h 30min).

To continue the traverse, follow the rim of the Garbh Choire for 1½km, first S then SE to descend abruptly (still SE) down steep bouldery ground to reach the Bealach Breabag. From there climb NE to Sron Coire na h-Iolaire (955m) which is a splendid viewpoint above Loch Ericht. Ahead, the spine of the hill stretches NNE for 3½km above 800m, dropping to 860m before rising to Beinn Bheoil. (14½ km; 1030m; 5h). Follow the ridge N for a further 2km, then descend NW to reach the path returning to Loch Pattack and Dalwhinnie. Altogether a very long expedition of 45km, half of which can be done by bicycle.

The ascent of Ben Alder from Corrour Halt follows the same route as for Beinn Eibhinn to the Uisge Labhair, and continues up that stream for 5km. Cross the stream to the foot of Ben Alder's broad west ridge, which is followed to the top. (16km; 750m; 4h 50min).

Ben Alder from Carn Dearg   *J. Renny*

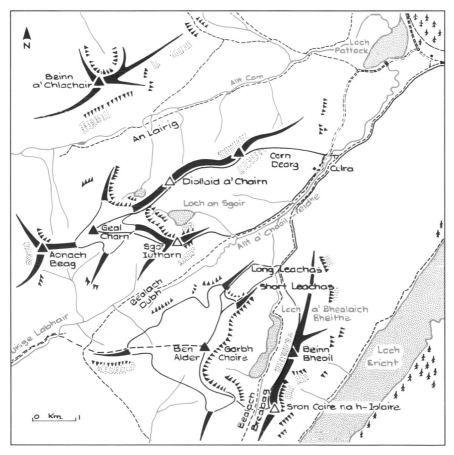

A'Mharconaich, with Sgairneach Mhor to its left, from Drumochter Lodge   D.J. Bennet

SECTION 5

The Drumochter Mountains

Sgairneach Mhor; 991m; (OS Sheet 42; 599731); M151; *big stony hillside*
Beinn Udlamain; 1010m; (OS Sheet 42; 579740); M119; *gloomy mountain*

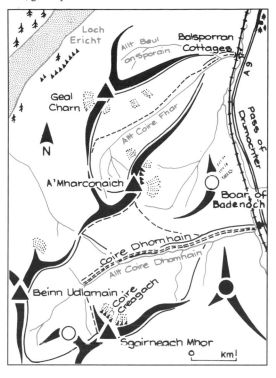

These two mountains lie between the Pass of Drumochter and Loch Ericht. Sgairneach Mhor is prominently seen from the A9 road east of Dalnaspidal as a high rounded mass, and it is also well seen from further north near the summit of the pass from where its most obvious feature is the steep north-facing Coire Creagach which often holds snow until early summer. Beinn Udlamain, on the other hand, although the highest of this group of mountains, is screened by its satellites and is only visible from the A9 directly opposite the foot of Coire Dhomhain. The two mountains lie on either side of the head of this corrie, and can be conveniently climbed together in a single expedition.

Leave the A9 at a derelict house opposite the entrance to Coire Dhomhain and cross the railway line to join the track up the corrie on the north side of the Allt Coire Dhomhain. (There is a passage under the railway a few hundred metres south). Follow the track up Coire Dhomhain for 1½km, then cross the stream and climb S up grass and deep heather to a col on the east ridge of Sgairneach Mhor.From this col the ridge is rounded and easy-angled at first, but becomes steeper and narrower before reaching the summit along the edge of Coire Creagach. (5km; 550m; 2h 10min).

If the Allt Coire Dhomhain is in spate and difficult to cross, it may be necessary to walk 3km up the corrie almost to the end of the track before crossing the stream and climbing the ridge on the west side of Coire Creagach.

From the summit walk SW for almost ½km before turning W to the 810m col at the head of Coire Dhomhain. The slopes of the descent are featureless, and in misty weather care should be taken not to be diverted S by the fall of the ground. From the col continue W up a short steeper slope to reach the south ridge of Beinn Udlamain, and follow the remains of a fence north up this ridge to the summit. (8½km; 750m; 3h 10min).

Descend NE along the broad ridge, following the fence for 2km until the 860m col is reached. From there descend SE down easy slopes to reach the track in Coire Dhomhain.

It is easy to include A'Mharconaich in this traverse by climbing NE from the 860m col, still following the fence until it goes off leftwards. The summit of A'Mharconaich is at the north-east end of the level summit ridge. From there descend steeply SE towards the Boar of Badenoch col and Coire Dhomhain.

Geal-charn; 917m; (OS Sheet 42; 597783); M272; *white hill*
A'Mharconaich; 975m; (OS Sheet 42; 604763); M178; *the horse place*

These mountains, which lie north-west of the Pass of Drumochter, are the continuation northwards of the two described above. Geal-charn is a rounded hill formed by a broad ridge running from south-west to north-east, and high on its shoulder there are some tall slender cairns, clearly visible from the A9 road and looking like giant climbers. A'Mharconaich is a fine looking mountain seen from the road, with a very steep east face forming a high corrie just under the summit. They are both accessible from the road, which is 425m above sea level, so their traverse is a pleasant and undemanding day.

Leave the A9 road at Balsporran Cottages, 3km north of Drumochter Pass, and cross the railway. Follow the path W, crossing the Allt Beul an Sporain, and then climb directly up the broad north-east ridge of Geal-charn through deep heather. Above about 650m

a faint path on the south-east side of the ridge leads up past the tall cairns to the flat shoulder of the hill at 850m. Finally a broad stony slope leads to the summit of Geal-charn. (3½km; 500m; 1h 40min).

Descend the stony ridge SW then S for 1½km to the col at the head of Coire Fhar at 740m. From there ascend SE up grassy slopes to reach the flat summit plateau of A'Mharconaich, where the summit is at the north-east end. (6½km; 730m; 2h 40min).

Descend N, steeply at first down rocky ground, then easily along the north-east ridge which leads directly back to Balsporran Cottages, with rough ground of peat bog and heather near its foot. This rough ground can be avoided by leaving the ridge to cross the Allt Coire Fhar to the path on its north side. However, if this stream is in spate, the crossing should be made high up as there is no bridge across it.

Carn na Caim from the Allt Coire Chuaich bothy   *H.M. Brown*

A'Bhuidheanach Bheag; 936m; (OS Sheet 42; 661776); M235; *the little yellow place*
Carn na Caim; 941m; (OS Sheet 42; 677822); M226; *cairn of the curve*

These two hills are the highest points on the large undulating plateau which extends NE from the Pass of Drumochter to Loch an t-Seilich in the Gaick Forest. Both are flat-topped and their most characteristic features when seen from the A9 road which runs along their western flank are the many gullies and corries descending from the plateau in shallow curves. A'Bhuidheanach Bheag lies well back from the edge of the plateau and its summit is not visible from the road. Carn na Caim, on the other hand, is on the western edge of the plateau and, viewed from Dalwhinnie, it is the obvious rounded summit whose north and west sides are scalloped by shallow corries.

The two hills may conveniently be climbed together. The recommended route of ascent starts from the A9 road ½km south of the road junction to Dalwhinnie, close to a large lay-by. From that point ascend by an old rough road which climbs SE to a disused quartz quarry on the edge of the plateau. Continue to the 902m knoll a few hundred metres south-east of the quarry.

To climb A'Bhuidheanach Bheag first, descend S to a shallow col and contour to the east of two lesser knolls to reach the wide 830m col at the head of Coire Chuirn. The bearing from there to the summit of A'Bhuidheanach Bheag is due south, and in misty conditions accurate map and compass work is essential as the plateau lacks any distinctive features. Alternatively, one can follow an old fence from the col; it initially goes SE, but leads eventually to the summit. (6½km; 620m; 2h 30min).

To reach Carn na Caim, return to the 902m knoll. Continue NE over another knoll (914m) then slightly downhill for 1km and up again for the same distance to the summit. (11½km; 780m; 4h).

To return to the day's starting point, head S of W along the plateau and descend steeply W, crossing the Allt Coire Uilleim where it flows out of its narrow corrie, and continue across the more gentle lower slopes to the A9 road.

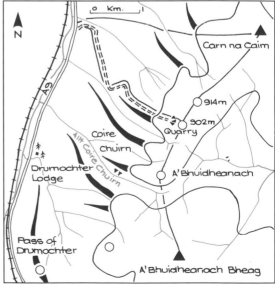

Meall Chuaich from Loch Insh   *D.J. Bennet*

Meall Chuaich; 951m; (OS Sheet 42; 716879), M209, *hill of the quaich*

Meall Chuaich lies at the northern end of the group of hills which form a large undulating plateau to the east of the A9 road near Dalwhinnie. This plateau extends for 15km NE from the Pass of Drumochter to Loch an t-Seilich in the Gaick Forest. Its roundness and isolation are the distinctive features of Meall Chuaich, making it a prominent landmark, and as there are no higher hills in its vicinity, it is a very good viewpoint.

Leave the A9 road some 4km north of the turn-off to Dalwhinnie and just south of Cuaich cottages, where a private road is barred by a locked gate. Walk along this road and in a short distance join another road and follow it E along the aqueduct which transfers water from Loch Cuaich to Loch Ericht. Continue past a small hydro-electric power station until ¼km from the dam at Loch Cuaich, and there turn SE onto a rough track to a small bothy. From the bothy continue along the track towards Coire Chuaich for ½km,

cross the Allt Coire Chuaich and then climb NE up the steep heathery hillside, aiming for the crest of the broad ridge above where the going becomes much easier on grass and heath. Continue along the flat shoulder above Stac Meall Chuaich and finally climb a steeper stony slope to the mossy summit of Meall Chuaich. (7km; 610m; 2h 40min).

To descend, either return by the route of ascent or alternatively drop down NW from the summit, easily at first and then down very steep slopes north-east of Stac Meall Chuaich to cross the Feith na Braclaich. Reach a track which is followed SW along the side of Loch Cuaich to rejoin the route of ascent.

An alternative approach to Meall Chuaich is up Glen Tromie, but it is longer and less interesting. The road up the glen is private and a bicycle is essential for the 10km from Tromie Bridge to Bhran Cottage. From there the ascent to Meall Chuaich goes up the long and featureless north-east ridge.

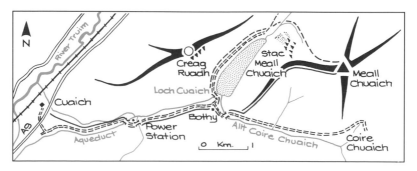

Looking up Glen Fender to Beinn a'Ghlo   D.J. Bennet

SECTION 6

The Grampians: Blair Atholl to Braemar

Beinn Dearg from the south   R. Simpson

Beinn Dearg; 1008m; (OS Sheet 43; 853778),
M121; *red hill*

A pointed hill rising above a multitude of flat or
rounded hills and peaty plateaux, Beinn Dearg stands
north-east of Bruar Lodge in the middle of the Atholl
deer forest, 12km north of Blair Atholl. It is a lone
granite peak surrounded by a vast area of schist hills.

The approaches to Beinn Dearg are from the south,
starting from Blair Atholl, Bruar or Calvine, and they
are all long. The route from Calvine up Glen Bruar
follows a long-established right of way, the Minigaig
route, but it is rather uninteresting and not recommended. Its one advantage is that it is possible to use
a bicycle on the very rough road right to the foot of
the hill.

The Glen Banvie route starts from Old Blair, 1km
north of Blair Atholl. Walk up the private road on the
north-east side of the Banvie Burn, and continue up
the east side of the Allt an t-Seapail to the bothy beside
the Allt Sheicheachan. The path continues along the
north-west side of this burn to a height of 800m on
Meall Dubh nan Dearcag. From there an easy broad
ridge leads N to the summit of Beinn Dearg up dwarf
heath and the reddish-coloured screes which
obviously give the hill its name. (14km; 890m;
4h 40min).

An alternative route of similar length and character
also starts at Old Blair, but follows the high road on
the west side of Glen Tilt through Blairuachdar Wood
and up the Allt Slanaidh by a track ending at a bothy.
Continue up the burn, bearing N across the west side
of Beinn a'Chait, then descend slightly to the col at the
head of the Allt Sheicheachan and join the route described above on the final ascent up the south ridge
of Beinn Dearg. (13km; 890m; 4h 30min).

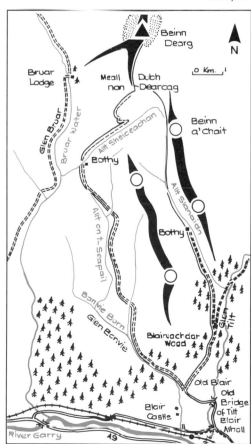

Carn Liath from the road to Shinagag   *W.D. Brooker*

Carn nan Gabhar; 1129m; (OS Sheet 43; 971733); M29; *hill of the goats*
Braigh Coire Chruinn-bhalgain; 1070m; (OS Sheet 43; 946724); M63; *upland of the corrie of the round blisters*
Carn Liath; 975m; (OS Sheet 43; 936698); M175; *grey hill*

A beautiful, mysterious stony mountain of many remote peaks and corries, Beinn a'Ghlo *(hill of the veil or mist)* is the finest mountain in the Mounth between Drumochter and Aberdeen, with the sole exception of Lochnagar. It rises to the north-east of Blair Atholl, a complex range of summits, ridges and corries which looks particularly fine seen from the Cairngorms.

The general orientation of the range is from south-west to north-east, rising above the farms and policies on the north side of the River Garry between Killiecrankie and Blair Atholl. On its north-west side the range is bounded by the long straight trench of Glen Tilt, and on its south-east by the shallower valley of Glen Girnaig. Far to the north-east the mountain ends above the deep and narrow defile of Glen Loch, holding the curiously named Loch Loch.

The highest summit, Carn nan Gabhar, is the remotest, 12km from Blair Atholl as the crow flies, and the finest way to it is the traverse of the other two Munros *en route*, starting with Carn Liath. From Killiecrankie the pointed hill of Carn Liath, with its grey screes, looks more prominent than the higher tops beyond it. It is best approached from Blair Atholl by the narrow public road on the south side of Glen Fender which ends near Loch Moraig, where cars can be parked.

From there walk along the track ENE towards Glen Girnaig for 2km to a little bothy, and then strike NE directly up the ever-steepening slopes of Carn Liath. (4½km; 640m; 2h 10min).

Follow the twisting ridge NW then NE down to the col at 760m, and continue up the broad ridge of heath and stones to Braigh Coire Chruinn-bhalgain. (7½km; 950m; 3h 20min). There is a fine view down into Glen Tilt from this summit.

Continue NE along the ridge for 1km before turning E to descend a grassy slope to the next col at 847m. Climb ESE to the col between Carn nan Gabhar and Airgiod Bheinn (1061m; *silver hill*), and finally go NE along the broad easy-angled ridge to the top where there are two large cairns. The highest point is at the north-east end of this nearly level summit ridge, at a cairn about 200 metres north-east of the trig point and 9m higher. (11km; 1230m; 4h 30min).

The return to Loch Moraig can either be made by retracing the outward route along the ridges, or by descending the stony south-west shoulder of Airgiod Bheinn and traversing rough heathery terrain SW round the base of Carn Liath to reach the track between Glen Girnaig and Loch Moraig.

Carn nan Gabhar from the south ridge of Braigh Coire Chruinn-bhalgain   *W.D. Brooker*

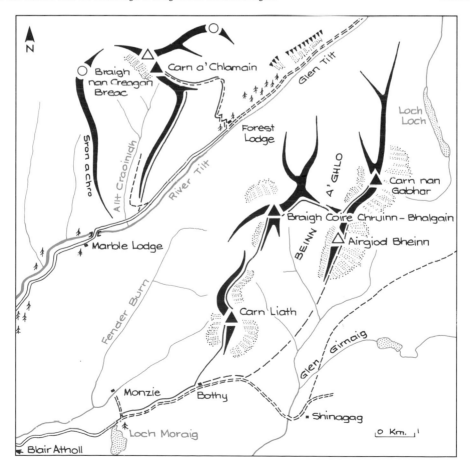

Carn a'Chlamain from the south   W.D. Brooker

Carn a'Chlamain; 963m; (OS Sheet 43; 916758); M188; *hill of the kite or buzzard*

This hill is the highest point of the undulating plateau, intersected by two or three deep glens, on the north-west side of Glen Tilt. Carn a'Chlamain has a pointed summit, with a prominent path of grey screes on its south-west side, rising slightly above the level of the plateau, which makes it recognisable.

The approach is up Glen Tilt, and it is possible on enquiry at the factor's office at Blair Castle to obtain permission to drive up the private road from Old Bridge of Tilt to Forest Lodge. Alternatively, the walk or cycle ride up this very beautiful glen is full of interest and variety and these are aesthetically the better ways to approach the hill.

If a car is taken, drive to Forest Lodge. At the end of the lodge wood a path zigzags up the steep hillside on the north-west side of the glen, offering an easy

way up. This path, continuing at an easier angle beyond the edge of the plateau, passes close to the summit of Carn a'Chlamain on its north side. (4km; 660m; 2h).

If one is walking up Glen Tilt, either the road on the west side of the river or the right of way which follows a footpath N from Fenderbridge on the east side of the glen may be taken. Go as far as the bridge over the Allt Craoinidh, 1km beyond Marble Lodge, at the foot of the long south ridge of Carn a'Chlamain. There is a fair path up the broad crest of this ridge which gives good walking on short grass and heather, heading NNE then NW to join the previous route just before the summit of Carn a'Chlamain is reached. (12½km; 820m; 4h 10min).

Map on page 99.

An Sgarsoch; 1006m; (OS Sheet 43; 933837); M124; *the place of the sharp rocks*
Carn an Fhidhleir; 994m; (OS Sheet 43; 905842); M145; *hill of the fiddler*

These two very remote hills stand in one of the wildest and most inaccessible parts of the Highlands, more or less at the centre of the headwaters of the rivers Feshie, Geldie and Tarf. They are both smooth, gently sloping hills, with rough heather and peaty ground on their lower slopes, but excellent walking on mossy turf on their upper parts.

They are a long way from any starting point, and a bicycle is a great help in reaching them along rough roads which, although private and not accessible to cars, nevertheless follow long-established rights of way. The three possible access points to which cars can be driven are Linn of Dee, Achlean farm in Glen Feshie and (with permission) Forest Lodge in Glen Tilt. The Linn of Dee approach is described first as for most of the way from there to the two hills there is a

track which makes for fast walking, and although it is rough and stony in places, it is negotiable by bicycle for much of its length.

From Linn of Dee the route follows the track on the north bank of the River Dee to White Bridge, and then along the Geldie Burn to the ruined Geldie Lodge. From there a bulldozed track climbs WSW and is followed to its highest point. Continue SW across peaty ground and climb the north-east slopes of Carn an Fhidhleir, up grass and heather,to reach the north ridge near the summit. (18½km; 630m; 5h 10min).

Descend SSE along the broad ridge for 1km and then drop down the east side of the ridge to reach the 710m col. From there climb NE up a broad ridge to the large cairn on the flat summit of An Sgarsoch. (22km; 930m; 5h 10min).

Looking north-west from Beinn a'Ghlo towards the hills beyond Tarf Water   W.D. Brooker

The easiest way back is due N, avoiding the steep north-east corries which may hold snowdrifts well into summer. Keep west of Scarsoch Bheag across peaty ground and reach the bulldozed track leading down to Geldie Lodge.

The route from Forest Lodge in Glen Tilt starts up the zigzag path to Carn a'Chlamain (see previous page). Once fairly level ground is reached at about 750m, bear N across rough terrain of peat and heather over the col between Carn a'Chlamain and Conlach Mor and descend to Tarf Bothy. This old shooting lodge is now in a ruined state, but one room is still weatherproof.

From the bothy cross the Tarf Water and head N. To find the best ground for walking it is preferable to go up the very broad south ridge of An Sgarsoch rather than follow the shallow glen of the Allt a'Chaorainn. (From Forest Lodge: 11½km; 930m; 4h 10min). Traverse to Carn an Fhidhleir across the 710m col by reversing the route described above, and descend the long south ridge of this hill over two or three knolls down to the Tarf Water. A short stop at the bothy will be needed before making the last climb over the hills to return to Forest Lodge in Glen Tilt.

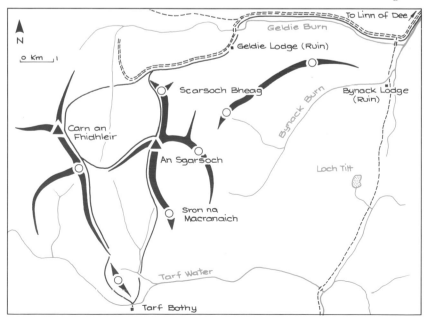

Carn an Righ from the north-east   *H.M. Brown*

Glas Tulaichean; 1051m; (OS Sheet 43; 051760); M77; *from glas-thulchan, green hills*
Carn an Righ; 1029m; (OS Sheet 43; 028773); M98; *hill of the king*

These two hills stand rather remotely between Glen Shee and Glen Tilt, and can most easily be reached up Glen Lochsie, an offshoot of Glen Shee. There is a private road from Spittal of Glenshee for 2km to Dalmunzie Hotel in Glen Lochsie. Cars should not be driven as far as the hotel without permission, but should be parked near the start of this private road at (105702).

Glas Tulaichean is a typical green Mounth hill, with crisp mossy turf and heath giving excellent walking on its upper slopes, and with grassy corries to the east. Carn an Righ is much more remote, the western outlier of the group of hills which extends west from the Cairnwell pass to the head of Glen Tilt and includes Glas Tulaichean and Beinn Iutharn Mhor. It is a rounded hill, with much scree on its slopes.

From Spittal of Glenshee walk up the private road past Dalmunzie Hotel and Glenlochsie farm and along the track of the old railway which used to link Dalmunzie with Glenlochsie Lodge, a former deer-stalking lodge now in ruins. From this ruined lodge climb NNW towards Glas Tulaichean, avoiding the glens and streams which are peaty and wet, and climbing along the crest of one of the two broad ridges which lead to the summit. (9½km; 710m; 3h 20min).

To continue to Carn an Righ, go down the north ridge of Glas Tulaichean for 1km and then descend NW to reach the path on the south side of of Mam nan Carn. Follow this path W for 1km to the col due east of Carn an Righ and climb to the summit up slopes of short heath and grass, mixed with stony patches. (13½km; 1000m; 4h 40min).

On the return journey retrace the outward route for

2km and reach the 800m col at the foot of the north ridge of Glas Tulaichean. Cross this col and descend by the Glas Choire Bheag into Gleann Taitneach where a bulldozed track has replaced the former path down this steep-sided glen. At its foot there are spots where people once had their farms.

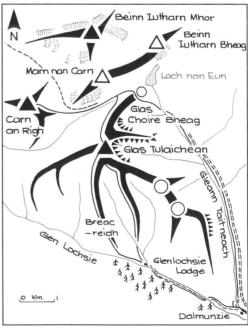

Looking up Glen Ey to Beinn Iutharn Mhor   G. Nicoll

Beinn Iutharn Mhor; 1045m; (OS Sheet 43; 045792); M85; *probably from Beinn Fhiubharainn Mhor, big hill of the edge-point*

Carn Bhac; 946m; (OS Sheet 43; 051832); M216; *hill of peat-banks*

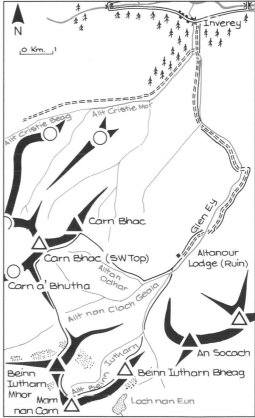

Beinn Iutharn Mhor is a green rounded hill, the highest in the Mounth between Beinn a'Ghlo and Glas Maol. It rises boldly in the view from upper Glen Ey, thrusting its big shoulders out into the glen, which offers the most interesting approach.

From Inverey cycle or walk up the road which starts on the east side of the Ey Burn (locked gate). This road climbs through decaying birch woods past The Colonel's Bed, and higher up through beautiful grassy haughs to the ruined Altanour Lodge, 8km from Inverey. From there walk up the Allt Beinn Iutharn for a further 2½km, and then strike SSW up the shoulder of Beinn Iutharn Bheag (953m); the western edge of the steep north-east corrie is the easiest route.

From Beinn Iutharn Bheag there is a short drop to a col above Loch nan Eun, and then a gentle rise to the flat top of Mam nan Carn (986m). Again there is a short drop NW to a col below the mainly mossy and grassy slopes leading to the summit of Beinn Iutharn Mhor. (15km; 900m; 4h 50min).

From there the route to Carn Bhac goes NE along a fairly level ridge for 1km, then NW down stony slopes to a col and over a slight rise before the climb to the 920m south-west top of Carn Bhac. Finally an easy walk for 1½km NE leads to the summit, 5km from Beinn Iutharn Mhor. (20km; 1080m; 6h 20min).

The name Carn Bhac applies to both tops, although on the OS 1:50,000 map it appears to refer to the lower south-west top only, and the higher top is not named. The best descent route is ESE down the Alltan Odhar to reach Altanour Lodge.

On the broad summit ridge of An Socach, looking towards the east top   *D. Green*

An Socach; 944m; (OS Sheet 43; 080800); M221; *the projecting place (from soc, a beak or snout)*

An Socach is a broad ridge rising between upper Glen Ey and the Baddoch Burn, several kilometres west of the A93 road from Perth to Braemar. The ridge is about 2km long between the east and west summits. The west summit is the higher, but its height is not shown on the OS 1:50,000 map. On this map the name appears incorrectly to apply only to the east top (938m).

The shortest approach to An Socach is from the summit of the A93 road at the Glenshee Ski Centre. Follow the bulldozed track (or the ski trails) NW into Butchart's Corrie past several ski tows and bear W up to the col between The Cairnwell and Carn Aosda. Descend W from the col, traversing the heathery slopes and peat bo˙s north of Loch Vrotachan to reach the Baddoch Burn. Once on the north-west side of the burn climb WNW on a rising traverse to reach the col at the middle of An Socach's summit ridge. Finally go 1km W along the level stony ridge to the summit. (6½km; 560m; 2h 30min).

The 938m east top is 2km away, with very little drop along the ridge, and it can easily be included in the return.

A more attractive approach to An Socach, avoiding the ski slopes, is up the Baddoch Burn from Glen Clunie. A road and then a bulldozed track lead far up into the glen to the point where the previous route is joined. It is equally possible to leave the track lower down the glen and climb the long east ridge to the east top.

Another feasible route is from Glen Ey, particularly if one cycles to Altanour Lodge. From there the summit can be climbed by its short steep north ridge.

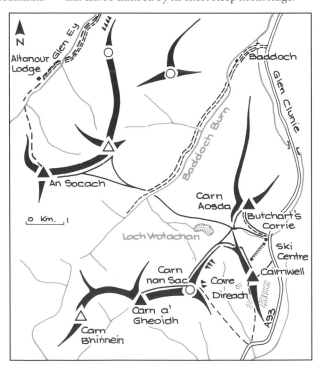

The Cairnwell from Glen Shee   *H.M. Brown*

The Cairnwell; 933m; (OS Sheet 43; 135773); M242; *from the Gaelic Carn Bhalg, hill of bags (referring to its shape)*
Carn Aosda; 917m; (OS Sheet 43; 134792); M270; *hill of age*
Carn a'Gheoidh; 975m; (OS Sheet 43; 107767); M177; *hill of the goose*

These three hills lie on the west side of the A93 road from Perth to Braemar, and are most easily accessible from the summit of that road where the Glenshee Ski Centre has its many tows, lifts and bulldozed pistes.

The Cairnwell may be a dull-looking hill from that point on the road, but it stands out boldly in the view up Glen Shee from the south. Carn Aosda rises to the north of The Cairnwell, a heathery hill with pale grey screes on its bald top. The flanks of both these hills are scarred by bulldozed pistes, ski tows and lifts right up to their summits. Carn a'Gheoidh, on the other hand, lies well to the west of its two neighbours, hidden from the road and unspoiled by ski developments.

The Cairnwell and Carn Aosda are the two most accessible Munros in Scotland, particularly The Cairnwell for there is a chairlift which operates in summer as well as winter and goes up to 910m, a short distance from the summit. However, no true Munro-climber would use this form of uplift.

Going to The Cairnwell first, and starting just south of the Ski Centre, steepish slopes of short dry heather and, higher up, wind-clipped heath and occasional patches of grey screes lead to the big cairn where there is also a small hut. (0.6km; 270m; 40min). It is a very good viewpoint, offering fine panoramas of the Cairngorms and down towards Central Scotland.

Descend NNW past the top of the chairlift and along the broad ridge with snow-fences. After 1km, just before reaching the Cairnwell-Carn Aosda col, diverge W and drop down to another col at 810m which is the lowest point between The Cairnwell and Carn a'Gheoidh. Continuing SW, the walking is easy up a gentle slope of crisp mossy heath along the edge of the Coire Direach rocks, past Carn nan Sac (920m) and west to Carn a'Gheoidh across a little plateau. (4½km; 440m; 1h 50min).

Return along the same route to the Cairnwell-Carn Aosda col and climb NE then E along the broad ridge of wind-clipped heath, passing the top of the ski tow in Butchart's Corrie, to reach the flat stony summit of Carn Aosda. (9km; 570m; 3h). Descend S between the pistes and snow-fences and return to the road by the bulldozed tracks at the foot of Butchart's Corrie.

If one wants to avoid the pistes, tows and noise of Butchart's Corrie, there are alternative ways to The Cairnwell and Carn a'Gheoidh. The starting point for these routes is about 2½km south of the summit of the A93 road. From there The Cairnwell can be climbed directly up its broad south ridge, and the best route to Carn a'Gheoidh goes NW up the shoulder of Carn nan Sac.

The White Mounth from the River Dee   *A. Watson*

SECTION 7

The South-east Grampians: Glen Shee to Mount Keen

Looking south from Glas Maol to Creag Leacach   *J. Renny*

Lying to the east of the A93 road over the Cairnwell Pass, the sprawling Mounth plateau extends from Creag Leacach in the south-west and Driesh in the south-east for 20km to the north- facing corries of Lochnagar. Never dropping below 800m, the outline of its continuous high ground widens and narrows in accordance with the glens and corries which bound the edge of the plateau: Callater on the west , Muick, Clova and Isla on the east. North of the Tolmount drove route, which crosses the Mounth from Callater to Glen Doll, the underlying granite yields a poorer soil and sparser vegetation than the grassier tundras to the south which are based on varied metamorphic rocks. No fewer than thirteen Munros and sixteen Tops are scattered across the Mounth, and easy high-level walking connects them all so that they may be climbed in various combinations. The routes suggested in the following descriptions involve a variety of approaches by different glens, and do not include any particularly long days.

Glas Maol; 1068m; (OS Sheet 43; 166765); M67; *greenish grey bare hill*
Creag Leacach; 987m; (OS Sheet 43; 155745); M157; *slabby rock*

These hills lie east of the A93 road over the Cairnwell Pass at the south-west corner of the great Mounth plateau. The bald dome of Glas Maol rises just south of the point where the plateau is pinched between the Garbh-choire and the Caenlochan Glen to form a narrow isthmus joining it to Cairn of Claise. Spurs project from the dome NW to Meall Odhar (922m) and SE to Little Glas Maol (973m). The main ridge extends SSW to Creag Leacach and beyond it for a further 5km over a series of lesser tops towards Glen Shee.

Start from the car park near the summit of the A93, and ascend to the east where a bulldozed track leads over a knoll and into a dip holding sundry buildings at the foot of the Meall Odhar ski-tows. In summer these have an abandoned and desolate atmosphere. Continue up the stony slope, keeping to the right of the ski-tow, and cross Meall Odhar to a flat col. From there a short but steep pull up 100m, with the edge of the Glas Choire just to the left, brings one to the dome of Glas Maol. The summit cairn is ½km south-east across the stony plateau. (3½km; 440m; 1h 30min).

The summit is wide, but from a short distance east of the cairn a fine grassy ridge carrying the Monega drove road drops towards Little Glas Maol and along the curving rim of the Caenlochan Glen. To the south-west of the summit schistose screes blanketed in moss slope down towards the Creag Leacach ridge. A dry stone dyke is a useful guide, and it can be followed down to the col and from there SW to Creag Leacach. The ridge is quite narrow for this part of the Grampians, and even rocky in places, although broken into large scree and boulders. The summit of Creag Leacach is 1km beyond the col. (6km; 520m; 2h 20min).

Continue down the widening stony ridge to the South-west Top (943m) and then leave the crest to go NW down a fairly steep slope to the saddle south-east of the outlying knoll of Meall Gorm. From there descend NNE down grassy slopes to the floor of the corrie below. Go downstream, crossing to the north side to join a path and cross the Allt a'Ghlinne Bhig by a footbridge to reach the A93. Walk up this road for 2km to return to the starting point.
Map on page 109.

Carn an Tuirc from Cairn of Claise

J. Renny

Carn an Tuirc; 1019m; (OS Sheet 43; 174804); M112; *hill of the boar*
Cairn of Claise; 1064m; (OS Sheet 43; 185789); M68; *hill of the green grassy place*
Tolmount; 958m; (OS Sheets 43 and 44; 210800); M199; *Doll mounth or hill, (i.e. leading to Glen Doll)*
Tom Buidhe; 957m; (OS Sheets 43 and 44; 214788); M200; *yellow hill*

Of these four hills, Carn an Tuirc and Cairn of Claise overlook the head of Glen Clunie a few kilometres north-east of the Cairnwell Pass, showing shallow grassy corries and rounded shoulders to the A93 road. Tolmount, a few kilometres east, stands at the head of Glen Callater with a steep craggy face above this glen, and Tom Buidhe to its south is a rounded swelling on the Mounth plateau. The four can be climbed in a round tour from the head of Glen Clunie.

Leave the A93 road 2km north of the Cairnwell Pass at (148800) and descend a short distance to cross the Cairnwell Burn by the old bridge, a remnant of the 18th century military road. Follow the Allt a'Gharbh-choire E for 1km by a rather indistinct path shown on the OS 1:50,000 map and cross the tributary coming down from the north-east. Then climb E across the hillside over heather, grass and areas of boulders to reach the flat stony summit of Carn an Tuirc. (3km; 510m; 1h 40min).

Continue E across the summit stonefield and, where the slope steepens towards Coire Kander, turn SE down a wide grassy ridge to the saddle from where Cairn of Claise lies 1½km SSE. Climb the easy slope to reach a line of fence posts which lead to the summit. (5½km; 620m; 2h 20min). A pleasant walk ENE down grassy slopes leads to a shallow peaty col from which a wide incline (it is hardly a ridge) leads to Tolmount. (8½km; 700m; 3h 10min). The summit is garnished with broken granite slabs and stands near the steep headwall of Glen Callater.

To the south the subdued eminence of Tom Buidhe swells from the tableland. It is best approached by returning down the wide incline and skirting round the upper part of the shallow green corrie, one of the sources of the River South Esk, which separates Tolmount from Tom Buidhe. A short ascent SE up a grassy slope studded with a few boulders leads to the rounded summit of the latter. (10km; 790m; 3h 40min).

Return due W along the highest ground over Ca Whims. After about 2km bear WSW, contouring at about 970m between the upper slopes of Cairn of Claise on one's right and steepening ground dropping towards the Caenlochan Glen on one's left. This traverse is across tussocky grass and blaeberry, but it leads in about 2km to the smooth ground of the watershed where the Mounth plateau is reduced to quite a narrow ridge between the Caenlochan Glen and the Garbh-choire.

Go SW along this ridge, following a fence line, to reach the path of the Monega road, the highest drove route in the Highlands, which comes up from Glen Isla over Little Glas Maol. The path crosses the ridge and leads NW down the spur of Sron na Gaoithe towards Glen Clunie. Follow it, and leave the crest of the spur to descend its north flank just before reaching the rocky knob at its termination.

Below this the path disappears, but an easy grass slope leads down to the Allt a'Gharbh-choire which must be crossed to reach the bridge at the starting point of the route.

Carn an Tuirc from Glen Clunie   H.M. Brown

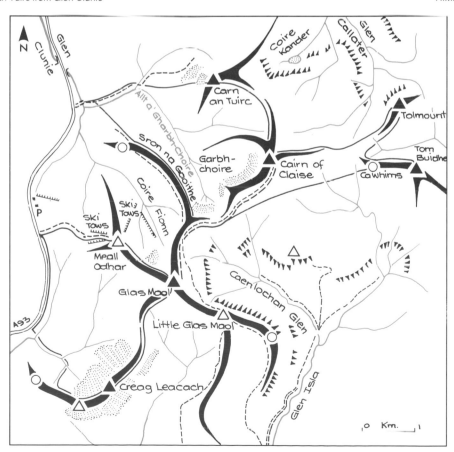

The White Mounth from the road to Glen Gairn   W.D. Brooker

Carn an t-Sagairt Mor; 1047m; (OS Sheets 43 and 44; 208843); M81; *big hill of the priest*
Carn a'Coire Boidheach; 1118m; (OS Sheet 44; 226845); M33; *hill of the beautiful corrie*

Between the north-facing corries of The Stuic and Lochnagar and the deep valley of Loch Muick and the Dubh Loch is the corner of the high Mounth plateau known as The White Mounth. To its east the summit of Lochnagar, Cac Carn Beag, is its highest point, while in the middle Carn a'Coire Boidheach rises only marginally higher than the top of The Stuic just to its north. Westwards the plateau begins to rise and fall into individual hills of which Carn an t-Sagairt Mor (or Cairn Taggart to give its anglicised name) is the highest.

It is possible to climb these hills in a single long day from Glen Muick and include Lochnagar, Cairn

Bannoch and Broad Cairn. However, this involves a walk of nearly 30km, and it is more usual to enjoy them in shorter sections by the routes described here and in the following pages.

For these two hills, start at Auchallater farm on the A93 road in Glen Clunie and follow the private road up Glen Callater for 5km to Lochcallater Lodge. (This is the first part of the Tolmount road which leads to Glen Clova). Just outside the lodge enclosure a path strikes uphill before turning SE to traverse the hillside above Loch Callater, gaining height gradually. It turns NE below the small rocky bluff of Creag an Loch to gain a col below the west slope of Carn an t-Sagairt

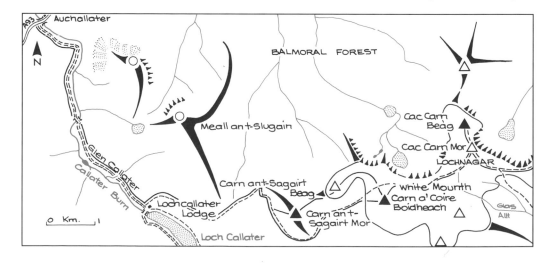

Mor. Follow the path up this slope until it starts to contour around to the south-east, and then climb directly to the summit by the line of a fence. (9km; 680m; 3h 10min).

Continue NE, descending about 80m and reascending the same height to pass over Carn an t-Sagairt Beag (1044m) and reach the rim of the plateau ¾km beyond. The Stuic rises a little higher, ½km east along the edge of the cliffs, and is well worth visiting for the view over its rocky corries to the Dee valley far below.

From there an easy walk south for ½km over the sparse stony tundra of the high plateau brings one to Carn a'Coire Bhoidheach. In thick weather, with snow on the ground, careful navigation is needed to find the summit of this very flat-topped mountain. (11½km; 880m; 4h 10min).

Return by descending W to intersect the path which leads SW across the head-streams of the Allt an Dubh-loch and round the south side of Carn an t--Sagairt Mor on the way back to Glen Callater.

Broad Cairn and Creag an Dubh-loch from the track on the south side of Loch Muick   I. Brown

Cairn Bannoch; 1012m; (OS Sheet 44; 223826); M114; *hill of the point*
Broad Cairn; 998m; (OS Sheet 44; 240815); M139

The glacial valley which bites into the eastern part of the Mounth plateau to the south of Lochnagar forms a deep trough containing Loch Muick. Upstream the valley floor rises to a smaller upper basin holding the Dubh Loch. Broad Cairn stands at the southern edge of this upper basin; Creag an Dubh-loch, its northern extension, has a great face of overlapping slabs. Cairn Bannoch is set back from the west side of the basin and is only distinguished from the other tops in this corner of the plateau by its small yet prominent summit cone.

From the car park at the end of the public road up Glen Muick walk SW past Spittal of Glenmuick and in 1km take the path to the right which crosses the outflow of Loch Muick to reach the road on the west side of the glen. Continue along the lochside to the Glas-allt-Shiel wood, and emerge on its far side by a footpath. In another 100 metres take the right fork of the path and go up the glen of the Allt an Dubh-loch. On the right the Stulan burn cascades down its rocky bed in an attractive waterfall, while below on the left the Dubh loch stream sluices over red granite slabs in a succession of waterslides.

Abruptly the Dubh Loch comes into view and the path peters out on the north side of the loch, however continue to its head and upstream until the north-west end of Creag an Dubh-loch is outflanked and Cairn Bannoch can be seen. After crossing the tributary that tumbles down over the slabs of Eagle's Rock, cross to the south side of the Allt an Dubh-loch and ascend by another tributary between Creag an Dubh-loch and Cairn Bannoch until it is easy to climb to the summit cone of the latter with its broken granite tor. (11½km; 610m; 3h 40min).

Go SE for 1km along the undulating plateau to Cairn of Gowal (983m), and then E across a wide col leading to a gentle ascent of the boulderfield summit of Broad Cairn. (14km; 710m; 4h 20min).

Descend E down granite boulders to a rough path, which becomes a bulldozed track, and in a further 1km reach a wooden shed. Continue E for 300 metres, then bear left along the path which slants down to reach Loch Muick near its head. The path continues along the south shore of the loch through scattered birches and joins a bulldozed road leading back to Spittal of Glenmuick. Map on page 113.

The north-east corrie of Lochnagar   *R. Robb*

Lochnagar; 1155m; (OS Sheet 44; 244861); M19; *named after Lochan na Gaire in the NE corrie, meaning little loch of the noisy sound*

Located entirely in the royal estate of Balmoral, this fine and complex mountain lies south of the Dee valley, and north-west of Loch Muick. Its summit crowns the northern rim of the great Mounth plateau which from there sweeps far southward to Glen Shee and the Angus glens. The true nobility of Lochnagar is best appreciated from the north, from Deeside or even better from the B976 road from Crathie to Gairnshiel, from where its sharp summit and flanking corries can be seen rising above the lower slopes mantled by the ancient pinewoods of the Ballochbuie Forest.

The usual route to Lochnagar starts at the car park at the end of the public road up Glen Muick. Walk SW along the private road for 250 metres to Spittal of Glenmuick and turn right along the edge of the plantation to reach the other side of the glen at Allt-na-giubhsaich. Continue W along a path on the south side of the burn through the pinewoods to reach a track which is followed W for almost 3km to the col at the head of Glen Gelder.

There take the rough and much eroded path WSW across a slight dip and then uphill for 1¼km to the last waterpoint of the Foxes' Well to the left of the path. The slope relents for a short distance before the steep ascent known as The Ladder, and a short diversion west to the col just south of Meikle Pap gives a splendid view of the great north-east corrie of Lochnagar.

If there is old hard snow covering the steep slope of The Ladder it may be safer to keep to the right among the boulders near the edge of the corrie, and at the top the summit ridge is reached. A short descent across a wide col and a climb of 70m lead to the almost level roof of the mountain. Finally, an airy walk of 1km along the rim of the great north-east corrie past the cairn of Cac Carn Mor and round the deep inden-

tation of the Black Spout ends at the summit cone of Cac Carn Beag, as the highest point of Lochnagar is called, where the trig point stands on top of a granite tor. (9km; 800m; 3h 20min).

The quickest descent is by the route of ascent, but an enjoyable alternative is by the path down the Glas Allt past a pretty waterfall and then by steep zigzags

At the top of the Lochnagar cliffs   *D.J. Bennet*

Lochnagar from Aberarder in Deeside   A. Watson

to the wood of Glas-allt-Shiel. From there return to Spittal of Glenmuick either by the road along the north-west side of Loch Muick and the path across the outflow of the loch, or by Allt-na-giubhsaich.

There are no restrictions on climbing Lochnagar by the ascent route described above during the stalking season, but other routes should be avoided at that time.

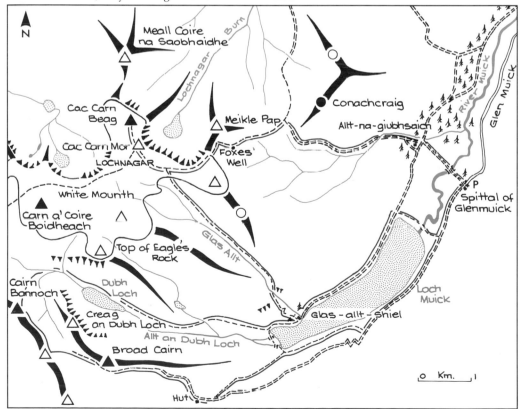

Driesh above the forested hillsides of Glen Doll   J. Renny

Driesh; 947m; (OS Sheet 44; 271736); M213; *from Gaelic dris, a thorn bush or bramble*
Mayar; 928m; (OS Sheet 44; 241738); M248; *meaning obscure*

The straightest and deepest of the Angus glens, its sides scalloped by many corries, Glen Clova slices north-westwards into the Eastern Grampians. At its head it divides into two branches, the northerly one being the glen leading to Bachnagairn, the southern one being Glen Doll. Both these glens are hemmed in by steep slopes and rocky bluffs, and on its south side Glen Doll opens out to form the wide amphitheatre of Corrie Fee. The two hills described here stand above this amphitheatre, Driesh to its south-east and Mayar to its south-west. Mayar is the southernmost hill of the Mounth plateau, marking the point where its gently undulating expanse changes to the rounded hills of the Angus glens.

There are extensive coniferous plantations in upper Glen Clova and Glen Doll, and the route to Driesh and Mayar starts at the Forestry Commission car park ½km past Braedownie farm. Go W along the road past the youth hostel at Glendoll Lodge as far as the bridge at (276763), cross it and shortly reach the start of the old hill path to Kilbo in Glen Prosen. This path leads SW uphill until it crosses the Burn of Kilbo and emerges from the forest at a deer fence. Continue up the path along the steep side of the Shank of Drumfollow to the col between Driesh and Mayar. Turn SE then E to reach the summit of Driesh in 1½km of easy walking over a subsidiary top. (5½km; 700m; 2h 30min).

From Driesh one can see into the upper reaches of the Clova glens and identify the lines of the old drove roads crossing to Glen Muick and Braemar, and all the summits of the Mounth from Mount Keen to Glas Maol can be seen on a clear day.

Mayar is reached by returning to the col and following the line of the fence west over pleasant grassy tundra. (9km; 860m; 3h 30min). On a clear day the position of this hill at the edge of the Mounth is obvious, for to the north is its wide plateau while to the south are the many low rounded hills between Glen Isla and Glen Prosen.

Grassy slopes lead down NNE for 1km to the head of Corrie Fee where the Fee Burn tumbles down the steep headwall. Descend on the south-east side of the burn past small waterfalls to reach a path which in turn is followed ENE down the lower corrie, over a stile and into the Glendoll Forest. The path develops into a forest road which leads downhill across the White Water and past the youth hostel to reach the car park.

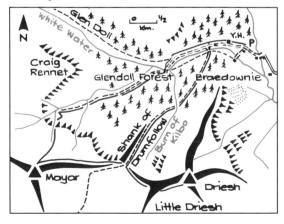

The path from Mount Keen to Glen Mark over the Knowe of Crippley   W.D. Brooker

Mount Keen; 939m; (OS Sheet 44; 409869); M229; *from Gaelic monadh, meaning hill*

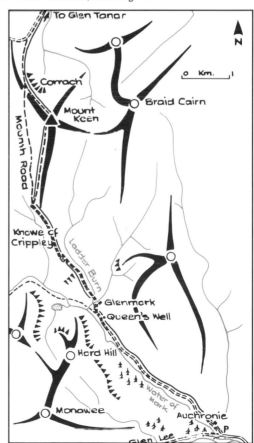

This is the most easterly of all the Munros, and one of the most solitary. Its pointed dome is on the spine of the Mounth between the Dee valley and the Vale of Strathmore, and it is the highest summit east of Loch Muick. There are two commonly used approaches to Mount Keen, from Glen Esk to the south-east and Glen Tanar to the north-east.

The Glen Esk route starts at a car park where the glen divides into its two upper reaches, Glen Lee and Glen Mark. Go W to the road junction and take the right fork up Glen Mark, continuing for 3½km to the Queen's Well, a monument which commemorates a visit by Queen Victoria.

Bear right (north) past the last house in the glen and follow the track up the narrow glen of the Ladder Burn, climbing its west slope to emerge onto an undulating high moorland near the Knowe of Crippley. The blunt cone of Mount Keen rises to the north, and the track to it reaches a fork. The traditional Mounth Road goes due N and another path, more frequently used today, bears to the right to ascend Mount Keen. Just before the summit cairn there is a boundary stone with a large **B** carved on it. (9km; 680m; 3h 10min).

The other route to Mount Keen starts at the end of the public road up Glen Tanar. From the car park at Glen Tanar House go past a sawmill and through a gate to the estate road up the north side of the Water of Tanar. This road passes through fine native pines for 6km, and for another 4km goes up the open glen, crossing the river twice. Cross the Water of Tanar for a third time at (407896) and ascend the Mounth Road southwards by a bulldozed track through heather-clad slopes. After climbing for 2km diverge SE along the path which goes above the headwall of the Corrach to the top of Mount Keen. (13½km; 760m; 4h 20min). Both these routes follow rights of way.

The Cairngorm Mountains from Morrone   *W.D. Brooker*

SECTION 8

The Cairngorm Mountains

Ben Macdui from Braeriach   *N. Ritchie*

The vast high mountain range of the Cairngorms is divided into three main blocks or massifs by two major passes, the Lairig Ghru and the Lairig an Laoigh, which go from south to north across the range through glacially carved valleys. To the east of the Lairig an Laoigh lie Beinn Bhreac, Beinn a'Chaorainn and the huge plateaux of Beinn a'Bhuird and Ben Avon. The middle block consists of the high ground above Strath Nethy and the deep basin of Loch Avon; it extends over Cairn Gorm to Ben Macdui and round to Beinn Mheadhoin in a great horseshoe, with off-shoots to Derry Cairngorm, Bynack More and Carn a'Mhaim. To the west of the Lairig Ghru the largest of the three blocks extends from the rim of the mighty amphitheatre of An Garbh Choire across the grassy plateau of the Moine Mhor (the great moss) to Glen Feshie; it includes Braeriach and Cairn Toul which face Ben Macdui across the Lairig Ghru, and further south and west The Devil's Point, Beinn Bhrotain, Monadh Mor and, overlooking the Feshie, Mullach Clach a'Bhlair and Sgor Gaoith.

Largely of intrusive granites, the Cairngorms are characterised by poor acid soils and bleak stony tundra, albeit richer and grassier on the western massif. Consequently the most obviously impressive features tend to be in the corries and penetrating valleys where cliffs, streams and lochans create variety and interest. The high plateaux might be thought at first sight to tend towards monotony, but it is there that one finds a little piece of the arctic in Scotland, a fascinating landscape with vast spacious views.

Some of the summits of the Cairngorms may be approached from either Deeside or Speyside. Since both approaches are frequently used, brief descriptions of access routes from the two directions are included where appropriate.

In Deeside the common starting point for several of the peaks is the car park near the Linn of Dee at the end of the public road up Deeside. From there one rough private road continues up the River Dee towards the Lairig Ghru and distant passes leading to Glen Tilt and Glen Feshie; another private road leads north-west up Glen Lui to Derry Lodge and is the most important access route on the south side of the Cairngorms. Both these roads follow rights of way and bicycles can be used along them to save some time reaching the mountains.

From Speyside the Cairngorms appear as a great scarp, scalloped by corries and sliced through by the deep cleft of the Lairig Ghru, with the dark forests of Glen More, Rothiemurchus and Inshriach in the foreground. There are a number of suitable starting points for the mountains, those most frequently used for the central massif being the car parks at the end of the roads to the ski slopes in Coire Cas and Coire na Ciste. The western summits may be reached by the narrow public road up the east side of Glen Feshie to its end at Achlean farm.

Attractive approaches through Rothiemurchus Forest to Gleann Einich and the entrance to the defile of the Lairig Ghru may be made from Coylumbridge, the end of the public road near Whitewell and the western corner of Loch Morlich. Another pleasant way of reaching the Lairig Ghru and Braeriach is by the path leading south-west through the Creag a'Chalamain gap from the car park at the big bend in the ski road near the upper limit of the forest below Coire Cas.

Ben Avon, Leabaidh an Daimh Bhuidhe; 1171m (OS Sheets 36 and 43; 132019); M16; *bed of the yellow stag*

One of the most unusual mountains in Scotland because of the many strange granite tors along its skyline, Ben Avon is also one of the biggest in terms of its area of high ground, being a vast plateau stretching 12km from Glen Quoich in the south-west to Inchrory in Glen Avon far to the north-east. It is the most easterly mountain of the main Cairngorm range, and the most prominent of them when seen from lower Aberdeenshire or Banffshire.

Ben Avon can be reached from three points: Inchrory in Glen Avon to the north, Corndavon Lodge high up the River Gairn to the east, and Invercauld Bridge near Braemar to the south. All these routes are long, and the use of a bicycle along the private approach roads will save some time and shorten walking distances.

The Invercauld Bridge route, which is probably the most frequently used, starts from the A93 road a few kilometres east of Braemar. Turn up the public road to Keiloch where cars should be left. Continue on foot or by bicycle for 5½km along the private road past Alltdourie into Gleann an t-Slugain, and onwards by the path past the ruins of Slugain Lodge to reach Glen Quoich. The path continues up the east side of this glen to end just beyond the huge boulder of Clach a'Cleirich. From there it is an easy climb up the narrowing grassy glen to the col at 970m called The Sneck, where a fine view opens out to the north into the wild corrie of Slochd Mor. Climb E up slopes of gravel and turf to the plateau of Ben Avon, and then go 1½km NE across the level tundra to the large summit tor, whose top is reached by an easy scramble. (16km; 850m; 5h).

To vary the return route, one can keep high along the plateau on the east side of Glen Quoich, going S to the Top of Carn Eas (1089m), then SE to Creag an Dail Mhor (972m) before descending SW to Glen Quoich and the ruined lodge in Gleann an t-Slugain.

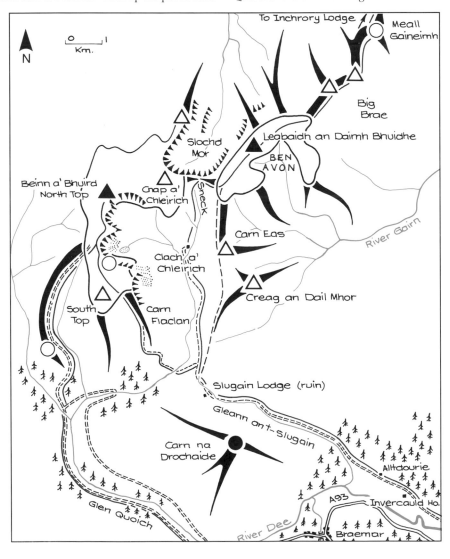

Ben Avon seen from Beinn a'Bhuird above Coire an Dubh Lochain   *D.J. Broadhead*

The northern approach is from Tomintoul. Cars should be left 1km beyond the village at the Queen's View car park at (165176) and the old road along the east side of Glen Avon followed on foot or bicycle for 13km past Inchrory Lodge to a point ½km beyond the Linn of Avon.

From there pleasant heathery ground leads up the northern spur of Meall Gaineimh to gain the north-eastern corner of the vast tor-studded plateau of Ben Avon. Finally, the route goes SW across this undulating plateau for another 5km to the summit. (20½km; 870m; 6h).

The summit rocks of Ben Avon   *H.M. Brown*

The South Top of Beinn a'Bhuird above the pinewoods of Glen Quoich   *A. Watson*

Beinn a'Bhuird; 1196m; (OS Sheets 36 and 43; 093006); *from beinn bord, meaning table-hill*

This vast mountain between Glen Quoich and Glen Avon has the biggest high tableland in the Cairngorms, and although it sweeps down gently on its west side to lower peaty glens and plateaux, on the east and north-east it plunges in spectacular cliffs to great wild corries.

One possible approach is from Invercauld Bridge, a few kilometres east of Braemar. It follows the same route as described on the previous pages for Ben Avon as far as the entry to Glen Quoich 1km beyond the ruined Slugain Lodge. There a path breaks off to the west towards Quoich Water, crosses the stream and on the far bank continues NE high up past Carn Fiaclach, from where easy slopes of short grass and gravel lead up to the edge of the plateau of Beinn a'Bhuird.

Once on the plateau, it is a short distance south-west to the South Top (1179m), but this is a diversion from the route to the summit. The walking along the plateau is excellent, on dry ground with grand views at times into the great east-facing corries: Coire na Ciche, Coire an Dubh Lochain and Coire nan Clach. In misty weather in summer the cliff-edge on the right can be useful for navigating, but remember that snow wreaths and unstable cornices sometimes remain along the edge long into summer. The cliffs lead to the North Top, which is the true summit, although marked by only a small cairn in the middle of the featureless plateau. (16km; 980m; 5h 10min).

The grassy swelling of Cnap a'Chleirich (1172m) rises from the plateau to the east, and the return journey can be varied by crossing this Top, descending E to the saddle called The Sneck, and then turning S to reach Clach a'Cleirich and the path which leads down Glen Quoich to Gleann an t-Slugain.

A quite different route to Beinn a'Bhuird starts at the Linn of Quoich, which can be reached by car from Braemar via the Linn of Dee. Walk up the track on the south-west side of the Quoich Water through fine stands of Old Caledonian pines, and after 6km cross the west tributary of the Quoich Water. Keep on north, following the bulldozed track through the highest trees and then climb by a few zigzags onto the ridge of An Diollaid. The track leads high onto Beinn a'Bhuird, ending only about 1½km SSW of the summit, which is easily reached across the plateau. (14km; 870m; 4h 40min). Although shorter than the Gleann an t-Slugain route and having the merit of passing through the Old Caledonian forest in Glen Quoich, this route is rather spoiled by following a bulldozed track almost the whole way to the summit.

Map on page 118.

Looking south from Bynack More to Beinn a'Chaorainn and the Lairig an Laoigh pass (right)   *A. Watson*

Beinn Bhreac; 931m; (OS Sheets 36 and 43; 058971), M245; *speckled hill*
Beinn a'Chaorainn; 1082m; (OS Sheets 36 and 43; 045013); M58; *hill of the rowan*

These two hills occupy a large area of high ground on the east side of upper Glen Derry with, between them, the vast expanse of the Moine Bhealaidh, a flat featureless plateau at about 850m altitude. From Derry Lodge or Luibeg, Beinn Bhreac stands out prominently above the Old Caledonian pine forest of Derry, a broad heathery hill speckled with grey screes that obviously give its Gaelic name. Beinn a'Chaorainn is a conical stony hill rising at the head of Glen Derry, just above the Lairig an Laoigh pass, towards which its western slopes drop steeply in broken crags.

The car park near Linn of Dee is the starting point for this expedition, as well as for others to the mountains round Glen Derry and the southern end of the Lairig Ghru. The first 5km are along the private road as far as Derry Lodge. From there take the bulldozed track up the east side of Glen Derry for about 2km to its highest point at about 500m. Then strike NE uphill through the trees and over heather slopes to the 673m col between Meall an Lundain and Beinn Bhreac, and finally climb NNE on wind-clipped heath up the broad ridge to the summit of Beinn Bhreac. (10km; 590m; 3h 10min).

Continue NW then N across the grassy, peaty plateau of the Moine Bhealaidh, usually known as the yellow moss. Stay near the watershed as this gives the driest ground, dropping only to about 850m. The route offers spacious views towards Ben Macdui and Beinn a'Bhuird. After 4km the ground becomes firmer and the going is easy on heath, gravel and stones up the broad ridge to Beinn a'Chaorainn. (15km; 820m; 4h 50min).

The easiest return to Derry Lodge goes SW for 1½km, then steeply down W to the summit of the Lairig an Laoigh at 740m. There is a fine view northwards through the pass to the distant tors on Bynack More, the Barns of Bynack. Follow the path south down Glen Derry until it becomes a bulldozed track, and continue along this track for a further 1km until it begins to climb uphill to the left. At that point diverge to the right along a footpath, cross the Derry Burn by a footbridge and go down the west side of the burn, a more pleasant way to return to Derry Lodge than along the bulldozed track.

If a bicycle is used, it can be taken about 4km beyond Derry Lodge as far as the Glen Derry flats. From there it may be preferable to continue up Glen Derry to the summit of the Lairig an Laoigh and climb Beinn a'Chaorainn first. The 4km high-level walk south across the Moine Bhealaidh gives splendid views beyond the pine woods of the Dubh Gleann and Glen Quoich to Lochnagar. From Beinn Bhreac return to Glen Derry down the lower part of Coire an Fhir Bhoga.

Map on page 122.

Ben Macdui; 1309m; (OS Sheets 36 and 43; 989989); M2; *hill of the son of Duff*
Carn a'Mhaim; 1037m; (OS Sheets 36 and 43; 994952); M93; *hill of the pass*
Derry Cairngorm; 1155m; (OS Sheets 36 and 43; 017980); M20; *blue hill of Derry*

The central group of the Cairngorms, lying between the defiles of the Lairig Ghru and the Lairig an Laoigh, has as its highest point the great dome of Ben Macdui. From it two long high ridges thrust southwards separated by Glen Luibeg. The eastern ridge includes Derry Cairngorm and ends above the woods of Glen Derry; the western one is Carn a'Mhaim, whose crest, one of the narrowest of Cairngorm ridges, is joined to Ben Macdui by a high col.

These three mountains can all be climbed from Derry Lodge, either singly or together, and the following description is for the complete traverse, a long day's hillwalking which can be shortened by starting or finishing the circuit at intermediate points.

Start from the Linn of Dee as described on the preceding page up the private road to Derry Lodge and cross the Derry Burn by the footbridge west of the lodge. Go W along the north side of the Lui by the path through splendid scattered native pines for 3km to the Robbers' Copse where the Lairig Ghru and Glen Luibeg paths diverge. At this point the direct route to Ben Macdui goes N along the path beside the Luibeg Burn and up the Sron Riach ridge. (15km; 950m; 5h).

The route to Carn a'Mhaim crosses the Luibeg Bridge, below which the boulder debris is evidence of the power of the flood which carried away the earlier bridge after a cloud-burst. Leave the Lairig Ghru path to climb the south-east ridge of Carn a'Mhaim. There is a grassy col between its two boulder-clad tops, of which the north-west one is the summit. (11½km; 700m; 3h 50min).

Continuing to Ben Macdui, go NNW down the narrow ridge, passing several rocky knobs and small tors until after 2km a wide col is reached at 800m. Beyond it climb the steep side of Ben Macdui up the Allt Clach nan Taillear *(the tailors' burn)*, or the slopes to its south-east, to reach the flatter summit dome and the huge cairn at its highest point. (16km; 1210m; 5h 40min).

Descend 1km E to the edge of Coire Sputan Dearg and turn NE down the ridge along the edge of this corrie to the col which is the watershed between the Luibeg Burn and Loch Etchachan. This is an excellent point from which to appreciate the grandeur of the central Cairngorms, with their deep glaciated hollows, granite slabs, snow beds, streams and lochs.

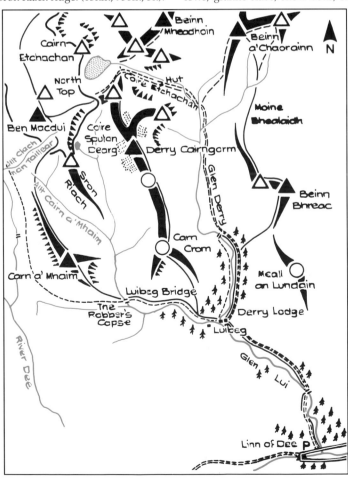

Carn a'Mhaim and Ben Macdui from the south   *A. Watson*

From the col contour SSE round the side of Creagan a'Choire Etchachan (1108m) and descend a little to reach the saddle on its south side. Then go SE up the boulder-strewn elongated cone of Derry Cairngorm. (21km; 1350m; 7h).

Continue SSE along the broad ridge, keeping slightly on its east side above Glen Derry, and climb 50m to Carn Crom. From there descend SE to the Derry woods and the road back to the Linn of Dee.

Ben Macdui can also be climbed from the north, from the direction of Cairn Gorm, and this route is described on pages 124 and 125.

Derry Cairngorm from Beinn Mheadhoin   *D. Scott*

Hell's Lum Crag and Cairn Gorm from the headwaters of the Garbh Uisge Beag   *H.M. Brown*

Cairn Gorm; 1245m; (OS Sheet 36; 005040); M5; *blue hill*

Standing at the highest point on the northern edge of the central Cairngorm massif, Cairn Gorm itself is prominently visible from Aviemore and is easily identified by the lines of its ski pistes in winter, and the summer scars of these developments. Its rounded summit rises above the bowl of Coire Cas, with the narrow Coire na Ciste to the north-east, and the fine rocky cirques of Coire an t-Sneachda and Coire an Lochain, the Northern Corries, to the south-west.

The easy access provided by the ski road into Coire Cas makes Cairn Gorm one of the easiest and most climbed of all Munros. It is possible to go by car and chairlift to within 160m of the summit, but no self-respecting Munroist would do this. However, most climbers use the access road and start their climb from the car park at a height of 625m.

To avoid the unsightly pylons and snow-fences of Coire Cas, climb steeply NE for a short distance to join the path up the broad ridge of Sron an Aonaich. Follow this much trodden path SE to the hemispherical dome of the Ptarmigan restaurant, and for a further 1km south to the summit of Cairn Gorm. (3km; 620m; 1h 50min). Various structures for weather recording and radio relay are sited on the boulder-clad summit area, and once every half hour the weather instruments emerge automatically from their housing to sample the elements for a few minutes.

Several possibilities exist for continuing the day's walk rather than returning directly by the route of ascent. Descend ½km west by stony slopes to the broad col at the head of Coire Cas. From there a quick return to the car park may be made down the Fiacaill a'Choire Chais in little more than half an hour. Alternatively, continue S then SW following a worn path

across the stony plateau, along the rim of Coire an t-Sneachda and over the Top of Stob Coire an t-Sneachda (1176m) to the next col. From there a path, known as The Goat Track, drops steeply in zigzags north into Coire an t-Sneachda, and a pleasant walk down to the mouth of this corrie and then north along a well-made path leads back to the car park.

To extend the walk further, one can climb from the col at the head of Coire an t-Sneachda for ½km to Cairn Lochan (1215m), a fine summit right on the edge of the vertical cliffs of Coire an Lochain. The high-level circuit of the Northern Corries can be completed by going W along the edge of the corrie past spectacular cliff scenery and descending NW then N to a level grassy area known as the Miadan. Continue N down the ridge separating Coire an Lochain from the Allt Creag an Leth-choin (or Lurcher's Gully as it is more commonly known) and follow the path NNE below the corries back to the car park.

Ben Macdui can also be climbed from the direction of Cairn Gorm, and this is probably the most popular route. Certainly the Coire Cas car park is a good deal nearer to Ben Macdui than the Linn of Dee, and also a lot higher. However, this route goes for several kilometres across a high and exposed plateau, and cannot be recommended in bad weather.

From the col at the head of Coire an t-Sneachda (reached either direct from the car park or over the top of Cairn Gorm) bear SSW along a path which climbs a little and then descends very gradually across grassy slopes to Lochan Buidhe at the lowest point of the plateau. At 1125m it is the highest body of water in the British Isles, and it is the only landmark in this wide expanse of stony tundra. Continue SSE for another 2km, keeping just west of the rounded spine of the plateau to reach the summit of Ben Macdui. (By Cairn Gorm: 9½km; 930m; 3h 40min. Direct by Coire an t-Sneachda: 8km; 730m; 3h). Return by the same route to the col at the head of Coire an t-Sneachda, down this corrie and so back to the car park.

No restrictions on access by these routes in the stalking season.

Ben Macdui from Braeriach   *D.J. Broadhead*

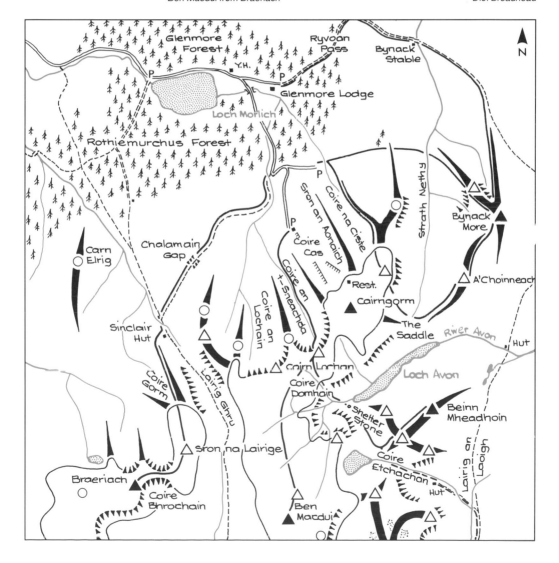

Looking across Loch Avon to Beinn Mheadhoin   *J.E.S. Bennet*

Beinn Mheadhoin; 1182m; (OS Sheet 36; 024017); M12; *middle hill*

Beinn Mheadhoin is on the east side of the central Cairngorms, separated from Ben Macdui by the hollow of Loch Etchachan, and from Cairn Gorm by the deep trough holding Loch Avon. It is rather an inaccessible mountain, in the centre of the massif as its name implies, and not easily seen from either the Dee or the Spey valleys, although it is just visible from the latter through the defile of Strath Nethy. It is well seen from Glen Derry, and also from the Cairn Gorm plateau across Loch Avon, and the granite tors along its summit ridge give it a distinctive appearance.

The nearest approach is from the car park at the foot of Coire Cas on Cairn Gorm, and the route from there involves first crossing the plateau south-west of Cairn Gorm and descending to Loch Avon before climbing Beinn Mheadhoin itself. There is thus a good deal of up and downhill effort on both the way there and back, and particularly in winter the route is a serious one, calling for mountaineering experience.

From the Coire Cas car park there are two possible routes to the head of Loch Avon:

1. Ascend the Fiacaill a'Choire Chais ridge on the south-west side of the corrie to reach the plateau ½km west of Cairn Gorm and descend SSE down Coire Raibert, following a rough path down the east side of the stream in the lower part of the corrie to reach Loch Avon.

2. Take the path SW from the car park into Coire an t-Sneachda, going right up to the innermost southwest corner of the corrie. Climb the path (The Goat Track) to the col on the plateau and descend SSE down Coire Domhain where there is a path down the

steep slope between cliffs.

Thus one enters the place which well merits its description as the 'heart of the Cairngorms'. The Loch Avon basin is ringed by precipitous slopes and high crags, and at its upper end streams from the plateau above cascade down granite slabs in a profusion of white torrents. Continue round the head of Loch Avon where the crossing of the Feith Buidhe may cause a problem, particularly if it is swollen by melt water in spring. Pass below the Shelter Stone and the great cliffs of the Sticil and Carn Etchachan and climb SE up a slanting path towards Loch Etchachan. Before reaching the loch bear E up to the South-west Top of Beinn Mheadhoin (1163m) and finally go NE along the broad crest past several granite tors or barns to the largest of these, which forms the summit. (9km; 960m; 3h 40min).

On the return to Coire Cas by either of the routes described above there is a further 410m of ascent from Loch Avon to the Cairn Gorm plateau.

No restriction on access by these routes during the stalking season.

An easier but longer approach may be made from Linn of Dee via Derry Lodge, using the route described for Beinn Bhreac. Leave upper Glen Derry by the path which climbs NW through Coire Etchachan to pass the outlet of Loch Etchachan and join the route described above for the final stages of the ascent to the summit plateau. (17km; 860m; 5h 20min). A bicycle can be used for the first 10km as far as the Glen Derry flats.

Maps on pages 122 and 125.

Bynack More; 1090m; (OS Sheet 36; 042063); M52; *meaning obscure*

Ben Bynack or Caiplich as it was once known forms the north- eastern outpost of the central Cairngorms, separated from Cairn Gorm itself by Strath Nethy. When seen from Nethybridge or other nearby viewpoints in Strath Spey it appears as a shapely pointed mountain rising above the dark Forest of Abernethy, rather isolated from the rest of the Cairngorms.

The traditional approach to Bynack More is from Loch Morlich through the Ryvoan Pass, and it is possible to drive to Glenmore Lodge, park a few metres beyond it and start from there. Continue on foot through the picturesque Ryvoan Pass with

Bynack More from the top of Shelter Stone Crag   D.J. Bennet

its beautiful Lochan Uaine, the aptly named green lochan, and ½km further on take the track going east to cross the River Nethy at Bynack Stable. Beyond this point the track becomes a path, climbing SE over the lower shoulder of Bynack More towards the Lairig an Laoigh. Follow this path for 3km almost to its highest point and then bear S up the north ridge to the summit. (10km; 750m; 3h 30min).

Two other routes to Bynack More from the Cairn Gorm access road have become popular, being shorter and more interesting, though crossing rougher, pathless and more demanding terrain. Both start from the car park at the foot of Coire na Ciste, and their combination gives a good circular traverse.

The lower route heads ENE across the heather-clad hillside for 2km above a small plantation to the col just south of Pt.737m. Descend steeply E down heather and gravelly scree to Strath Nethy, cross the river and

climb the north-west ridge of Bynack Beg (964m). Continue SE across boulders and granite outcrops to the upper slopes of Bynack More. (6km; 790m; 2h 40min).

The higher route goes up the ridge flanking Coire na Ciste on its east side to reach the flat col 1km NNE of Cairn Gorm. Descend diagonally SE down steep slopes to reach The Saddle at the head of Strath Nethy. From there a broad ridge leads NE over A'Choinneach (1017m) to a grassy plateau from which rise the upper slopes of Bynack More. On the ridge crest above are the tors of the Little Barns, and beyond them, 40m down on the east side at (045058), are the Barns of Bynack proper. They are huge and impressive granite castles well worth the short diversion required to visit them before going on to the summit. (9½km; 960m; 3h 50min).

Map on page 125.

Bynack More (left) and Cairn Gorm (right) from the north   I. Brown

Braeriach from Ben Macdui   *A. O'Brien*

Braeriach; 1296m; (OS Sheets 36 and 43; 953999); M3; *brindled greyish upper part*

Mighty Braeriach forms a high peninsula of the great western Cairngorm plateau, joined to Cairn Toul around the rim of An Garbh Choire. When seen from the vicinity of Aviemore it appears as the western part of the Cairngorm scarp, lying to the right of the cleft of the Lairig Ghru, its northern slopes scalloped by three graceful corries. The hidden south-east face of the mountain is even more impressive, for on that side the precipices of Coire Bhrochain drop from the summit sheer into the depths of An Garbh Choire.

Although the mountain can be climbed from Gleann Einich or, more distantly, from Glen Feshie, the usual route is from the road to the ski slopes on Cairngorm. Start at the car park near the edge of the trees at the first big bend on the road (985074) and descend S along a good path to a footbridge over the Allt Mor. Cross this stream and continue S then SW on a path high on the opposite bank. The path deteriorates, but leads SW to the prominent notch of the Chalamain Gap and through this little gorge, cut out by glacial melt water. Continue SW downhill to reach the Lairig Ghru path, cross the stream and climb up to the knoll on which is the site of the Sinclair Hut. (At the time of this revision it is expected that the hut will be demolished in early 1991).

To the south-west a path leads up the hillside to the broad base of the Sron na Lairige ridge which is climbed for 400m, steeply at first, then less so. A line along the east edge of this ridge gives some striking views down into the Lairig Ghru. Traverse the gravelly tundra of the crest over the Top of Sron na Lairige (1148m),

then descend SSW to a wide col and finally climb 140m, SW at first to reach the cliff-top of Coire Bhrochain, and finally W along the edge of the corrie to the summit. (10½km; 1000m; 4h).

The cairn stands on the brink of the 200m granite cliffs of Coire Bhrochain, and looks out across the great amphitheatre of An Garbh Choire to Cairn Toul and Sgor an Lochain Uaine, with between them the high hanging corrie holding the Lochan Uaine. To the south-west the plateau stretches for many kilometres, gradually dropping towards the Moine Mhor. The return is best made by the same route. There are no restrictions on access by this route in the stalking season.

Map on page 125.

The summit cliffs of Braeriach   *H.M. Brown*

Cairn Toul and Sgor an Lochan Uaine from Braeriach   *D.J. Bennet*

Cairn Toul; 1293m; (OS Sheets 36 and 43; 963972); M4; *from Gaelic carn an t-sabhail, hill of the barn*
The Devil's Point; 1004m; (OS Sheets 36 and 43; 976951); M127; *from bod an deamhain, penis of the demon*

The west side of the deep valley of the Lairig Ghru is dominated by the plateau of Braeriach which curves round the huge amphitheatre of An Garbh Choire before continuing over the shapely peaks of Sgor an Lochain Uaine *(The Angel's Peak)* and Cairn Toul, whose corries hang high above the valley floor. Southwards from Cairn Toul the crest, now forming a broad ridge, drops to the col at the head of Coire Odhar before thrusting outward to The Devil's Point. This remarkable feature is a spur truncated by the streams of ice which once flowed down Glen Dee and Glen Geusachan, and it now forms a prominent landmark with its great headland of granite slabs.

The southern approach to Cairn Toul and The Devil's Point starts at the Linn of Dee and follows the same route as that for Ben Macdui and its neighbours, namely the private road up Glen Derry to Derry Lodge, followed by the path up Glen Luibeg to the Luibeg bridge. From there the way to Cairn Toul continues W, rising slightly round the southern base of Carn a'Mhaim along a well-worn path which in a few more kilometres drops to join the path in Glen Dee leading N to the Lairig Ghru.

Continue only about 200 metres past the path junction and then diverge W to cross the River Dee by a cable bridge to reach Corrour Bothy. This one-time stalker's bothy is now the best-known Cairngorm refuge for climbers and walkers. A well-worn path leads W behind the bothy up the grassy banks of the Allt a'Choire Odhair and reaches the col at the head of this corrie by steep zigzags. Any potentially dangerous snow slope is probably best avoided on the south side of the corrie. From the col an easy walk

heading SE then bearing round E leads to the tip of The Devil's Point. (15½km; 700m; 4h 40min). It is a splendid viewpoint above the River Dee.

Return to the col. From there a broad grassy ridge rises N around the shallow bowl of Coire Odhar, then swings NW, becoming stonier, to Stob Coire an t-Saighdeir (1213m). Beyond this Top the ridge curves round the Soldiers' Corrie, dropping slightly and then climbing more steeply up the last 120m to the summit of Cairn Toul. (18½km; 1120m; 6h). Return to the Linn of Dee by the same route.

Sgor an Lochain Uaine is less than 1km north-west of Cairn Toul, and is a fine point from which to appreciate the grandeur of An Garbh Choire and its wild recesses. Returning from this peak to the head of Coire Odhar it is possible to traverse below Cairn Toul at about 1150m and thus avoid some climbing.

The alternative approach to Cairn Toul is from Achlean in Glen Feshie. From the end of the public road near the farm follow the path across the level moor east, then uphill into the National Nature Reserve. The path continues up Coire Fhearnagan high on the north side of the Allt Fhearnagan and eventually reaches the crest of the Glen Feshie ridge just south of Carn Ban Mor. Leave the path and aim direct towards Loch nan Cnapan on a gradually descending course ESE across the Moine Mhor. This wide expanse is different from the higher stony plateaux further east, being mainly grassy with some extensive areas of peat bog and many streams meandering southwards across the featureless landscape to join the River Eidart. From Loch nan Cnapan, which is more or less at the low point in the centre of

The Devil's Point   *H.M. Brown*

the Moine Mhor, bear ENE across the plateau and then up gradually steepening slopes to reach Sgor an Lochain Uaine on the edge of An Garbh Choire. From there descend SE for 120m to the col and climb the west ridge of Cairn Toul. (12km; 1250m; 4h 50min).

This may be a shorter route than the one from the Linn of Dee, but it goes for a long way over high and featureless ground that needs accurate navigation in bad visibility, and is very exposed to the elements in stormy weather.

Looking east across the Moine Mhor to the distant outline of Braeriach and Cairn Toul   *D.J. Broadhead*

The view south-west from Ben Macdui over the summits of the Devil's Point, Beinn Bhrotain and Monadh Mor   *A. Watson*

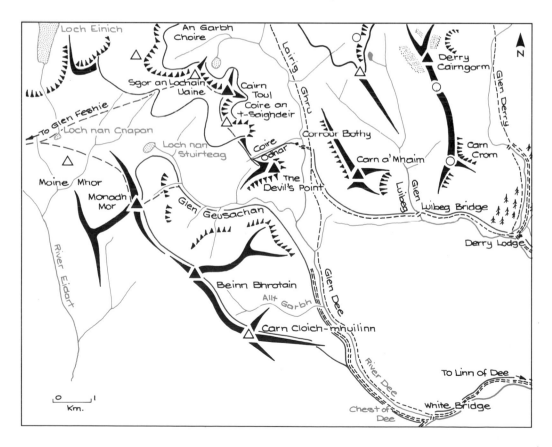

Beinn Bhrotain and the east face of Monadh Mor from Loch nan Stuirteag   *J. Renny*

Monadh Mor; 1113m; (OS Sheet 43; 938942); M39; *big hill*
Beinn Bhrotain; 1157m; (OS Sheet 43; 954923); M18; *hill of the mastiff*

These two rounded mountains are the southern extension of the great Braeriach - Cairn Toul plateau, separated from it by Glen Geusachan, and separated by the River Eidart from the Glen Feshie hills. Their grandest features are the steep faces overlooking Glen Geusachan which form a discontinuous line of slabby buttresses and gullies extending for several kilometres. At its north end Monadh Mor merges into the undulating expanse of the Moine Mhor, the great moss, a vast lonely basin of peat and tundra which sweeps across from the crests of Braeriach and Cairn Toul to the edge of Glen Feshie.

Two routes are possible for the ascent of these two mountains, from Linn of Dee and from Achlean farm in Glen Feshie. The Linn of Dee route is a good deal longer, but it is possible to use a bicycle from there for a long way up the Dee to the foot of the mountains.

From the Linn of Dee walk or cycle up the right of way along the north side of the River Dee to reach White Bridge. Continue along the south-west side past the Chest of Dee, where the river plunges over granite slabs, to reach a conifer plantation and some ruined shielings. Thus far the road is rough and stony, but possible for a bicycle. Beyond, it deteriorates and ends ½km north of the crossing of the Allt Garbh at the boundary of the National Nature Reserve.

Continue up the pathless west bank of the River Dee, choosing the best line possible over rough ground, and enter Glen Geusachan. This remote and enchanting glen is flanked by the imposing slabs of Beinn Bhrotain and The Devil's Point, and directly ahead rises Monadh Mor with a prominent plaque of slabs below and to the right of its summit. These may be outflanked on the right by following the stream up

to the outflow of Loch nan Stuirteag, and then heading back SSW to the summit of Monadh Mor. (18km; 750m; 5h 20min). A more direct ascent of the east face can be made through a wide gap in the slabs on that side, but it is steep and should be avoided if there is snow to be climbed.

The elongated whaleback summit of Monadh Mor is almost completely flat, dipping gradually NNW towards the Moine Mhor. Continue S for ¾km to a slightly lower cairn, and then SE by grassy tundra for another 1km, descending quite steeply at the end to reach a narrow col at 975m. From there climb SE up a boulder-strewn slope for about 800 metres to reach the summit of Beinn Bhrotain. (21km; 930m; 6h 20min).

Descend SE over (or round) the Top of Carn Cloich-mhuilinn (942m) and down its long east ridge. Before the glen is reached, drop down on the south flank of this ridge to avoid slabs and boulders at its foot, and reach the road back to Linn of Dee at the conifer plantation.

The route from Achlean in Glen Feshie is the same as that for Cairn Toul described previously as far as Loch nan Cnapan at the centre of the Moine Mhor. From there bear ESE across the Allt Luineag, or possibly go a little further south to climb the knoll of Tom Dubh (918m), which is a very remote and insignificant Top of Braeriach. The rounded NNW ridge of Monadh Mor is reached and followed to the summit. (11km; 950m; 4h 10min). Continue to Beinn Bhrotain as above. (14km; 1130m; 5h 10min), and return by the same route.

Maps on pages 131 and 134.

The Glen Feshie hills from Ruthven Barracks   *D.J. Bennet*

To the west of the main Cairngorm mountains which enclose the Lairig Ghru, the Moine Mhor (or great moss) extends for several kilometres, forming a wide shallow basin whose western edge is the long broad ridge of the Glen Feshie hills. This range rises in the north above the pine woods of Loch an Eilein and Inshriach, and extends 18 kilometres south to end above the desolate upper reaches of Glen Feshie. At its north end the ridge is quite well defined, particularly on its east side which falls steeply into Gleann Einich in a long series of buttresses and gullies from Sgoran Dubh Mor and Sgor Gaoith down to Loch Einich. Further south the crest broadens out to form a plateau between Coire Garbhlach and the River Eidart in the south-west corner of the Moine Mhor.

From the west and south-west the range of the Glen Feshie hills looks like a long level plateau, the dips between the summits being almost imperceptible,

and on that side the deep gash of Coire Garbhlach is the most prominent feature. This corrie is particularly interesting because it lies on the geological boundary between the granites of the Cairngorms and the schistose rocks into which they have been intruded. The north side of the corrie is of granite with heather streaked screes and an inner recess formed by the typically bowl-shaped Fionnar Choire. The rest of the corrie is cut in schist, with a narrow V-shaped entrance, steeply sloping stream bed with waterfalls and a botanical variety derived from lime-rich soils.

Despite its length and height, there are only two Munros in this group: Sgor Gaoith and Mullach Clach a'Bhlair. They are both usually climbed from Glen Feshie, where a narrow public road goes south from Feshiebridge up the east side of the glen to end at Achlean farm.

Mullach Clach a'Bhlair; 1019m; (OS Sheets 35, 36 and 43; 883927); M111; *summit of the stone of the plain*

Between the indentations of Coire Mharconaich on the east and Coire Garbhlach on the west the high plateau extends south in a featureless tableland of grassy tundras. At its south-west corner it swells upward slightly to reach its highest point at the summit of Mullach Clach a'Bhlair, seen from Glen Feshie as a wide gentle dome.

The end of the public road on the east side of Glen Feshie near Achlean farm is the nearest starting point for the ascent of Mullach Clach a'Bhlair and for other expeditions onto the Moine Mhor. Three routes are possible, each one with its own character: the pine woods of Glen Feshie, the narrow recesses of Coire Garbhlach and the open spaces of the Moine Mhor.

The Glen Feshie route goes past the farm and along paths on the east bank of the River Feshie for 4km. There may be a problem crossing the Allt Garbhlach in spate, in which case it might be better to cross the Feshie and walk up the private road on its west side. At Carnachuin bridge a track leads SE across the level floor of the glen among stately scattered pines, and swings E upwards along the north bank of the Allt Coire Chaoil. Follow this track to gain the narrow ridge on the brink of Coire Garbhlach at which point there is a fine view down into the corrie.

This point can also be reached more quickly by leaving the path ¾km south of Achlean and bearing SE across the nearly level moor, following a narrow path through the heather. Cross the Allt Garbhlach near the upper edge of Coille an Torr and climb SE up deep rough heather for 1km to reach the 800m spur and continue E slightly downhill to join the track on the edge of Coire Garbhlach.

The track continues uphill along the corrie rim until it reaches the plateau and forks, its right branch making a sweeping curve across the tundra and passing within 300 metres of the small summit cairn of Mullach Clach a'Bhlair. (10km; 700m; 3h 20min. 6½km; 750m; 2h 50min by the more direct route).

Although undistinguished in itself, there are few better places than this from which to appreciate the scale and character of the vast tract of hill and moorland which extends south across the wide trough of the upper Feshie and beyond the An Sgarsoch ridge to Glen Tilt, and north-east over the Moine Mhor to the uptilted rim of Braeriach and Cairn Toul.

Another route goes right up Coire Garbhlach from its mouth along a narrow path on the north bank of the Allt Garbhlach. High up, the Fionnar Choire gives an easy exit onto the plateau, while the two streams which tumble down into the true head of Coire Garbhlach give steeper climbs. Once on the plateau bear SSE to join the track which, as noted above, leads close to Mullach Clach a'Bhlair.

The third way is to follow the path from Achlean east up Coire Fhearnagan to its high point just south of Carn Ban Mor (1052m), which can easily be included in the day's walk.

From there go S along the plateau, keeping to the highest and driest ground to avoid some wet areas of peat bog, and join the track near the head of Coire Garbhlach.

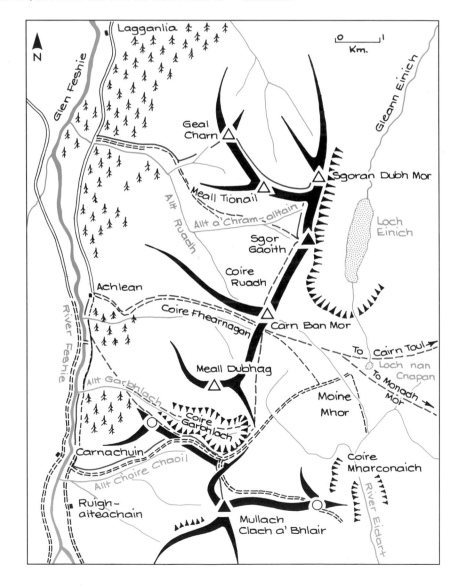

On the Glen Feshie hills near Carn Ban Mor   *J.S. Stewart*

Sgor Gaoith; 1118m; (OS Sheets 36 and 43; 903989); M34; *peak of wind*

This is the highest point of the ridge which extends from Carn Ban Mor to Sgoran Dubh along the west side of the Einich glacial trough. The east side of this ridge between Sgor Gaoith and Sgoran Dubh Mor forms a magnificent series of ridges, buttresses and gullies above Loch Einich in a wild and remote setting, but the approach from that side of the mountain is long and there are no easy routes up the steep slopes above the loch. The usual routes of ascent are from Glen Feshie, either starting from Achlean and traversing Carn Ban Mor, or by an alternative route up Coire Ruadh which is described below.

Leave the road on the east side of Glen Feshie at (852013) near the bridge over the Allt Ruadh and go E along a forest track for ½km. Cross the deer fence and continue uphill along the track through pine trees high on the north side of the narrow valley of the Allt Ruadh. After crossing a small side stream and passing through the last scattered pine trees the path continues across the open hillside to a stile over another deer fence. Once over it cross the Allt Coire na Cloiche and follow the path S, at first over rather boggy ground, but as the path climbs gradually round the lower slopes of Meall Tionail it gives good going. Eventually the path reaches the Allt a'Chrom-alltain and disappears. Cross to the south side of the burn and ascend E for 400m up broad slopes of grass and heath to reach the ridge. The summit of Sgor Gaoith is on a little promontory, right on the brink of the crags which plunge for 500m to Loch Einich far below. (7km; 830m; 3h).

The descent may be varied by going N for 1½km along the broad ridge, crossing the saddle at 1053m and climbing to the Top of Sgoran Dubh Mor (1111m). From the rocks of its summit tor descend SW for ¾km to reach the start of the spur which projects northwest towards Geal-charn (920m), once classified as a Munro in its own right, but now just a Top. Follow the undulating crest of this spur over Meall Buidhe (976m) for 2½km to the stony summit of Geal-charn. Descend SW down slopes of boulders, grass and heather to rejoin the Coire Ruadh path at the stile over the upper deer fence.

The summit of Sgor Gaoith   *D.J. Bennet*

Creag Meagaidh from Coire Ardair W.D. Brooker

SECTION 9

The Monadh Liath and Creag Meagaidh

Geal Charn from the south across the headwaters of the River Spey   D.J. Bennet

Geal Charn; 926m; (OS Sheet 35; 561988); M256; *white hill*

Geal Charn is the westernmost of the Monadh Liath Munros, and has many of the characteristics of these hills. Its most interesting feature is the eastern corrie, with its high lochan above Glen Markie and the ice-carved window in the innermost recess of the corrie forming a steep-sided col between Geal Charn and its neighbour Beinn Sgiath. To the north-west the hill merges into vast undulating moorland typical of the western Monadh Liath.

The approach to the hill is along the narrow public road west from Laggan Bridge on the north side of the River Spey. This road leads towards the Corrieyairack Pass, a famous right of way and military road of the 18th century.

One route to Geal Charn is up Glen Markie from the Spey Dam, there being a track up the glen for 3½km on the east side of the Markie Burn. Follow the track and the path beyond it to the foot of the Piper's Burn, the stream flowing down from Lochan a'Choire. Cross the Markie Burn and climb NW into the corrie, keeping well to the NE of the lochan until above the level of the crags. Then go SW across the featureless grassy plateau to the huge, finely built summit cairn which stands a few hundred metres west of the rim of the corrie. (7½km; 650m; 2h 50min).

If the Markie Burn is in spate, the preceding route may not be possible. In that case proceed further west along the public road to Garva Bridge and start from there. The ascent is easy and involves no awkward stream crossings. Follow a track north for ¾km, then aim for the footbridge over the Feith Talagain at (525959) and continue up the path on the south-east side of the stream. At its end cross the Allt Coire nan Dearcag and climb the heathery south-west ridge of Geal Charn direct to its summit. (7½km; 630m; 2h 50min).

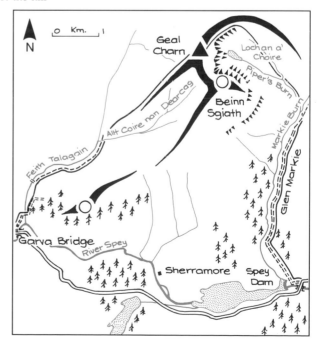

The south top of Carn Dearg from Carn Macoul   *D.J. Bennet*

Carn Dearg; 945m; (OS Sheet 35; 635024); M219; *red hill*
A'Chailleach; 930m; (OS Sheet 35; 681042); *the old woman*
Carn Sgulain; 920m; (OS Sheet 35; 684059); M263; *hill of the basket, or of the old man*

The Monadh Liath range is an extensive undulating plateau on the north-west side of the Spey Valley above Newtonmore and Kingussie. This desolate high moorland extends a long way north and west across the headwaters of the River Findhorn towards Loch Ness, but it is mainly the south-east corner near Glen Banchor that holds much interest for the hillwalker and cross-country skier, for it is there that the four Munros of the Monadh Liath are to be found. Of the four, Geal Charn on the west side of Glen Markie is described separately on the previous page.

From a viewpoint on the A9 road opposite Newtonmore, Carn Dearg and A'Chailleach show up clearly, for they have well-defined summits and prominent east-facing corries. Carn Sgulain, on the other hand, is rather inconspicuous, appearing as little more than a high point on the horizon, almost hidden behind A'Chailleach. The starting point for all three hills is 2km from Newtonmore where the road up Glen Banchor changes from being public to private at the foot of the Allt a'Chaorainn.

The route to Carn Dearg continues up Glen Banchor for 1km and then takes the rough track NW up the Allt Fionndrigh. Go for 3½km up this track, then cross the stream by a footbridge and follow a faint path SW through a gap onto the broad ridge above Gleann Ballach. Continue NW up rough heathery ground on the north-east side of the glen for 2km towards its head. Cross the stream and climb an easy grassy slope above broken rocks (appearing from below as a slanting shelf) in a south-west direction to reach the broad ridge of Carn Dearg ½km

north of the top. A short climb up this ridge leads to the summit cairn which is perched right on the edge of the east corrie. (9km; 650m; 3h 10min). This corrie is mostly steep grass, with a few small crags, and a shorter route could be made more directly up the east face of Carn Dearg from Gleann Ballach, but it is very steep and cannot be regarded as an easy alternative.

The way to A'Chailleach and Carn Sgulain goes up the rough track on the east side of the Allt a'Chaorainn. Continue up the glen for a short distance following the scar in the heather made by tracked vehicles, then cross the stream and climb NW to a tiny stalker's bothy on the slopes of A'Chailleach. Keep on uphill in the same direction to reach the broad south-west ridge of the hill, and climb this easy-angled ridge to the big cairn of A'Chailleach at the edge of its east corrie. (6km; 630m; 2h 30min).

Descend N into the deep little glen of the Allt Cuil na Caillich, and climb rough tussocky grass and peat NNE to Carn Sgulain. A line of fence posts across its flat summit makes finding the cairn easy, even in thick weather. (8km; 750m; 3h 10min).

The most direct return to Glen Banchor goes down the Allt Cuil na Caillich, on its right (south) bank at the point where it cascades down through crags to join the Allt a'Chaorainn. Cross this stream to its east side where there is a sheep track for a long way down the glen.

It is quite possible to traverse these three hills in a single expedition. The plateau between Carn Dearg and Carn Sgulain is an undulating featureless expanse of grass, moss and stones, giving fairly easy

The approach to the Monadh Liath up Glen Banchor   *D.J. Bennet*

walking past a series of minor tops and cairns and at least one tiny lochan. (Others may appear in wet weather). Even in the thickest weather there are no route finding problems, for a line of fence posts goes all the way from Carn Ban, ¾km NNW of Carn Dearg, to Carn Sgulain. The distance for the complete circuit, starting at and returning to the road at the foot of the Allt a'Chaorainn, is 24km.

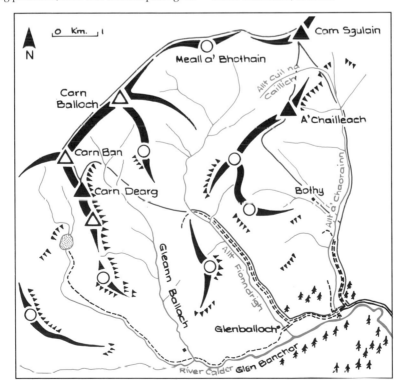

Creag Meagaidh from Coire Ardair   *A. Tibbs*

Creag Meagaidh; 1130m; (OS Sheets 34 and 42; 418875); M26; *bogland rock*

This is a massive and magnificent mountain with a rather complicated topography. From its high central plateau several steep-sided ridges radiate outwards enclosing some very fine corries, of which Coire Ardair to the north-east is the most impressive. This corrie provides a superb approach to the mountain and some of the best winter climbing in Scotland. It is quite difficult to get a good impression of Creag Meagaidh from the south, for example from the A86 road along the side of Loch Laggan, and one has to walk up towards Coire Ardair from Aberarder farm to appreciate the grandeur of the mountain.

There are two very fine walking routes to the summit which, if combined into a traverse, make a magnificent mountain expedition. However, as the finishing point of this traverse is 8km from the start, two cars would be useful.

The first route starts at the Nature Conservancy Council car park at Aberarder, half way along Loch Laggan. Walk up the road to the farm and continue along the path behind the farm, heading WNW at first, then NW and climbing high above the Allt Coire Ardair through scattered birches. In about 3km the corrie bears round towards the west and as the path passes through the highest group of birch trees the great cliffs of Coire Ardair come into view.

Continue along the path on the north side of the burn to the outlet of Lochan a'Choire which is in a superb situation under the cliffs. Bear W, climbing across grassy slopes, then up screes and boulders into the steepening, narrow corrie leading to the obvious col called The Window which separates Creag Meagaidh from Stob Poite Coire Ardair. From the col climb S up steep slopes to reach the grassy plateau of Creag Meagaidh and cross this, S at first, then SW and finally W to the summit. (9km; 880m; 3h 30min).

The return to Aberarder may be made by the same route, but a better way is to go E across the plateau, first to the Top of Puist Coire Ardair (1070m), then along the narrower ridge with good views on the left down into Coire Ardair. Bear ENE and cross the flat-topped dome of Sron a'Choire (1001m) and descend E down a wide shallow corrie towards Aberarder. There is a footbridge across the Allt Coire Ardair to the west of the farm.

The second route starts at Moy, 2km west of the west end of Loch Laggan and 8km from Aberarder. Leave the road on the west side of the Moy Burn and cross gently rising moorland to the steep craggy ground below Creag na Cailliche. Climb through the broken rocks and reach the crest of the long ridge on which there is a substantial wall. This ridge is followed all the way to the summit. (6km; 880m; 2h 50min).

The Coire Ardair cliffs of Creag Meagaidh   *M. Shaw*

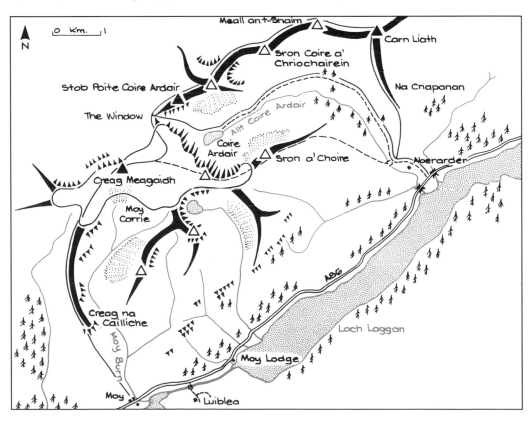

Stob Poite Coire Ardair

D.J. Bennet

Carn Liath; 1006m; (OS Sheet 34; 472903); M123; *grey hill*
Stob Poite Coire Ardair; 1053m; (OS Sheet 34; 429889); M75; *peak of the pot of the high corrie*

These two mountains lie on a long, fairly level ridge which forms the north bounding wall of Coire Ardair. They are best combined in an east to west traverse which gives a fine high-level walk with excellent views of the impressive cliffs at the head of the corrie. The traverse can in fact be easily combined with the ascent of Creag Meagaidh, which is described on the previous pages.

The best starting point is from the A86 road at Aberarder about half way along Loch Laggan. From the Nature Conservancy Council car park, walk up the private road past Aberarder, and once on open ground beyond the farm leave the path to Coire Ardair and climb north towards Na Cnapanan, which appears from below as an obvious shoulder. Above it the slopes rise steadily but less steeply for almost 400m over grass, heather and patches of boulders to the flat stony summit of Carn Liath. (3½km; 750m; 2h).

Turn west and follow the broad mossy ridge, gradually descending to a col and climbing again to the Top of Meall an t-Snaim (969m). Continuing WSW, the ridge narrows and drops to a well-defined notch followed by a short steep rise to the next Top, Sron Coire a'Chriochairein (991m). Thereafter the ridge continues around the edge of this corrie to the level crest of Stob Poite Coire Ardair, the summit cairn being at the west end. (8km; 980m; 3h 30min).

Continue WSW down the smooth ridge for barely ½km and then turn south to descend more steeply to the narrow pass called The Window. From that point Creag Meagaidh can be climbed and the return to Aberarder by the ridge over Puist Coire Ardair and Sron a'Choire completes an excellent traverse.

Alternatively, the direct return from The Window to Aberarder goes east from the pass, at first quite steeply down a bouldery corrie, then more easily across grassy slopes above Lochan a'Choire to reach the path down Coire Ardair to Aberarder.

Map on page 141.

Stob Poite Coire Ardair from the birch woods at the foot of Coire Ardair

Beinn a'Chaorainn from Luiblea in Glen Spean   D.Scott

Beinn a'Chaorainn; 1052m, (OS Sheets 34 and 41; 386851); M76; *hill of the rowan*
Beinn Teallach; 915m; (OS Sheets 34 and 41; 361860); M276; *forge hill*

These two mountains are north of the Laggan Dam on opposite sides of the glen of the Allt a'Chaorainn. Beinn a'Chaorainn, which is much the finer of the two, has three tops of similar height on its north-south spine, the highest being the middle one. The western slope is uniformly steep, but not rocky, while the eastern face is steep and rocky, forming the fine Coire na h- Uamha.

The eastern and northern corries of Beinn Teallach are steep, but to the south and west there are long, easy-angled slopes which give the mountain an uninteresting appearance from those directions.

Start the traverse from the A86 road at Roughburn, ½km north-east of the Laggan Dam. Follow a forest road NW for ¾km to a junction where a road runs across the hillside in both directions. Turn west for 200 metres to a firebreak which is marked by a small cairn on a rock. Walk north up the firebreak to reach the upper deer fence where there is a gate. From the gate climb north, turning Meall Clachaig to the west, and then ascend NE up easy slopes to the South Top (1050m), and thence ½km along the broad ridge to the summit of Beinn a'Chaorainn. (4½km; 800m; 2h 20min).

Continue along the ridge to the North Top (1045m) and from there descend NNW for 1km, then west to the col at the head of the Allt a'Chaorainn glen, which is marked by a large cairn. Climb the slopes to the west to reach the north-east ridge of Beinn Teallach, which is followed to the summit. (9km; 1100m; 3h 50min).

The descent from Beinn Teallach follows the easy-angled south shoulder of the hill. There is no bridge across the Allt a'Chaorainn and as the stream may be difficult to cross in spate it may be advisable in such conditions to descend east into the glen ½km south of the summit, cross the stream and continue down its east bank. To avoid the extensive forestry plantations lower down the glen, contour SE below Meall Clachaig to join the route of ascent at the gate in the deer fence.

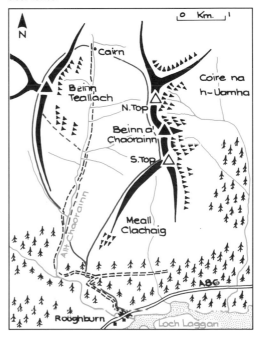

Luinne Bheinn   *J. Renny*

SECTION 10

Loch Eil to Glen Shiel

Looking towards the summit of Gulvain from the South Top   *I. Brown*

Gulvain; 987m; (OS Sheets 40 and 41, 003876), M156; *from Gaelic, either gaorr, filth or gaoir, noise*

Gulvain, or Gaor Bheinn, is a secretive mountain hidden in the jumble of hills between Loch Eil and Loch Arkaig. It is rather a remote peak, and apart from the route described below it is quite complicated to reach. The highest point (987m) is on OS Sheet 41, so beware of mistaking the OS trig point (961m) on Sheet 40 for the summit. Gleann Fionnlighe gives a pleasant approach, with the route of ascent in view ahead for a long way. Being a solitary peak, the summit is a rewarding panoramic viewpoint.

Start from the A830 road from Fort William to Mallaig 1km west of the west end of Loch Eil, and follow the rough track up the east side of the Fionn Lighe river. After 2km this track crosses to the west bank, passes Wauchan cottage and continues for another 4km to a bridge over the Allt a'Choire Reidh. On the other side of this stream the ascent of the south-west ridge of Gulvain begins. It is unrelentingly and uniformly steep, but as long as the crags to the west are avoided, it is a straightforward ascent on grass.

A craggy knoll (855m) is passed, and beyond it the South Top (961m), the trig point, is reached just over ½km further on. Continue NNE from there, dropping 60m to a saddle, and climb the narrowing ridge to the summit, which has a substantial cairn. (10½km; 1050m; 4h 10min). Return by the route of ascent.

Other approaches to Gulvain are much longer and less attractive scenically than the one described above. From the east end of Loch Arkaig there is a long and rather uninteresting walk up the rough track in Glen Mallie leading to the north-east ridge of the mountain. It is, however, possible to cycle for a long way up the glen. From Strathan at the head of Loch Arkaig one has to cross an intermediate ridge and drop down into Gleann Camgharaidh before reaching the steep flank of the north ridge, all across rough trackless terrain.

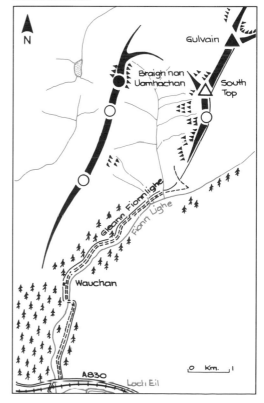

Streap and Sgurr Thuilm from the north-east   *I. Brown*

Sgurr Thuilm; 963m; (OS Sheet 40; 939879); M189; *peak of the rounded hillock*
Sgurr nan Coireachan; 956m; (OS Sheet 40; 903880); M202; *peak of the corries*

These Munros are just two of many peaks in an area of unusually rough and steep complexity, belonging in character if not geographically to the Rough Bounds of Knoydart further north-west. For the sake of the wild scenery, the summits are best traversed from east to west, but the route is as easy in reverse. The approach from Glenfinnan has been rather tamed by afforestation and road-making, but it is still the easiest and most popular route.

The National Trust for Scotland's Visitor Centre at Glenfinnan is worth a visit, and it is interesting to re-call that after his defeat at Culloden the fugitive Prince Charles spent a night out on Sgurr Thuilm, an unlikely Munroist.

Park a short distance off the A830 road up the road to Glen Finnan and walk up the west side of the River Finnan, the road passes under the spectacular railway viaduct and continues well up the glen which is now extensively tree-planted. In 3½km pass below Corry-hully Lodge and reach Corryhully bothy beside the river. It is possible to cycle to this point.

Continue along the track northwards to its crossing of the stream that drains the deep-set Coire Thollaidh and Coire a'Bheithe. There are bridges over all the potentially dangerous streams. A few hundred metres beyond aim for the spur that leads to the Druim Coire a'Bheithe and follow this long grassy ridge NE then N to Sgurr Thuilm, whose cairn is at the north end of the flat summit area in a command-ing position overlooking Glen Pean. (9km; 960m; 3h 40min).

Return S then SW for a short distance before conti-nuing the traverse west. There are many ups and downs over Beinn Gharbh and Meall an Tarmachain,

and much bare rock is exposed, but the easiest way is along the crest with a line of old fence posts to guide one in thick weather. It is a grand highway. Sgurr nan Coireachan, though lower than Sgurr Thuilm, is prob-ably a better viewpoint, with an unrestricted outlook to the west. (13km; 1360m; 5h 10min).

Descend SE and climb again to Sgurr a'Choire Riabhaich. The ridge over this point is steep-sided and rocky, and care is needed on the descent in bad visibility. Keep close to the crest to minimise difficul-ties. Lower down the ridge becomes broader and grassy; aim to reach the stalker's path on its east side at (917859) and follow it down to the road in Glen Finnan.

An alternative and equally fine traverse of these two mountains can be made from Strathan at the head of Loch Arkaig, and this route takes one into the extra-ordinarily wild corries on the north side of the ridge. The road along the north side of Loch Arkaig is public to within 1km of Strathan, and there seems to be no objection to cars being taken along this last kilometre of rough road and parked near the bridge over the River Dessarry. Going to Sgurr Thuilm, continue WSW along the road up Glen Pean for 1km, cross the River Pean and climb directly up the long north-east ridge of Sgurr Thuilm. (5km; 960m; 2h 50min).

Coming back from Sgurr nan Coireachan, return to Meall an Tarmachain and descend very steeply NE down the wild Coire nan Gall to Glen Pean. In spate conditions the crossing of the River Pean may be dif-ficult or impossible, as also may be the crossing of the Allt a'Chaorainn at the foot of Sgurr Thuilm's north-east ridge, so this traverse should not be attempted when the streams are in spate.

The ridge from Sgurr Thuilm to Sgurr nan Coireachan seen from the north   G.S. Johnstone

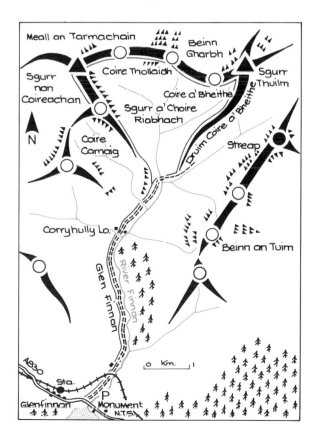

Sron a'Choire Ghairbh from the head of Gleann Cia-aig   *J. Renny*

Sron a'Choire Ghairbh; 935m; (OS Sheet 34; 222945); M237; *nose of the rough corrie*
Meall na Teanga; 917m; (OS Sheet 34; 220925); M271; *hill of the tongue*

These two mountains are elusively situated west of Loch Lochy in the Great Glen, and dominate the view across that loch from the A82 road north of Spean Bridge. They are bold, deeply-corried hills, and their lower slopes above Loch Lochy are heavily forested. These forests, now mature, are being felled and replanted. The hills are usually climbed together, and the traverse can be started either at Kilfinnan near Laggan Locks at the north-east end of Loch Lochy, or at the foot of Gleann Cia-aig near the east end of Loch Arkaig, and this route is described first. The times and distances for both routes are approximately the same.

The Gleann Cia-aig start is from the narrow B8005 road just before it reaches the east end of Loch Arkaig. From the car park at the Eas Chia-aig waterfalls follow the signposted 'Forest Walk' footpath up through the trees until it reaches a forestry road (about 15 minutes). Turn N and follow this road, then a path up Gleann Cia-aig to a footbridge across the Abhainn Chia-aig at (188929). Beyond this point the footpath shown on the 1:50,000 map is virtually non-existent, so continue ENE up the Allt Cam Bhealaich to reach another path just west of the Cam Bhealach. From this pass (615m) climb the stalker's path which zigzags N up the steep grassy hillside (further than the 1:50,000 map shows) to end almost on the ridge. Finally an easy walk for a few hundred metres NW along this broad mossy ridge leads to Sron a'Choire Ghairbh. (9½km; 880m; 3h 40min).

Having returned down the stalker's path to the Cam Bhealach, climb S below the screes of Meall Dubh to gain the col between that hill and Meall na Teanga. A steep climb up mossy boulders leads to the crest of Meall na Teanga at a small cairn, and the larger summit cairn is a few hundred metres further south. (11½km; 1200m; 4h 40min). It is a splendid viewpoint.

To return to Gleann Cia-aig, descend SW from Meall na Teanga and climb a narrow rocky ridge to Meall Coire Lochain, whose top is reached suddenly at the edge of a broad grassy ridge. Go W along the crest of the Meall Odhar crags and descend easy grassy slopes, still heading W, to reach the path in Gleann Cia-aig 3½km north of the day's starting point.

For the northern approach, drive along the narrow public road from Laggan Swing Bridge to Kilfinnan and park just before reaching the farm. Continue on foot along the upper Forestry Commission road through an area of forest which has recently been clear-felled. After 3km take a path which climbs W through the forest and emerges into a steep-sided glen leading to the Cam Bhealach, where the preceding route is joined. Unless a complete traverse to Gleann Cia-aig is intended, it is necessary to return from Meall na Teanga to the Cam Bhealach on the way back to Kilfinnan.

The best expedition on these hills is the complete traverse from Kilfinnan to Gleann Cia-aig or vice versa, but this requires the assistance of a friendly car driver. If doing this traverse from north to south, the descent from Meall Coire Lochain can be shortened by going WSW down the broad ridge of Leac Chorrach, past the 585m knoll to the edge of the Clunes Forest at (200890). At that point it is easy to reach the end of a forest road which leads down to Clunes.

Meall na Teanga and Meall Coire Lochain, with distant Ben Nevis between them, from Sron a'Choire Ghairbh   R. Wood

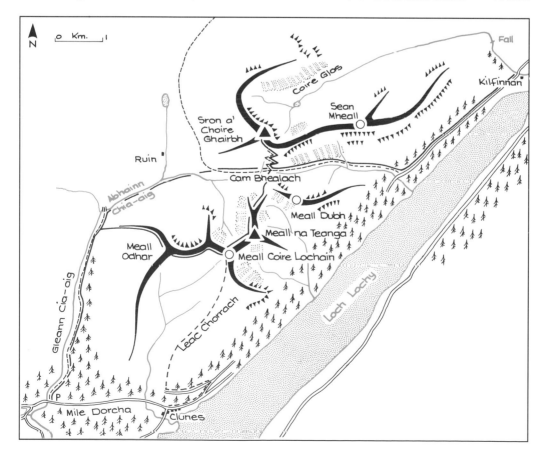

Gairich from the east end of Loch Quoich   *N. Ritchie*

Gairich; 919; (OS Sheet 33; 025995); M265; *roaring*

Gairich is the isolated peak which looks well in the view westwards along Loch Garry. It stands boldly on the south side of Loch Quoich, with lonely Glen Kingie to its south, and gives an easier day's climb than most peaks in the wild westland.

The starting point for the ascent is the dam at the east end of Loch Quoich, which is reached along the unclassified road which branches off the A87 beside Loch Garry and goes west to Kinloch Hourn. From the south end of the dam follow a path south and after 600 metres join the old stalker's path whose first few hundred metres are now submerged by the raised water level of Loch Quoich.

Take this path south over the boggy moors, dropping a little to the upper limit of the Glen Kingie forest where another stalker's path leads west up the Druim na Geid Salaich. This path peters out on the broad, easy crest leading to Bac nam Foid. The lochan shown on the map does not seem to exist, except possibly in the wettest of weather.

At the foot of the final steep rise to Gairich the path reappears, but goes off leftwards onto the south face. Abandon it and follow another path on the crest which gives a short steep climb with some rocky steps. The spacious summit dome has a large cairn. (8km; 730m; 3h).

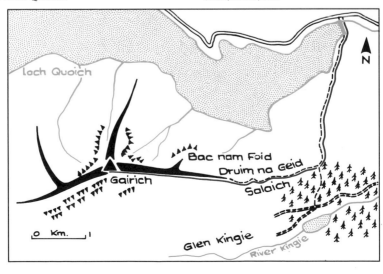

Sgurr Mor across Loch Quoich   J.S. Stewart

Sgurr Mor; 1003m; (OS Sheets 33 and 40, 965980); M128; *big peak*

This mountain is situated in very remote country, part of the long ridge from Gairich to Sgurr na Ciche which runs from east to west on the south side of Loch Quoich, and which is barred by the loch from easy access on the north. South of Sgurr Mor is desolate Glen Kingie, and one has to pass through the hills on the south side of this glen to find the nearest point of access, at the western end of Loch Arkaig.

The public road along the north side of Loch Arkaig ends near the west end of the loch, but there seems to be no objection to driving one kilometre further and parking near Strathan. This is the nearest point of access by car to all the mountains west and north-west from Loch Arkaig towards Loch Nevis and Knoydart.

Walk up the private road to Glendessarry, and from there take the stalker's path which leads N up to the pass at about 360m between Druim a'Chuirn and Fraoch Bheinn. This path is not so clear on the Glen Kingie side, and at the point where it turns NE towards Kinbreak bothy descend NW to cross the River Kingie and gain another stalker's path on its north side. In spate conditions it may be necessary to go up the glen for some distance to find a safe crossing place. The path climbs steadily, then dog-legs back up to the col (662m) between An Eag and Sgurr Beag. This is one of the country's most dramatic man-made paths; continue along it over Sgurr Beag, down steeply to the col at 750m and steeply up again to Sgurr Mor. (10km; 1200m; 4h 20min).

The route described above can be used for the return. However, it is quicker, if there are not problems crossing the River Kingie, to continue about 350 metres east along the nearly level summit ridge of Sgurr Mor and go down the south-east ridge, still on

the stalker's path, to the col below Sgurr an Fhuarain. Descend S down 500m of steep grassy slopes to cross the Kingie and return over the pass to Glendessarry and Strathan.

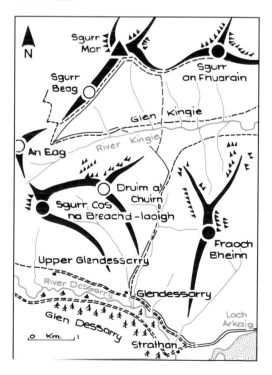

Garbh Chioch Mhor, Sgurr na Ciche and Ben Aden from Spidean Mialach   D.J. Bennet

Sgurr nan Coireachan; 953m; (OS Sheets 33 and 40; 933958); M207; *peak of the corries*
Garbh Chioch Mhor; 1013m; (OS Sheets 33 and 40; 909961); M113; *big rough place of the breast*
Sgurr na Ciche; 1040m; (OS Sheets 33 and 40; 902966); M89; *peak of the breast*

These grand mountains are in the heart of the remote wilderness between Loch Arkaig, Loch Quoich and Loch Nevis, an area which fully lives up to the name and character of The Rough Bounds of Knoydart. The day spent traversing them will be a memorable one, and one calling for Munro experience, for it is a serious expedition in rugged terrain. It is worth waiting for a clear day, if that is not expecting too much in a corner of Scotland that has the reputation for the country's highest rainfall.

The approach is from Strathan at the west end of Loch Arkaig, as described for Sgurr Mor. Walk up the private road on the north side of Glen Dessarry to the house at Upper Glendessarry. Continue along a path which climbs the hillside behind the house for a short way, then contours along the glen just above the forest. There is a footbridge across the Allt Coire nan Uth, well hidden from sight and not shown on the OS map, which is essential if the burn is in spate. (This point can also be reached along the forest road on the south side of Glen Dessarry and across the river by a narrow

bridge).

Once across the Allt Coire nan Uth leave the path to climb N up the steep grassy ridge to Sgurr nan Coireachan, an unrelenting 750m grind. The ridge narrows and is edged with crags near the top, but there is no difficulty if the crest is followed. (8km; 900m; 3h 20min).

Sgurr na Ciche and Garbh Chioch Mhor from Bidean a'Chabair   D.J. Broadhead

The continuation of the traverse goes WSW steeply down to the Bealach Coire nan Gall (733m). Westwards from there the Garbh Chiochs live up to their name, for the ridge is a succession of rocky outcrops, and Coire nan Gall on its north side is one of the roughest corries outside Skye. However, navigation along the ridge is simplified by there being a well-built dry stone dyke to follow. Garbh Chioch Bheag (968m) is passed on the way to the summit of Garbh Chioch Mhor. (10½km; 1200m; 4h 20min).

Keep following the wall W then NNW down to the col (845m) below Sgurr na Ciche. This pass is called Feadan na Ciche, the *'whistle'* or *'chanter'* of the peak; an apt description on a windy day. The upper slopes of Sgurr na Ciche are a maze of crags and boulders, and a faint path zig-zags up this very rough ground to reach the summit ridge just east of the top. (11½km; 1400m; 5h).

To return to Strathan, retrace the route to the Feadan na Ciche col and descend the narrow boulder-filled gully SW towards Coire na Ciche. At the foot of this gully (about 670m) traverse SE almost horizontally below the crags of Garbh Chioch Mhor and descend grassy slopes by a little stream to the Bealach an Lagain Duibh, the pass at the head of Glen Dessarry. Follow the path (often rather wet and muddy) down this glen to rejoin the outward route at the Allt Coire nan Uth.

Sgurr na Ciche from the south-west   D. Rubens

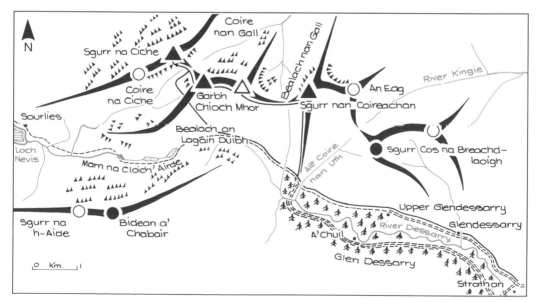

Looking up the south-east ridge of Meall Buidhe from Sgurr Sgeithe   H.M. Brown

The next three mountains to be described are in the Knoydart peninsula, one of the wildest and most inaccessible parts of the Scottish Highlands. No roads penetrate into this area, and access is either by boat or on foot along one of the rights of way which go west from the nearest road-ends. Because of the remoteness of Knoydart, the climbing of its mountains entails finding overnight accommodation in the area. Wild camping is possible almost anywhere except near the habitations at Inverie and Barrisdale.

The following routes of access to Knoydart are possible:

1. By mail boat from Mallaig to Inverie (Mon, Wed, Fri). Contact Bruce Watt Cruises, The Pier, Mallaig, Inverness-shire. Tel. 0687 2233.

2. From the road-end at the west end of Loch Arkaig by the right of way through Glen Dessarry to the head of Loch Nevis, and then over the Mam Meadail to Inverie.

3. From the road-end at Kinloch Hourn by the right

of way along Loch Hourn to Barrisdale, and then over the Mam Barrisdale to Inverie.

4. By private arrangement a boat may be hired at Arnisdale or Corran on the north side of Loch Hourn to cross the loch at Barrisdale.

Accommodation may be available at the following places:

1. Inverie. Inverie Guest House, The Pier House and Torry Cottage offer accommodation. For further information contact the Factor's Office, Knoydart Estate, Inverie, by Mallaig, Inverness-shire. Tel. 0687 2331.

2. Barrisdale. There is a bothy beside the keeper's house, but accommodation is very limited. Contact the Keeper, Barrisdale, by Glenelg, Inverness-shire.

3. Sourlies. This small bothy at the head of Loch Nevis has space for only a very few people.

Climbing routes are described starting at Inverie, as this is the most easily accessible place in Knoydart using public transport.

Meall Buidhe; 946m; (OS Sheets 33 and 40; 849990); M215; *yellow hill*
Luinne Bheinn; 939m; (OS Sheet 33; 869008); M230; *perhaps hill of anger, or hill of mirth or melody*

These two fine and complex mountains are in the heart of Knoydart, and their traverse is one of the roughest hill walks in Scotland. From Inverie take the estate road up the glen of the Inverie River for 3½km until just beyond the knoll on which stands the Brocket Memorial. Follow the right-hand track across the river and continue along the right of way up Gleann Meadail to the pass at its head, the Mam Meadail (c. 550m). The slopes on the north side of the pass are craggy, but any difficulties can be avoided by keeping slightly to the east, aiming for the little col west of Sgurr Sgeithe. From there climb the south-east

ridge of Meall Buidhe, which is narrow and rocky in places and leads in ½km to the South-east Top (c. 940m). The summit is ½km further north-west along a broad grassy ridge. (10½ km; 960m; 4h). If only climbing this mountain, a good alternative route for the descent is the long west ridge to rejoin the right of way near the foot of Gleann Meadail.

To continue to Luinne Bheinn return to the South-east Top, descend the narrow north-east ridge to the Bealach Ile Coire, and climb 90m to the rocky knoll of Druim Leac a'Shith. Continue over another rocky knoll and drop to the Bealach a'Choire Odhair (684m),

Luinne Bheinn from the north-east ridge of Meall Buidhe across the head of Coire Odhair   *D.J. Bennet*

the lowest point between the two Munros. (This up and down section of the ridge can be partly avoided by a rough traverse along discontinuous grassy rakes on its north-west side). Climb N to reach the east ridge of Luinne Bheinn a short distance south-east of its East Top (937m) which is sometimes mistaken for the summit. This lies about 450 metres further WNW, and only 2m higher, at a small cairn. (15km; 1400m; 5h 40min).

Follow the ridge WNW past another larger cairn, and when it steepens descend W to about 550m and make a descending traverse NNW to join the Mam Barrisdale path. In this way the traverse over the top of Bachd Mhic an Tosaich can be avoided. A good path leads down to Gleann an Dubh-Lochain and joins the estate road back to Inverie.

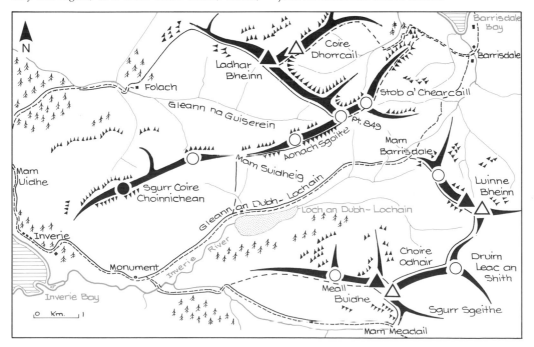

Ladhar Bheinn from Stob a'Chearcaill   *D.J. Bennet*

Ladhar Bheinn; 1020m; (OS Sheet 33; 824040); M108; *hoof or claw hill*

Ladhar Bheinn (pronounced Larven) rises in the northern part of the Knoydart peninsula, overlooking Loch Hourn. It is one of the finest mountains in Scotland, with narrow rocky ridges, spectacular corries and a setting which makes the views from it, or towards it, among the best in the land. The northern half of the mountain, from Coire Dhorrcail down to Li on the shore of Loch Hourn, is now owned by the John Muir Trust to be maintained in its natural state without any development.

The circuit of Coire Dhorrcail is the finest traverse of Ladhar Bheinn, but it is rather difficult of access from Inverie, being on the Loch Hourn side of the mountain. From Inverie the direct approach by Gleann na Guiserein is easier, but less interesting; however, a longer route up Gleann an Dubh-Lochain and the Aonach Sgoilte ridge is finer and includes the traverse along the headwall of Coire Dhorrcail. The ascent by this route and descent by Gleann na Guiserein is the best circuit of the mountain from Inverie.

Take the road up the Inverie River to Gleann an Dubh-Lochain as far as the outflow from Loch an Dubh-Lochain and climb steeply N to Mam Suidheag (490m). From there traverse ENE along the undulating crest of Aonach Sgoilte. This ridge is narrow, rocky in places and always interesting, and it leads to Pt.849m at the junction with the main Ladhar Bheinn ridge round the head of Coire Dhorrcail. A short diversion NE leads to Stob a'Chearcaill which is a splendid peak and viewpoint.

From Pt.849m descend NW to the Bealach Coire Dhorrcail and traverse over a series of rocky knolls and past the tops of the steep gullies that plunge down to the corrie. Finally climb to the junction of ridges at the western corner of Coire Dhorrcail and reach the top of Ladhar Bheinn a short distance along the nearly level summit ridge. (12km; 1250m; 4h 50min).

Continue WNW along the summit ridge past the 1010m trig point and for about 1½km further, possibly as far as the little lochan on its crest. From there descend SW steeply down grassy slopes to Folach in lonely Gleann na Guiserein, a sad, peaceful spot dominated by the steep flank of Ladhar Bheinn. Follow the path W then SW towards the Mam Uidhe and return to Inverie along the road across this pass.

The classic traverse of Ladhar Bheinn, namely the circuit of Coire Dhorrcail, is best done from Barrisdale. Take the stalker's path WNW from there for 1½km to the shoulder of Creag Bheithe, and then strike SW up this ridge, gaining superb views of Ladhar Bheinn across Coire Dhorrcail. Beyond a level section of the ridge the steep buttress of Stob a'Chearcaill rears up and for 100m there is a scramble up broken rock and grassy ledges, traversing to and fro to find the easiest line. From Stob a'Chearcaill continue SW along the narrow ridge to Pt.849m, and then go NW to Ladhar Bheinn, following the route described above. (From Barrisdale: 6½km; 1180m; 3h 30min).

Descend the north-east ridge over the Top of Stob a'Choire Odhair (960m) and continue down to a more level part of the ridge at about 400m where one should turn SE and drop down into Coire Dhorrcail to reach the stalker's path which leads back to Barrisdale.

Map on page 155.

Beinn Sgritheall across Loch Hourn   *D.J. Bennet*

Beinn Sgritheall; 974m; (OS Sheet 33; 836126); M180; *probably scree or gravel hill*

This grand peak, rising steeply above Loch Hourn, dominates the Glenelg peninsula and gives fine views across the loch to Knoydart, and beyond the Sound of Sleat to Rhum and Eigg. Its best features, the northern ridges and corries, are remote and hidden, and the southern flanks above Loch Hourn present a steep expanse of rotten crags and scree slopes that would deter the bravest. On closer acquaintance, however, Beinn Sgritheall proves to be one of the best of the solitary Munros.

The approach by road from Glen Shiel goes over the spectacular Bealach Ratagain and through Glenelg village to Arnisdale on the north shore of Loch Hourn, where the ascent begins. Climb NNE behind the village up the steep stream to the Bealach Arnasdail (c. 600m) which separates Beinn Sgritheall

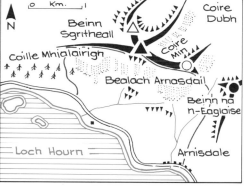

from its rocky lower neighbour, Beinn na h-Eaglaise. From the col climb WNW up steep scree to gain the East Top of Beinn Sgritheall (903m). Continue along the ridge for 1 km, a delightful walk with one short exposed section, to reach the summit trig point. (3½km; 1050m; 2h 40min).

An excellent traverse can be made, transport permitting, by continuing down the rockier west ridge to the lochan at its foot (816126). Find the start of a path just south-west of this lochan and descend steeply by it SE through the woods of Coille Mhialairigh and continue down the rough hillside to the road near Creag Ruadh, 3km from Arnisdale.

Approaching Beinn Sgritheall along the east ridge   *J. Henny*

Spidean Mialach and Gleouraich from the north, with Sgurr Mor appearing between them   H.M. Brown

Gleouraich; 1035m; (OS Sheet 33; 039054); M94; *possibly uproar or noise*
Spidean Mialach; 996m; (OS Sheet 33; 066043); M143; *peak of deer, or other wild animals*

The road westwards along the north side of Loch Quoich passes close below three fine peaks whose ascents are among the easiest in the Western Highlands. Not only are the distances from road to summits short, but stalker's paths give fast and easy walking onto the high ridges, and in some places along them. Gleouraich and Spidean Mialach, the eastern pair, are joined by just such a ridge and are separated from Sgurr a'Mhaoraich to the west by the deep trough of Glen Quoich into which the raised waters of Loch Quoich thrust a narrow arm.

Gleouraich and Spidean Mialach have two quite distinct aspects, dark rocky corries and steep spurs on their north side, and more gentle grassy slopes to the south. Their traverse is a delightful expedition combining good stalker's paths and a splendid undulating high-level ridge.

The start is from the road on the north side of Loch Quoich at a point about 4½km west of the Loch Quoich dam. A cairn on the west side of the Allt Coire Peitireach marks the overgrown start of a fine stalker's path which climbs to 850m on Gleouraich. This is one of the most impressive of all such paths, particularly high up where it traverses along the edge of the steep-sided south-west ridge, giving a feeling of exposure as one looks down to Loch Quoich hundreds of metres below. Beyond the end of the path, continue up the ridge to its junction with the north ridge, then turn SE up the crest to

the summit of Gleouraich. (3½km; 830m; 2h 10min).

Continue along the ridge to Craig Coire na Fiar Bhealaich (1006m). Beyond this Top a stalker's path zigzags down to the Fiar Bhealaich (c.740m), and from this col the ascent of Spidean Mialach is straightforward, following the scalloped cliff-edge of three successive corries. (7km; 1150m; 3h 30min).

Descend SW down easy slopes towards Loch Fearna, and when half way to it bear W into Coire Mheil. Reach the stalker's path in this corrie and follow it down to the road 400 metres east of the start.

Spidean Mialach from the north-west   R. Wood

Sgurr a'Mhaoraich from Loch Quoich   *J. Renny*

Sgurr a'Mhaoraich; 1027m, (OS Sheet 33; 984065); M101; *peak of the shellfish.*

Sgurr a'Mhaoraich is an isolated mountain which bulks large in any view up Loch Hourn, although to Loch Quoich it shows only its grassy side. Its hidden northern and western aspects hold vast flanks of black rock and a complex of ridges and steep corries. The traverse described below does justice to the mountain.

Leave the road to Kinloch Hourn at the start of a stalker's path 1km south-west of the bridge which spans the northern extension of Loch Quoich. Follow this path N up the Bac nan Canaichean ridge to Sgurr Coire nan Eiricheallach (891m), and a short distance further across a slight dip to its north-west top. There is another drop and then a rather contorted ridge leads to the summit of Sgurr a'Mhaoraich. There are outcrops of rock to either turn or scramble over, and at one point iron spikes driven into the rock are evidence of early fence building. (5km; 910m; 2h 40 min).

While easy descents can be made southwards or by the ascent route, it is more interesting to complete the circuit of Coire a'Chaorainn. Head NNW for 300 metres to a finger of rock, then descend steeply NNE to the Bealach Coire a'Chaorainn at the head of this long narrow corrie.

The traverse of Am Bathaich (910m) is rocky and narrow in places, and beyond it another stalker's path is found zigzagging steeply down the grassy east ridge to Glen Quoich. The private road in this glen is reached and followed south back to the Kinloch Hourn road.

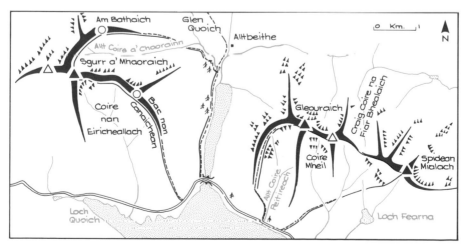

Aonach air Chrith from the west   *H.M. Brown*

Creag a'Mhaim; 947m; (OS Sheet 33; 088078); M214; *rock of the large rounded hill*
Druim Shionnach; 987m; (OS Sheet 33; 074085); M155; *ridge of the fox*
Aonach air Chrith; 1021m; (OS Sheet 33; 051083); M107; *trembling hill*
Maol Chinn-dearg; 981m; (OS Sheet 33; 032088); M166; *bald red head*

The South Glen Shiel Ridge, or the South Cluanie Ridge as it is sometimes known, is deservedly regarded as being one of the best of Scottish mountain ranges. It extends for 14km and has seven Munros in its length. Only once does the ridge drop below 800m, so it is a lofty highway. Strong walkers can traverse the whole ridge in a day, but others may prefer to take two days as described below. The north flank of the ridge is well seen from the A87 road through Glen Shiel; it is a succession of fine rocky corries carved along the hillside. The south side is a long uniform grassy slope dropping to Glen Quoich.

The first part of the ridge to be described is the eastern half, which is not far to the south of Cluanie Inn across the headwaters of the River Cluanie. Start just east of the Inn at the junction of the old road from Cluanie to Tomdoun, and walk up this road for 3km to the bridge over the Allt Giubhais, From there climb S to the easternmost peak of the ridge, Creag a'Mhaim. The going is pathless, but not particularly rough, and the crags shown on the OS 1:50,000 map near the summit present no problems. (5½km; 730m; 2h 30min).

A broad grassy ridge leads down to the first col, and on the way up to Druim Shionnach there is one surprisingly narrow section of ridge before the flat summit is reached. (7km; 850m; 3h). Navigation all along the ridge is simplified by having cliff-bitten corries on the north side, and bare grass slopes on the south.

The next 3km section of the ridge to Aonach air Chrith is bounded by the slabby crags of Coire an t-

Slugain. (10km; 1020m; 4h). Beyond, the crest of the ridge is narrower, but the traverse to Maol Chinn-dearg is perfectly easy. (12km; 1180m; 4h 40min).

The descent is down the north-east ridge, the Druim Coire nan Eirecheanach. It is steep at first, but becomes a very pleasant grassy crest with lower down a stalker's path leading back to the road in Glen Shiel 4km west of the day's starting point.

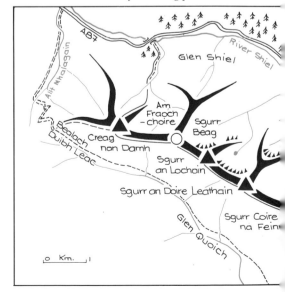

Sgurr an Lochain from the east   D.J. Bennet

Sgurr an Doire Leathain; 1010m; (OS Sheet 33, 015099); M116; *peak of the broad thicket*
Sgurr an Lochain; 1004m; (OS Sheet 33; 005104); M126; *peak of the little loch*
Creag nan Damh; 918m; (OS Sheet 33; 983112); M268; *rock of the stags*

The western half of the South Glen Shiel Ridge has two slightly lower summits to cross as well as its three Munros, so this traverse is just as long as the eastern section. The views are better, particularly to the south and west where great mountains such as Ladhar Bheinn and Beinn Sgritheall dominate the horizon.

The start is at the point where the eastern half traverse ended, a few hundred metres east of the summit of the A87 road on the watershed between the Shiel and Cluanie rivers. Follow the stalker's path south across the Allt Coire a'Chuil Droma Bhig, and follow its west branch onto the Druim Thollaidh. Climb up this ridge to reach the romantically named peak of Sgurr Coire na Feinne (the Feinne were the mythical warrior-heroes of early legends). The first Munro, Sgurr an Doire Leathain, is 1½km north-west along the main ridge with its summit on a grassy spur about 100 metres north of the ridge. (4½km; 800m; 2h 20min).

The next corrie is the only northern one on the ridge to hold a lochan, hence the name of the shapely Sgurr an Lochain, not the highest peak on the ridge, but the most distinctive. (6km; 910m; 3h).

Sgurr Beag is the next peak, a smaller one as the name implies, not a Munro and for this reason often traversed on its south side where a tiny stream high up on the grass slopes is a welcome source of water on a hot day. Drop to the next col, the lowest on the ridge at 726m and climb the last Munro, Creag nan Damh. (9km; 1210m; 4h 10min).

To return to Glen Shiel, two routes are possible. The first goes NE down a steep but quite easy ridge leading to the lower part of Am Fraoch-choire. In the corrie a stalker's path is reached at about 400m, and is followed down to the plantation in Glen Shiel near the site of the 1719 battle. The other longer route is to continue W along the main ridge to the Bealach Duibh Leac (c.725m). From there a path descends in steep zigzags to the Allt Coire Toteil and on its opposite side continues downhill beside the Allt Mhalagain to reach Glen Shiel a long way west of the day's starting point.

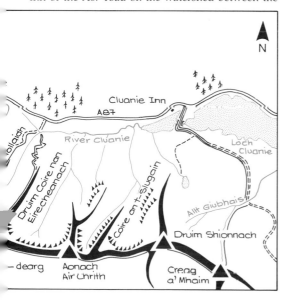

The Saddle from Sgurr na Sgine. The summit is on the left and the Forcan Ridge on the right   *D.N. Williams*

The Saddle; 1010m; (OS Sheet 33; 936131); M118
Sgurr na Sgine; 945m; (OS Sheet 33; 946113); M220; *peak of the knife*

The peaks to the north and south of Glen Shiel are certainly well known, but The Saddle is even more so for it combines in one mountain a complex of narrow ridges and deep corries that makes it one of the great Highland hills. With its neighbouring sharp peak Faochag *(the whelk)*, it forms the classic view down Glen Shiel from the site of the 1719 battle. More than one visit is needed to explore The Saddle fully, and here the description is restricted to the traverse of it and Sgurr na Sgine.

Start in Glen Shiel from the A87 road ½km south-east of the quarry at Achnangart. A good stalker's

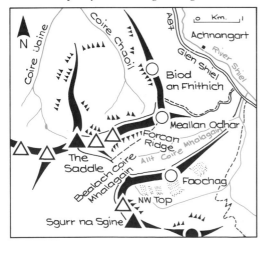

path is followed W to the col between Biod an Fhithich and Meallan Odhar. Continue S then SW to the foot of the narrow east ridge of The Saddle, the Forcan Ridge. This superb rock ridge involves some exposed scrambling, and a short tricky pitch to descend on the far side of Sgurr na Forcan, but it is not technically difficult. However, nervous or inexperienced hill-walkers may prefer the alternative route described below.

The crest of the Forcan Ridge sweeps up, narrowing to a knife-edge above the slabs of Coire Mhalagain before reaching Sgurr na Forcan (c.960m). Continue W, descending a short steep pitch with good holds and traversing the narrow ridge over the East Top (958m) to the summit cairn on top of a rocky crag. (5km; 1080m; 3h). The OS trig point is about 100 metres west along a level grassy ridge.

The alternative route bypassing the Forcan Ridge is to traverse below its south flank, following a dry stone dyke across the rough hillside to the little lochan at the Bealach Coire Mhalagain (696m). From there climb WNW on a rising traverse towards The Saddle, aiming for a point a short distance south of the summit to avoid steep ground below the summit itself. Finally climb N up a steep but easy slope to the trig point.

To continue to Sgurr na Sgine, descend this easy route from the trig point to Bealach Coire Mhalagain, and climb S to the North-west Top of Sgurr na Sgine (944m). Continue SE along the rocky ridge to the summit cairn perched right at the edge of the steep south-east face of the mountain. (7½km; 1330m; 4h).

Looking towards the summit of The Saddle from the upper part of the Forcan Ridge   *D.J. Bennet*

Return past the North-west Top and continue N then E to Faochag along a fine narrow crest. Descend the north-east ridge, a continuously steep but other-wise easy route which leads to Glen Shiel ½km up the road from the day's starting point.

The east face of Sgurr na Sgine   *H.M. Brown*

Mullach Fraoch-choire from Glen Affric   R. Robb

SECTION 11

Glen Affric and Kintail

Toll Creagach from Tom a'Choinich   H.M. Brown

Toll Creagach; 1054m; (OS Sheet 25; 194283), M73, *rocky hollow*
Tom a' Choinich; 1111m; (OS Sheet 25; 163273); M40; *hill of the moss*

These two hills are at the eastern end of the long range of mountains on the north side of Glen Affric, a range which stretches 25km from the forested lower reaches of Glen Affric and Cannich westwards to the Glomach chasm above Glen Elchaig. Toll Creagach is a hill of rounded outlines and a fairly level summit ridge 2km long, with the highest point at the east end. Tom a'Choinich has a more distinctive outline with a crescent-shaped ridge enclosing its east corrie. Between the two hills is the Bealach Toll Easa, across which goes the path which in former days led from Affric Lodge to Benula Lodge, the latter now submerged below the raised waters of Loch Mullardoch.

Although it is possible to climb these hills from Glen Cannich, this route is not recommended as the going along the south side of Loch Mullardoch through the pinewoods is trackless and very rough. It is better to approach from Glen Affric, leaving the road at the foot of Gleann nam Fiadh near the west end of Loch Beinn a'Mheadhoin. Walk up the track in this glen for 3km and then climb N up Toll Creagach, at first up steep slopes west of the shoulder of Beinn Eun, then more easily over grass and heath to the summit cairn a few metres west of the OS trig point. (5½ km; 830m; 2h 40min).

Go WSW along a broad ridge of grass and stones to the West Top (952m), then descend more steeply down a narrowing crest to the Bealach Toll Easa (873m). Continue W up the spur which rises in the centre of Tom a' Choinich's east corrie. This

spur is grassy at first, then it steepens and becomes rockier and leads directly to the summit. (9km; 1070m; 3h 50min).

The return to Gleann nam Fiadh may be made by the route of ascent to the Bealach Toll Easa and then down the path beside the Allt Toll Easa. Alternatively, descend the south-east ridge which is easy at first, but becomes rocky lower down where it is best to go E to join the Bealach Toll Easa path near its zigzags above the steep descent into the glen.

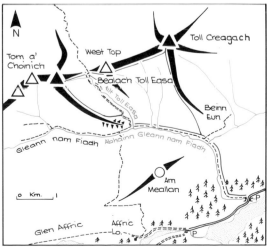

Mam Sodhail and Carn Eighe from Sgurr na Lapaich   *G.S. Johnstone*

Mam Sodhail; 1180m; (OS Sheet 25; 120253); M13; *hill of the barns*
Carn Eighe; 1183m; (OS Sheet 25; 123262); M11; *file hill*
Beinn Fhionnlaidh; 1005m; (OS Sheet 25; 115282); M125; *Finlay's hill*

Carn Eighe and Mam Sodhail, almost identical twins in height and appearance, are the highest mountains north of the Great Glen and dominate the high ground between Glen Affric and Loch Mullardoch. They form a great horseshoe around Gleann nam Fiadh, both throwing out long ridges to the east to enclose this glen. From Carn Eighe another important ridge goes north to end at Beinn Fhionnlaidh, a very remote mountain overlooking the head of Loch Mullardoch. The most familiar view of this group is from Glen Affric, from where Sgurr na Lapaich (one of the Tops of Mam Sodhail) is the most prominent peak, projecting far in front of its two higher neighbours. These are not particularly rocky mountains, but their ridges are steep-sided and their corries wild and craggy enough to make this a fine group whose traverse gives a long and serious mountain expedition. Beinn Fhionnlaidh is included as it is difficult to reach from any other glen, only Glen Elchaig offering a feasible but long approach, unless one has a canoe on Loch Mullardoch.

The closest starting point is at the end of the public road in Glen Affric, 1½km east of Affric Lodge, and from the lodge two alternatives exist for the ascent of Mam Sodhail. The quicker is along the right of way on the north side of Loch Affric to Coire Leachavie and up the stalker's path in this corrie. It ends on the south-west ridge of Mam Sodhail at 1086m, and the final ½km up the final slope is easy, past the remains of a stone shelter used by the men of the Ordnance Survey many years ago. The summit has a huge circular cairn which was an important point in the Ordnance Survey's primary triangulation of Scotland in the 1840's. (10km; 940m; 3h 50min).

Alternatively, a route for good weather goes N then W from Affric Lodge by a stalker's path for 2km. Leave the path and continue W across rising moor for 1½km to the foot of the south-east ridge of Sgurr na Lapaich and so directly to this Top (1036m). Continue W along a splendid 3½km ridge, following a path along the grassy crest. The ridge narrows and crosses Mullach Cadha Rainich (993m) before rising to Mam Sodhail.

Descend N for 140m to the col at 1044m and climb the opposite slope to Carn Eighe. (11 km; 1070m; 4h 20min). At this point a long diversion is needed to include Beinn Fhionnlaidh; descend NW and then traverse N along the grassy ridge over Stob Coire Lochan (917m) for 2½km to its summit (13½km; 1260m; 5h 10min). Return to Carn Eighe by the same way. (16km; 1640m; 6h 20min).

Now embark on the long east ridge of Carn Eighe, first ENE to Stob a' Choire Dhomhain (1148m), then ESE along a narrow rocky ridge which gives an enjoyable scramble if the crest is followed. Reach Sron Garbh (1132m) and descend quite steeply down its rocky north-east ridge where at one point a stalker's path has been so well constructed as to form a flight of stone steps. From the Garbh-bhealach (963m) go SE past two tiny lochans to reach a path which leads down to Gleann nam Fiadh. Two kilometres further down this glen the stalker's path south to Affric Lodge gives the shortest route back to the day's starting point.

To climb Beinn Fhionnlaidh by itself from any other starting point involves a long approach. It is possible to canoe along Loch Mullardoch and reach the foot of the hill which can be climbed up the long steep slopes above the loch. Starting from Killilan at the foot of Glen Elchaig, it is necessary to cycle 12km to Iron Lodge at the head of the glen and walk from there over the pass to the head of Loch Mullardoch. Cross the Abhainn a'Choilich (which may be impossible in spate) and climb the west flank of Beinn Fhionnlaidh.

An Socach; 920m; (OS Sheets 25 and 33, 088230); M264; *the snout*

This Munro is the lowest on the long chain of mountains on the north side of Glen Affric, and it is rather overshadowed by its big neighbours Mam Sodhail and Sgurr nan Ceathreamhnan. Its position is very isolated, 12 km up Glen Affric from the end of the public road in that glen, nearly the same distance over the hills from Cluanie Inn, and 3km from the remote Alltbeithe youth hostel, the loneliest in Scotland. The effort required to climb An Socach is more in the approach march than in the ascent of the hill itself. In shape it has three broad ridges converging at a flattish, bouldery summit, and the east-facing Coire Ghadheil has some small crags around its rim, but lower down it is a maze of eroded peat bog.

The approach from the car park at the west end of Loch Beinn a' Mheadhoin in Glen Affric is either along the right of way past Affric Lodge and on the north side of Loch Affric, or along the Forestry Commission road which crosses from the car park to the south side of the loch. It is quite possible to cycle along this road for 7km to Athnamulloch, where the River Affric is recrossed to join the right of way on the north side. Whichever way one choses, the approach up Glen Affric is scenically the best part of the day.

Beyond Athnamulloch the glen becomes bare, but the track continues and in 2½km the footbridge over the Allt Coire Ghadheil is reached. On the west side of the stream bear NW up easy slopes of grass and heather leading to the broad flat ridge which leads round the edge of Coire Ghadheil. After a long level section a final short rise leads to the summit. (13½km; 680m; 4h10min).

To vary the descent, go down the north-east ridge to the Bealach Coire Ghadheil and follow the good stalker's path down the east side of the corrie to Glen Affric.

From the bealach one can also continue the traverse to Mam Sodhail up another stalker's path which climbs diagonally NE to reach the south-west ridge of Mam Sodhail near a prominent cairn 1km from its summit.

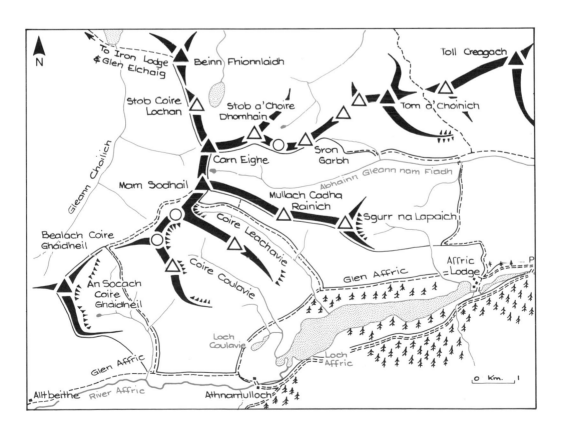

Sgurr nan Ceathreamhnan from A'Chralaig   *D.J. Bennet*

Sgurr nan Ceathreamhnan; 1151m; (OS Sheets 25 and 33; 057228); M21; *peak of the quarters*
Mullach na Dheiragain; 982m; (OS Sheets 25 and 33; 081259); M164; *perhaps summit of the hawk*

The long hill-range on the north side of Glen Affric culminates at its western end in the great massif of Sgurr nan Ceathreamhnan, a superb and complex mountain of many ridges, peaks and corries. In size it is the equal of several normal peaks, and from its summit long ridges radiate out to the north and east. The longest of these goes for 7km towards the head of Loch Mullardoch, and rises near its mid-point to the subsidiary peak of Mullach na Dheiragain, classified as a separate Munro, though very much a part of its higher neighbour.

Sgurr nan Ceathreamhnan is in a very remote and wild situation, surrounded by other mountains and many kilometres from the nearest public road. This remoteness adds to its character and makes it one of the great prizes for the hillwalker, involving a long approach from any direction unless one happens to be staying at the youth hostel at Alltbeithe in Glen Affric. Mullach na Dheiragain is even more remote and inaccessible.

It is not possible to drive up the private road in Glen Elchaig, but for those prepared to cycle for 8km up the glen and back again, this is probably the best approach for the traverse of both these mountains, and it is also possible to visit the Falls of Glomach to complete a superb expedition. The route described below involves at least one river crossing that may be difficult or impossible in spate conditions, possibly due to melting snow in Sgurr nan Ceathreamhnan's northern corries. The bridge across the River Elchaig at the outflow of Loch na Leitreach was destroyed by a spate in 1990, but it is expected that it will be rebuilt in 1991. Without it the following route is not possible except in very dry conditions.

If cycling, go for 8km as far as the path leading to this bridge. From there walk up the glen to Iron Lodge, and take the path east through the pass towards Loch Mullardoch until ½km beyond Loch an Droma. There branch S along the path to Gleann Sithidh and cross the Abhainn Sithidh, possibly with difficulty if this stream is in spate with rain or melting snow. From the end of the path climb steeply E up a grassy slope onto the north-west ridge of Mullach Sithidh (973m) and continue up the broad shoulder to this Top and ½km further to Mullach na Dheiragain. (10½km; 930m; 4h).

The long, and in places rough ridge is followed SW over Carn na Con Dhu (968m) to the Bealach na Daoine (840m), and from there a narrower rocky ridge with some easy scrambling leads to Sgurr nan Ceathreamhnan. (14½km; 1140m; 5h 10min).

Traverse the narrow summit crest to the West Top (1143m) and descend W, then NW along the broad grassy ridge round the rim of Coire Lochan. Continue NW, descending to Gleann Gaorsaic, cross the Abhainn Gaorsaic and continue down its left bank to reach the path near the Falls of Glomach. The Falls may be visited by a short diversion, and the descent continues along the path which traverses across the precipitous south-west flank of the Glomach chasm before dropping to the Allt a'Ghlomaich and Glen Elchaig.

A shorter route to Sgurr nan Ceathreamhnan, but less satisfactory for Mullach na Dheiragain, starts from Morvich or Dorusduain in Strath Croe (see pages 170 and 171). Follow the right of way to Glen Affric over the Bealach an Sgairne as far as the south end of Loch a'Bhealaich. From there climb NE to the col east of Sgurr Gaorsaic and up the south ridge of Sgurr nan Ceathreamhnan. (10km; 1300m; 4h 30min).

Looking towards Sgurr nan Ceathreamhnan from the Mullach na Dheiragain ridge   K.M. Andrew

The route from Alltbeithe youth hostel in Glen Affic goes north up the path in Coire na Cloiche to the col at the foot of the east ridge of Sgurr nan Ceathreamhnan. This ridge leads directly to the summit.

To reach Mullach na Dheiragain from the col, descend W across a steep hillside towards Loch Coire nan Dearcag and climb NW to the Bealach na Daoine where the route described above is joined.

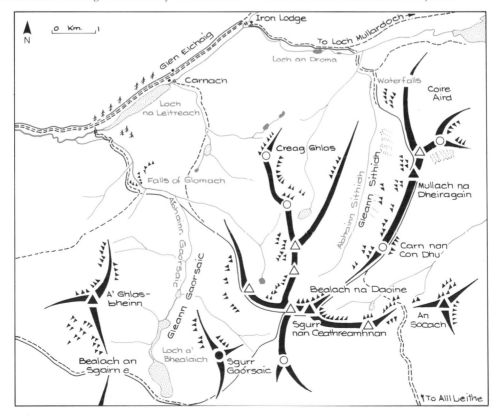

The north-eastern corries of Beinn Fhada from Sgurr Gaorsaic   H.M. Brown

Beinn Fhada; 1032m; (OS Sheet 33; 018192); M97; *long hill*
A'Ghlas-bheinn; 918m; (OS Sheet 33; 008231); M269; *the greenish-grey hill*

To the north of the Five Sisters of Kintail a single great mountain, Beinn Fhada, extends from Glen Affric to the head of Loch Duich. It is well named the long mountain, for it extends from east to west for almost 9km, and occupies an area equal to all the Five Sisters. The only roadside view of the mountain is from Loch Duich, from where the knobbly ridge of Sgurr a'Choire Ghairbh is seen. The summit, however, is far beyond and above this ridge. The south and west sides of Beinn Fhada above Gleann Lichd are uniformly steep and in places craggy, and the north side of the mountain is a succession of wild corries. By contrast, A'Ghlas-bheinn is a rather small and insignificant hill rising above the forest in Strath Croe. Beinn Fhada is in National Trust for Scotland property, and is accessible at all times of the year; A'Ghlas-bheinn is in the Inverinate estate.

The simple traverse of these two mountains starts in Strath Croe where there is a Forestry Commission car park at the end of the public road a few hundred metres west of Dorusduain. Cross the Abhainn Chonaig by a footbridge* at Dorusduain and follow the path E up Gleann Choinneachain below the steep and craggy north- west end of Beinn Fhada.

After crossing the stream which comes down from Coire an Sgairne take the stalker's path up this corrie onto the ridge of Meall a' Bhealaich at (011206). Go S along this ridge, which merges into the great summit plateau of Beinn Fhada, the Plaide Mhor, and continue SE along the edge of this plateau to the big summit cairn. (6km; 980m; 3h).

Return by the same route along the Meall a'Bhealaich ridge and go N to this outlying top. The direct descent from there to the Bealach an Sgairne is steep and rocky, and an easier way is to the east of the direct line to the pass, descending NE at first then down to the east of a prominent gully. (An alternative which may be preferable in bad conditions of visibility or rain is to return down Coire an Sgairne by the stalker's path of the uphill route to the junction with the main path in Gleann Choinneachain, and then to climb 1km up this path to the pass. This is a longer, but absolutely certain route).

From the Bealach an Sgairne climb the knobbly south-east ridge of A'Ghlas-bheinn, passing Loch a' Chleirich to the east. (11km; 1380m; 4h 50min). Descend WNW along a broad grassy ridge which steepens lower down near the forest. Keep on the crest of the ridge and aim for the point where the path from Strath Croe to the Bealach na Sroine emerges from the forest, and from there continue S through the forest along a track to Dorusduain.

An alternative route of ascent to Beinn Fhada which is better than the one described above, particularly if one is starting from Morvich, is to walk to the cottage at Innis a'Crotha and from there climb ENE up the grassy ridge of Beinn Bhuidhe. Towards the top of this ridge bear ESE and climb steeper, rockier slopes to the northern point of Sgurr a'Choire Ghairbh. This western outlier of Beinn Fhada forms a

This bridge was destroyed in a storm in 1990, but it is hoped that it will be rebuilt in 1991.

The cliffs of Sgurr a'Choire Ghairbh at the west end of Beinn Fhada   *D.J. Bennet*

fine undulating ridge with steep cliffs on its east side. Traverse S along it and drop down steeply to The Hunters' Pass; the descent is down a rocky pitch and may be awkward when wet or in winter conditions.

Beyond the pass climb SE up a narrow ridge to Meall an Fhuarain Mhoir (956m) which is at the western end of the Plaide Mhor. Cross this featureless plateau eastwards for 2km to the summit of Beinn Fhada.

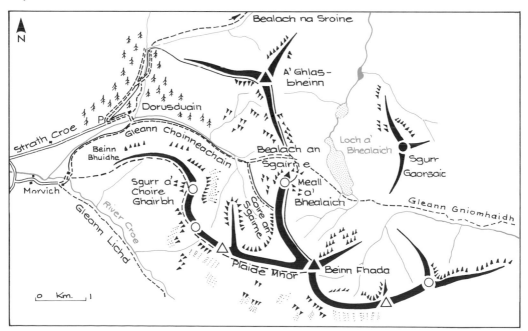

Sgurr nan Conbhairean from Carn Ghluasaid   *R. Robb*

Carn Ghluasaid; 957m; (OS Sheet 34; 146125); M201; *hill of movement*
Sgurr nan Conbhairean; 1110m; (OS Sheet 34; 130139); M42; *peak of the keeper of the hounds*
Sail Chaorainn; 1002m; (OS Sheet 34; 133155); M131; *hill (literally heel) of the rowan*

These three mountains are on the north side of Loch Cluanie mid-way between Loch Ness and Loch Duich. From the A87 road they do not look very impressive, for their southern slopes and corries are

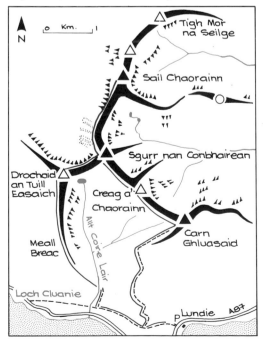

undistinguished and their tops hidden. Only when one is on the summits can their true character be appreciated, in particular the great wild eastern corrie in which rise the headwaters of the River Doe. The southern slopes by which the ascent is made are for the most part grassy.

Start the traverse at Lundie, 4km west of the Loch Cluanie dam. Follow the old military road W for ½km, then turn N along a fine stalker's path which leads right up to the flat plateau of Carn Ghluasaid. The summit cairn may be hard to find in the mist, it is about 50 metres back from the precipitous north face of the hill. (4km; 720m; 2h 10min).

Traverse W then NW along a broad ridge of moss and stones to Creag a' Chaorainn (999m), then W to the Glas Bhealach over a remarkably smooth expanse of grass, and finally climb NW to Sgurr nan Conbhairean. (7km; 990m; 3h 20min). Descend N along a curving ridge to the col at 910m and reach Sail Chaorainn by its easy-angled south ridge. (8½km; 1100m; 3h 50min).

Return by the same route towards Sgurr nan Conbhairean, whose summit can be bypassed on the west. Continue SW down a narrowing ridge to the col above Gorm Lochan, and climb a short distance further to Drochaid an Tuill Easaich (1000m), a Top not named on the OS 1:50,000 map. Turn S and descend the easy grass ridge which leads to the shoulder of Meall Breac. When the descent steepens, bear SE, cross the Allt Coire Lair to reach the path on its east side and go down it to the old military road which leads east back to Lundie.

A'Chralaig from Mullach Fraoch-choire   *K.M. Andrew*

A'Chralaig; 1120m, (OS Sheets 33 and 34; 094148); M32; *the basket or creel*
Mullach Fraoch-choire; 1102m; (OS Sheets 33 and 34; 095171); M46; *heather-corrie peak*

These two peaks are the high points of an 8km-long ridge extending north from the west end of Loch Cluanie to Glen Affric. A'Chralaig is a massive mountain; certainly this is the impression gained when looking from the south-west at the long grassy slopes rising high above Loch Cluanie. Mullach Fraoch-choire is more elegant, its summit being the meeting point of three narrow ridges, and it looks particularly fine seen from the pine woods round Loch Affric. The east side of the high ridge between them drops in a series of large grassy corries draining towards Glen Affric, while the west side is more uniformly steep above the deep glen of An Caorann Mor.

Start the traverse from the A87 road near the west end of Loch Cluanie where the track through An Caorann Mor leaves the road. Climb steeply NE up grassy slopes for 500m until the angle eases on the south ridge of A'Chralaig. Continue up this ridge, which becomes quite narrow and well-defined, and leads easily to the summit, crowned by a huge cairn visible for miles around. (3½km; 900m; 2h 20min).

Continue N along a grassy ridge to a col at 950m and climb the outlying Top, Stob Coire na Cralaig (1008m). The ridge becomes narrower, dropping NE across another col, then turning N to Mullach Fraoch-choire. The ascent to this peak is the best part of the traverse, along a narrow ridge broken into several rocky towers which give very pleasant and easy scrambling along their crests to the summit. (6km; 1110m; 3h 20min).

The return to Loch Cluanie may well be best made by the outward route over the summit of A'Chralaig. However, if circumstances dictate a quick descent to lower ground, the best route is back to the col ¼ km north-east of Stob Coire na Cralaig, then down NW (steeply at first) into Coire Odhar. Lower down this corrie, bear round SW to reach the path near the pass at the head of An Caorann Mor, and follow this path SSE to the road at Loch Cluanie.

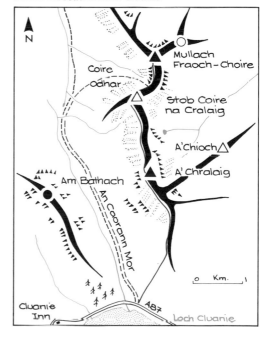

Ciste Dhubh from the south   *A. O'Brien*

Ciste Dhubh; 982m; (OS Sheet 33; 062166); M163; *black chest*
Aonach Meadhoin; 1003m; (OS Sheet 33; 049137); M129; *middle hill*

These two mountains lie to the north and north-west of Cluanie Inn at the west end of Loch Cluanie. They are separated by a col, the Bealach a'Choinich (567m) which is 3km north-north-west of the Inn. Ciste Dhubh is a pointed peak at the north end of the ridge which rises north of the bealach. The flanks of this ridge are very steep, and its crest narrow, and the summit is also steep and rocky, presenting a fine appearance from the south. Aonach Meadhoin and its slightly lower Top, Sgurr an Fhuarail (988m), lie to the south-west of the Bealach a'Choinich, and form a fine horseshoe ridge above Coire na Cadha. All these peaks have narrow, but perfectly easy ridges and give exhilarating high-level walking. From Cluanie Inn they give a fairly easy round traverse, which can be extended westwards by energetic hillwalkers to include the next two Munros on the north side of Glen Shiel.

Leave the A87 road ½km east of Cluanie Inn and go along the narrow strip of clear ground between the forest and the Allt a'Chaorainn Bhig. There is a path, but it becomes rather indistinct, however the going is easy up the grassy slopes on the east side of the stream leading to the Bealach a'Choinich.

A finer, but rather longer route to this col is along the narrow grassy ridge of Am Bathach. Start just east of the plantation at the foot of the south-east ridge and follow an old stalker's path up the first few hundred metres, then continue along the delightful undulating crest. A bit of extra effort, but well worthwhile.

The Bealach a'Choinich is a wide flat col, rather wet and peaty, and the south ridge of Ciste Dhubh rises abruptly from its north side. Climb a very steep grass slope for 150m until the gradient eases and a little rocky top is reached. From there the ridge goes N for 1km, level and very narrow, but perfectly easy and with a distinct path. There is a slight drop before the final rise to the summit of Ciste Dhubh. (5½km; 740m; 2h 30min).

Return to the Bealach a'Choinich and go SW up the north-east ridge of Sgurr an Fhuarail. The first part is a broad grassy slope, but higher up the ridge becomes better defined and leads directly to the sharp summit. Continue W along the fine narrow ridge, dropping to about 910m, then climb more steeply to Aonach Meadhoin. (9½km; 1230m; 4h 10min).

Sgurr an Fhuarail from the east, with Aonach Meadhoin just visible behind   H.M. Brown

The best return to Cluanie is back over Sgurr an Fhuarail and down its south-east ridge. There is a little top at 800m whose summit must be crossed as its flanks are very steep, and once past it an easy descent down grassy slopes leads to the road just west of the Inn.

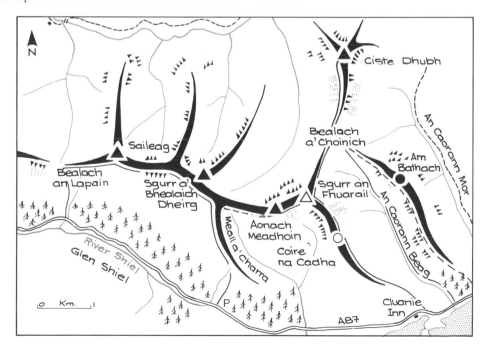

Looking west from Sgurr a'Bhealaich Dheirg to Saileag with the Five Sisters of Kintail beyond   J.S. Stewart

Sgurr a' Bhealaich Dheirg; 1038m; (OS Sheet 33; 035143); M92; *peak of the red pass*
Saileag; 959m; (OS Sheet 33; 018148); M195; *little heel*

Near its head Glen Shiel is densely forested along the lower slopes of the hills on its north side, and above the forest rise the smooth grassy flanks of Sgurr a' Bhealaich Dheirg and Saileag, two mountains which form a continuation of the Five Sisters of Kintail eastward beyond the Bealach an Lapain. They have some of the same character as the Five Sisters, long uniform slopes above Glen Shiel, and grand wild corries to the north overlooking Gleann Lichd. Their summit ridge and northern corries are in National Trust for Scotland territory.

Sgurr a' Bhealaich Dheirg has a level summit ridge ½km long, and at its south-east end a long spur projects north-east. The summit is a short distance along this spur. Saileag, 2km west, is mainly a grassy hill, "a mere swelling in the ridge", but its north-west face is steep and craggy. The two give a short and easy traverse from Glen Shiel, and can be combined with Aonach Meadhoin and Ciste Dhubh to give an excellent, but not unduly long day.

Start the traverse from the A87 road at its highest point between Glen Shiel and Loch Cluanie where there is a clear gap on the forested hillside. Climb N onto Meall a' Charra, and NW along the grassy crest of this spur to reach the main ridge ½km south-east of Sgurr a' Bhealaich Dheirg. (If traversing from Aonach Meadhoin, this point is reached along its east ridge and across the 831m col at its foot). Climb steeply up to the level ridge of Sgurr a'Bhealaich Dheirg and go for about 70 metres along its narrow north-east spur, following a low dry-stone wall to reach the summit where a large, finely built cairn stands astride the crest. (3km; 770m; 2h).

Return to the level ridge and go NW along it for about 400 metres, then turn W down the narrower continuation of the ridge where there is a fairly good path all the way down to the col and up a grassy rise

The summit of Sgurr a'Bhealaich Dheirg   H.M. Brown

to Saileag. (4½km; 900m; 2h 30min).

Go down an easy grassy slope WSW to the Bealach an Lapain, and from there descend steeply to Glen Shiel, following traces of a path, to reach the road 4km north-west of the day's starting point.

Map on page 175.

Sgurr nan Saighead and Sgurr Fhuaran from Beinn Bhuidhe   D.J. Bennet

For most of its length Glen Shiel is enclosed on the north-east side by a mountain range of awe-inspiring height and steepness, the Five Sisters of Kintail. They rise from glen to summit crests in uninterrupted slopes of heather, grass, scree and crag, riven by great gullies. The best-known view of the group is from the south side of Loch Duich, from where the mountains have a remarkable simplicity and symmetry of outline.

Of the Five Sisters, two are Munros and two are Tops.

The classic hillwalking expedition is the complete traverse, preferably from south-east to north-west; it is not an unduly strenuous day, but is does end at least 8km away from the starting point, so some suitable transport arrangement will be needed if a long walk through Glen Shiel is to avoided. Possibly the bus services through the glen might help.

The Five Sisters are National Trust for Scotland property, and access is possible all year.

Sgurr Fhuaran; 1068m; (OS Sheet 33; 978167); M66; *meaning obscure*

This is the highest and finest peak of the Five Sisters, and the outstanding landmark in this part of the Western Highlands. The most striking feature of Sgurr Fhuaran when seen from the foot of Glen Shiel is the long west ridge which rises from the River Shiel directly to the summit, bounded on both sides by great deep-cut ravines. In this view the height of the mountain is very obvious, and it is also evident that any ascent by this ridge, although very direct, is likely to be a long and unrelenting grind.

A more varied and interesting ascent traverses the peak of Sgurr nan Saighead *(peak of the arrows)* en route to Sgurr Fhuaran. Leave the A87 road near the head of Loch Shiel and cross the River Shiel by a suspension bridge just above the loch. Climb NE up a steep grassy slope to the 443m col just south-east of Sgurr an t-Searraich. Continue SE across level peaty ground to the foot of the WNW ridge of Beinn Bhuidhe (871m), which is the north-west peak of Sgurr nan Saighead. Climb this ridge direct to Beinn Bhuidhe, which is a superb viewpoint. The route continues along a fine narrow ridge, with a steep drop on the right, to the highest point of Sgurr nan Saighead (929m) and down across a grassy col, following a fairly well-defined path. Beyond the col, and below the steep final slope of Sgurr Fhuaran, the path bears right across the north-west face to reach the west ridge, which is followed to the summit. (5km; 1230m; 3h 10min).

The descent may be made by the same route, or more quickly down the west ridge.

Map on page 178.

Beinn Bhuidhe, the north-west peak of Sgurr nan Saighead   D.J. Bennet

Sgurr na Ciste Duibhe; 1027m; (OS Sheet 33; 984149); M102; *peak of the black chest*

This mountain near the south-east end of the Five Sisters range is less shapely than its neighbours, and it is difficult to get a good impression of it from Glen Shiel for it rises so abruptly in rough craggy slopes, presenting rather an unattractive appearance and discouraging any attempt at a direct ascent from the glen. Its south face is one of the highest and steepest mountainsides in Scotland, rising 1000m in a horizontal distance of 1½km, an average angle of 34 degrees.

The best starting point for the ascent of Sgurr na Ciste Duibhe is further up Glen Shiel, about 1¾ km east of the bridge at the site of the 1719 Battle of Glen-

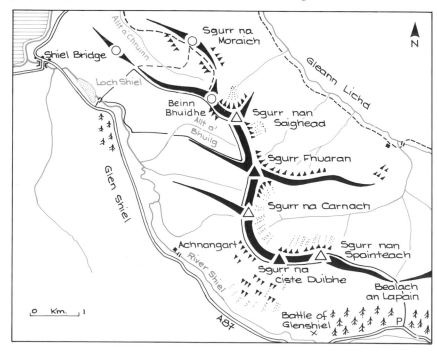

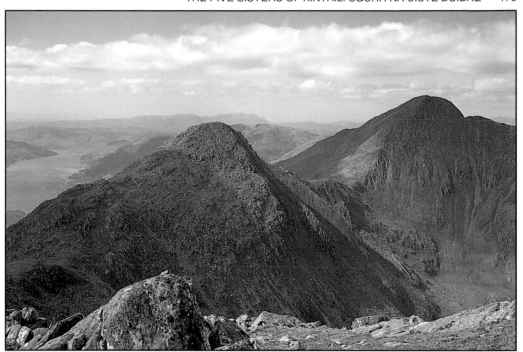

Sgurr na Carnach and Sgurr Fhuaran from Sgurr na Ciste Duibhe   H.M. Brown

shiel. At that point there is a wide gap between the rows of spruce trees on the north side of the glen. Climb steeply due N up this gap onto the open hillside, following a path worn by many hillwalkers. The ascent is continuously steep until the level grassy ridge is reached at the Bealach an Lapain (723m). Turn W and follow a well-defined path along the narrow grassy ridge, climbing gradually to Sgurr nan Spainteach (c. 990m), *peak of the Spaniards.*

Beyond this Top (which is not counted as one of the Five Sisters) the ridge drops more abruptly, with a short rocky pitch down to the next col. At this point, below Sgurr na Ciste Duibhe, the ridge has a curious double crest, with a hollow in between the two crests. This may be confusing in misty weather, but if the path is carefully followed there is no problem in climbing the final steep stony slopes to Sgurr na Ciste Duibhe, where there is a large cairn. (3½ km; 950m; 2h 30min). Descend by the same route.

If the traverse of the Five Sisters is intended, continue W then NW across the Bealach na Gaoithe (850m), then climb N up a broad ridge to Sgurr na Carnach (1002m), *peak of the stony ground.* Descend its rather steep north side, still following a broad, rather ill-defined ridge and reach the Bealach na Carnach (868m) at the foot of the south face of Sgurr Fhuaran. This slope is steep and bouldery, but a path zigzags up to the summit. (6km; 1300m; 3h 30min).

The descent to Glen Shiel can be made by either of the two routes described on page 177 for Sgurr Fhuaran.

The complete traverse of the Five Sisters involves also the northernmost of the five, Sgurr na Moraich (876m). This is the large rounded hill which rises directly above the head of Loch Duich. It is reached from Beinn Bhuidhe by descending NNE and climbing the south-east ridge of Sgurr na Moraich.

To return from there to Glen Shiel descend S to the Allt a'Chruinn and from there go W to reach the flat ground at the 443m col above Loch Shiel. Alternatively, descend WNW from the summit to reach the Allt a'Chruinn above the waterfall at the steep lower slope of the hill above the head of Loch Duich. Continue down the path on the north side of the stream to Ault a'Chruinn.

Sgurr nan Spainteach and Sgurr na Ciste Duibhe   H.M. Brown

Looking west from the Strathfarrar hills to Loch Monar, with Lurg Mhor and Bidein a'Choire Sheasgaich beyond

W.D. Brooker

SECTION 12

Glen Cannich to Glen Carron

An Socach from Loch na Leitreach in Glen Elchaig   D.J. Bennet

An Socach; 1069m; (OS Sheet 25; 100333); M64; *the projecting place, or snout*

Situated in the remote hinterland of southern Ross-shire between the upper reaches of Glen Cannich and Glen Elchaig, An Socach is a very inaccessible hill, many kilometres from the nearest public road. It might be thought of as a westward extension of An Riabhachan, but the col between the two is low enough to give An Socach the character of a separate mountain. Its summit ridge is an east-facing crescent enclosing Coire Mhaim, whose lower level is an extensive area of eroded peat bog. Around its western perimeter An Socach is grassy, and a curving ridge goes out to enclose Coire Lungard.

There are two very long routes to the mountain, from the Loch Mullardoch dam to the east, and from Glen Elchaig to the south-west.

From the Mullardoch dam, walk along the north shore of the loch following a fairly good path for most of the way for 8km to Benula Lodge. From there continue W up a stalker's path towards Coire Mhaim and climb the south-east ridge of An Socach, thereby avoiding the rough ground in the corrie itself. (13½km; 870m; 4h 30min).

It is not possible to drive up Glen Elchaig from Killilan and a bicycle is an asset for the 12km of private road (which is a right of way) to Iron Lodge. Otherwise the walk up the glen and back again in the evening makes for a very long day. From the road end near Iron Lodge continue along the path beside the Allt na Doire Gairbhe leading towards Pait Lodge. Near the south-west end of Loch Mhoicean climb SE to a col and then ENE up grassy slopes, along the level ridge round the head of Coire Lungard and finally up the broad west face of An Socach to the summit. (19½km; 1070m; 6h 10min. About 2h less by bicycle).

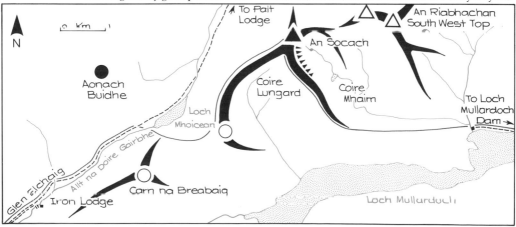

An Riabhachan from Sgurr na Lapaich   *A.J. Bennet*

An Riabhachan; 1129m; (OS Sheet 25; 134345); M28; *the brindled greyish one*
Sgurr na Lapaich; 1150m; (OS Sheet 25; 161351); M22; *peak of the bog*
Carn nan Gobhar; 992m; (OS Sheet 25; 182344); M149; *hill of the goats*

These three mountains, together with An Socach further west, form the main range between Glen Strathfarrar and Glen Cannich along the north side of Loch Mullardoch. An Riabhachan is a 4km long ridge with open grassy corries on all sides except at the north-east end where there is a steep rocky face above Loch Beag and Loch Mor. Sgurr na Lapaich is a more defined peak, visible from a long distance down Strath Glass, and having some steep corries on its east side. Carn nan Gobhar is a rounded and rather undistinguished hill with an outlying Top, Creag Dubh, 2km to its east.

The closest access to these mountains by road is from Glen Strathfarrar, particularly if it is possible to drive to the little power station in Gleann Innis an Loichel. If this approach is impossible (e.g. on Tuesdays under the present access arrangements, see page 185, or if the road is snow-bound) the alternative starting point at the road end in Glen Cannich at the Loch Mullardoch dam must be used.

From the power station in Gleann Innis an Loichel continue W along a track for 1km and then up the stalker's path WSW for a further 1½km before branching off left. Cross the stream (possibly difficult if in spate) and climb SW up a stalker's path which ends at the lip of An Riabhachan's north-east corrie, the Toll an Lochain, which is a grand wild place with dark crags overlooking two high lochans. Beyond the path the best way lies along the level ridge between the two lochans, then SE on a gradually rising traverse among huge fallen boulders towards the Bealach Toll an Lochain, the col at the head of the corrie.

From this col the ridge to An Riabhachan rises at a fairly easy angle, with one short narrow section, to the North-east Top (1117m), and then across level mossy ground to the summit. (8½km; 950m; 3h 30min).

Return to the col and climb the steep grassy south-west shoulder of Sgurr na Lapaich to the large circular cairn enclosing the trig point. (11½km; 1300m; 4h 50min). Descending E, it is best to keep just on the south side of the true east ridge, which forms a narrow rocky crest that would involve some scrambling. On the south side of this rocky ridge a slope of grass and boulders leads down easily to the next col.

The first part of the broad ridge leading to Carn nan Gobhar is littered with huge boulders, and higher up the angle steepens to the small cairn on the summit. (14km; 1500m; 5h 40min). The top of Carn nan Gobhar is a wide level ridge running south to north, with a big cairn about 200 metres SSE of and slightly lower than the small summit cairn.

To return to the day's starting point, descend more or less due N, at first down steep grassy slopes, then across several streams in the very rough and peaty Garbh-choire and finally over a little col to drop down through scattered birches on the steep hillside above the power station.

Approaching from the Loch Mullardoch dam, take the path for 1½km along the north side of the loch. Then climb the south-east ridge of Mullach na Maoile and continue NNE to Carn nan Gobhar, passing the large cairn shortly before reaching the summit. Continue to Sgurr na Lapaich by reversing the route described above.

Sgurr na Lapaich from the east ridge of An Riabhachan   G.F. Brunton

From its summit descend S to the Top of Sgurr nan Clachan Geala (1095m). From there the most direct return is down the south-east ridge of this peak to the Glas Toll, across the Allt Taige and on down the grassy hillside on a descending traverse SE. There is a path and occasional signs of a vehicle track on the hillside.

The inclusion of An Riabhachan in this traverse makes a very long day. It may be possible by prior arrangement with Cozac Lodge to hire a boat to reach Benula Lodge, and thereby avoid the long walk along the north side of Loch Mullardoch

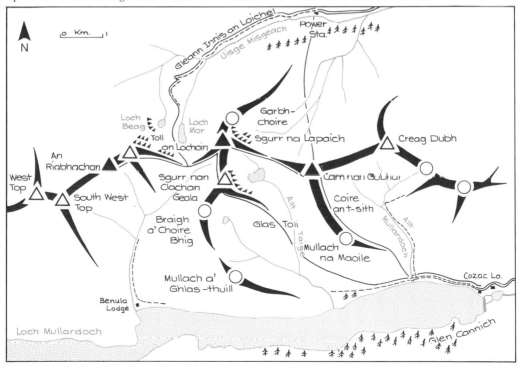

Looking west from Sgurr a'Choire Ghlais to Creag Ghorm a'Bhealaich   W.D. Brooker

Sgurr na Ruaidhe; 993m; (OS Sheet 25; 289426); M148; *peak of the redness*
Carn nan Gobhar; 992m; (OS Sheet 25; 273439); M150; *hill of the goats*
Sgurr a' Choire Ghlais; 1083m; (OS Sheet 25; 259430); M56; *peak of the greenish-grey corrie*
Sgurr Fuar-thuill; 1049m; (OS Sheet 25; 236437); M79; *peak of the cold hollow*

The four Munros on the north side of Glen Strathfarrar form a well-defined ridge several kilometres long which can be traversed in a single day, the only drawback being that the starting and finishing points on the road are about 6km apart. The two eastern hills, Sgurr na Ruaidhe and Carn nan Gobhar, are smooth and rounded and of no great distinction. Sgurr a'Choire Ghlais at the centre of the ridge is distinctly higher, steeper and more impressive, and at the west end Sgurr Fuar-thuill and its two adjacent Tops form an undulating crest with steep faces to the north. South-west of these, Sgurr na Muice (891m) can justifiably be regarded as the finest peak in this group by virtue of the great slabby face above the dark waters of Loch Toll a'Mhuic. It alone among these hills has any significant exposure of rock, elsewhere grass and heather predominate. Aesthetically the east to west traverse is preferable, leaving the best of the ridge and the finest views to the end of the day.

Leave the Strathfarrar road at the foot of the Allt Coire Mhuillidh and climb the zigzag track, followed by a stalker's path on the east side of the stream, for 2km. Beyond the first side stream climb NE up the grassy shoulder of Sgurr na Ruaidhe, which gives easy going all the way to the summit. (5km; 850m; 2h 40min). The upper slopes of this hill on its north and west sides are remarkably smooth and mossy. Descend these slopes WNW to a col at 780m, and then climb NNW then W to Carn nan Gobhar, which has a boulder-strewn summit with the cairn at its north edge. (7½km; 970m; 3h 20min).

Continue SW along the level mossy ridge, then descend W to the next col at 860m. From there climb Sgurr a'Choire Ghlais along the steep ridge on the edge of its northern corrie. The summit is crowned by two cairns and a trig point. (9km; 1120m; 4h). The ridge drops again to 900m before rising over Creag Ghorm a'Bhealaich (1030m), and continuing, now with a steep drop on the north side, to Sgurr Fuar-thuill. (11½km; 1350m; 4h 50min).

At the next col, just before Sgurr na Fearstaig (1015m), the top of a stalker's path is reached and it may be followed downhill. However, it is worth continuing along the ridge to the last Top for the westward view, and then going S along the ridge towards Sgurr na Muice for a few hundred metres until a short easy descent can be made E to join the stalker's path lower down. This path tends to disappear in the grassy corrie, but it reappears near Loch Toll a'Mhuic and thereafter gives a good fast descent to the glen.

It is only slightly longer, and on a fine evening would certainly be worthwhile, to continue along the southward running ridge to Sgurr na Muice, from where there is a splendid view westwards along the length of Loch Monar. From there descend S to the narrow col before Carn an Daimh Bhain and go ENE down a path below the south end of the Sgurr na Muice crags to join the main path by the Allt Toll a'Mhuic.

The road up Glen Strathfarrar is private, and a gate at Inchmore ½km west of Struy Bridge is kept locked.

Sgurr a'Choire Ghlais from Carn nan Gobhar   *G.F. Brunton*

An arrangement between the landowners and the Nature Conservancy Council (who administer a small Nature Reserve in the glen) allows access by car up this road. The keeper of the gate key lives in the cottage beside the gate.

The hours when it is normally possible to drive up the glen are: Weekdays (except Tuesdays) 9.00 a.m. to 6.00 p.m. Sundays 1.30 p.m. to 6.00 p.m. Tuesdays no access. Please do not call at the cottage between 1.00 p.m. and 1.30 p.m.

The above information is valid from Easter to the end of October. At other times of the year it is essential to telephone the keeper of the key (046 376 260) to check the situation as regards access.

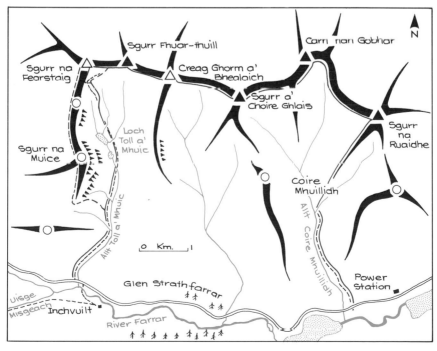

Lurg Mhor from Beinn Tharsuinn   *D.J. Bennet*

Five grand mountains lie to the south-east of Glen Carron in a fairly remote setting round the head of Loch Monar. Two of them, Lurg Mhor and Bidein a'Choire Sheasgaich, are among the least accessible, and hence most highly prized, of all Munros. The easiest approach to all five is from the A890 road at Craig in Glen Carron, 3½km east of Achnashellach. A private road crosses the railway at a level crossing there and goes east along the north side of the Allt a'Chonais through the Achnashellach Forest. Beyond the forest the road continues for several kilometres to Glenuaig Lodge, following the right of way between Glen Carron and Strathconon. It is possible to cycle along this road, which may be quite a help in view of the long distance to these mountains. 5½km from Craig, at the point where the glen turns east towards distant Strathconon, the climber reaches the parting of the ways: east to Maoile Lunndaidh, south to Sgurr Choinnich and Sgurr a'Chaorachain and south-west to Bidein a'Choire Sheasgaich and Lurg Mhor.

Bidein a'Choire Sheasgaich; 945m; (OS Sheet 25; 049413); M218; *peak of the corrie of the barren (or milkless) cattle*
Lurg Mhor; 986m; (OS Sheet 25; 065404); M158; *big ridge stretching into the plain*

These two mountains are the remotest of the group on the south-east side of Glen Carron, and there is very much the feeling of a real expedition to climb them. Some might prefer to take two days and stay in the remote and lonely Bearnais bothy (021430). Bidein a'Choire Sheasgaich is a very fine peak indeed, its sharp pointed summit being an easily recognisable landmark from many distant hills. Lurg Mhor is a long, rather level ridge, steep on the north side and narrow to the east where it joins the Top, Meall Mor (947m). This east ridge runs out for quite a long way above the west end of Loch Monar to lonely Pait Lodge. One of the best views of these two mountains is had from the east, looking along Loch Monar from the west end of the North Strathfarrar Ridge.

The start from Craig follows the route described above for 5½km up the Allt a'Chonais. Cross the footbridge at (074467), or ford the river just upstream, and follow the stalker's path SW to the Bealach Bhearnais. Continue SW, climbing onto the ridge of Beinn Tharsuinn and following its undulating crest to the summit (863m). Descend SW to the lochan on the crest of the ridge and continue down a short steep step to the col between the two tops of Beinn Tharsuinn. From there descend steeply SSW to the 550m Bealach an Sgoltaidh, the pass at the foot of the north ridge of Bidein a'Choire Sheasgaich.

This ridge rises very steeply and looks rather intimidating, encircled by crags. Climb directly uphill close to a dry stone dyke and scramble easily up the first band of rocks to reach a more continuous cliff. The most direct way up this is by an open gully directly above; it is steep, but grassy rather than rocky, and the way is obvious, trending slightly rightwards. An alternative route lies further left (E) following an inclined grassy ledge which narrows near its top. A third route is some distance to the west, up another steep grassy gully.

These three routes all lead to a level section of the ridge where there is a tiny lochan. Continue S over a knoll to a larger lochan and finally climb more steeply following a path up the narrowing ridge to the sum-

Bidein a'Choire Sheasgaich from Beinn Tharsuinn   D.J. Bennet

mit of Bidein a'Choire Sheasgaich. (From Craig, 12½km; 1300m; 5h).

Go S at first for a short distance along the summit ridge, then descend SE down a wide grassy slope to the next col at 740m. The ridge to Lurg Mhor is broad and bouldery, bounded on its north side by steep crags, and it leads directly to the summit. (From Craig, 14½km; 1550m; 5h 50min). Only the most dedicated of 'Top-baggers' are likely to continue the extra ¾km E to Meall Mor; the intervening ridge is narrow and rocky and gives a good scramble with one short pitch that cannot be easily avoided.

The return from Lurg Mhor to Craig is hardly less strenuous or time-consuming than the outward journey. One way is to reverse the traverse over Bidein a'Choire Sheasgaich and Beinn Tharsuinn, with all the climbing that that involves. The alternative is to descend NE from the col between Lurg Mhor and Bidein and lose a lot of height to about 350m, then traverse round below the rocky lower nose of Beinn Tharsuinn's south-east ridge and climb the long grassy slopes on the east side of that hill to the Bealach Crudhain. There the two routes rejoin, and one continues down to Craig. Altogether, it is a hard day's hillwalking that can be made easier with a bicycle.

For those spending two days on these mountains and staying overnight at Bearnais bothy, the best starting point is Achnashellach. Cross the River Carron, possibly by a wire bridge at (011482) if it is in spate, and follow the path up through the forest on the east side of Coire Leiridh. This path leads over the ridge and down to the bothy. From there cross the Abhainn Bhearnais, which may be very difficult if the river is in spate, and climb SE up Coire Seasgaich to the lochan high up on the north ridge of Bidein a'Choire Sheasgaich.

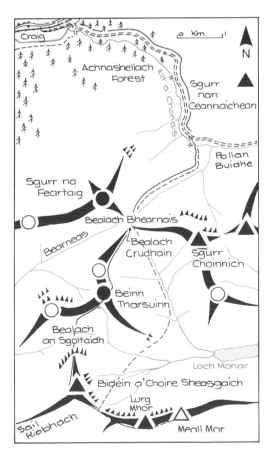

Sgurr a'Chaorachain from Sgurr Choinnich   W.D. Brooker

Sgurr Choinnich; 999m; (OS Sheet 25; 076446); M136; *moss peak*
Sgurr a'Chaorachain; 1053m; (OS Sheet 25; 087447); M74; *peak of the little field of the berries*

These two mountains are clearly seen as one approaches up the track along the Allt a'Chonais above the Achnashellach Forest. They are the two most accessible of the five in this group. Sgurr Choinnich presents a steep rocky front, and it has a level summit ridge, while Sgurr a'Chaorachain appears as a more rounded mountain. Between them is a fine little corrie, very rocky on its west side below the cliffs of Sgurr Choinnich, but less so on the east side. Not seen from this viewpoint is the third peak in this group, Bidean an Eoin Deirg (1046m). It has a pointed summit 2km east of Sgurr a'Chaorachain, and it appears as the finest of the group when seen from the east, for example in the view westwards along Loch Monar.

To reach this pair, cross the Allt a'Chonais by the footbridge at (074467) and take the stalker's path leading to the Bealach Bhearnais. A good traverse of Sgurr Choinnich (although not the shortest ascent) can be made by continuing up this path to the bealach, and then heading back E up the west ridge of the peak. This is a pleasant grassy ridge with a few little rocky steps, and it leads to the narrow level crest where the summit is perched on the edge of the steep north-east face. (From Craig, 9½km; 950m, 3h 50min).

Continue SE along the nearly level crest for about 200 metres, then turn NE down the steep ridge, quite rocky at first, to the Bealach Coire Choinnich (860m). From there climb ENE up a broad ridge, which is quite rocky in places, to the level stony summit of Sgurr a'Chaorachain. (From Craig, 11km; 1050m; 4h 20min).

On a good day it is well worthwhile going to the Top of Bidean an Eoin Deirg. The first 1km is along a

fairly level ridge which gives easy going on moss and flat stones. Then there is a short drop before the final

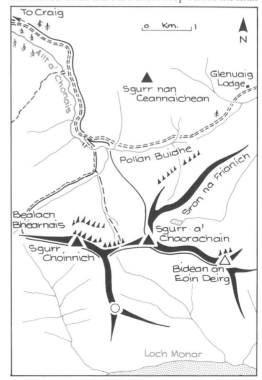

Sgurr a'Chaorachain from the east   *G.S. Johnstone*

climb. The north face of the peak drops very steeply for 400m and is not a good route of descent. It is best to return along the ridge to Sgurr a'Chaorachain.

From there the quickest descent is down the north ridge for about ¾km, then NW down steep but easy grassy slopes which lead to the Allt a'Chonais. Alternatively, return to the Bealach Coire Choinnich and descend N down the the corrie, keeping to the east side of the stream to avoid the small bands of rock below Sgurr Choinnich.

Bidean an Eoin Deirg   *D.J. Bennet*

Moruisg from Loch Gowan   *C. Pashley*

Moruisg; 928m; (OS Sheet 25; 101499); M252; *big water*
Sgurr nan Ceannaichean; 915m; (OS Sheet 25; 087481); M275; *peak of the merchants or pedlars*

These two mountains are on the south side of Glen Carron near the bleak upper reaches of that glen. Moruisg is long and flat-topped; its northern corries look out over featureless moorland to Achnasheen, and its north-west flank drops in concave grassy slopes to the River Carron. Sgurr nan Ceannaichean is a more interesting, though smaller mountain. Its west face is remarkably steep and craggy, and looks impressive from Glen Carron. Between the two the Coire Toll nam Bian is a deep hollow with a steep headwall of grass and broken crags.

The traverse of the two mountains is most easily done from Glen Carron, leaving the A890 road about 1½km west of the outflow of Loch Sgamhain. Cross the River Carron by a footbridge and follow the stalker's path towards the Alltan na Feola for a short distance. It is possible to leave the path anywhere and climb SE up the ever-steepening grass slopes of Moruisg, keeping north of an area of crags and selecting an easy line between the steep gullies which seam this side of the hill. Above these gullies the slope eases a bit and leads direct to the summit of Moruisg. (4½km; 780m; 2h 20min).

Go SW then S along the broad mossy ridge to Pt.854m, then descend more steeply SW to the col at 730m. Climb W up a broad grassy ridge for ½km, then SW to reach the summit of Sgurr nan Ceannaichean, which is a small plateau. The summit cairn is at its south-east edge. (7½km; 980m; 3h 20min).

Retrace the last part of the ascent route for ½km down the north-east ridge, then bear N down a steep broad ridge, avoiding a rocky bluff halfway down. Cross the Alltan na Feola to rejoin the stalker's path on its north-east bank, and follow it back to the day's

starting point.

Alternative descent routes from Sgurr nan Ceannaichean which make possible a complete traverse of these two hills are either down the stalker's path on the south-west side of the hill, or down steep stony slopes at the north end of the rocky west face. Both routes lead to the track beside the Allt a'Chonais which takes one back to Craig in Glen Carron.

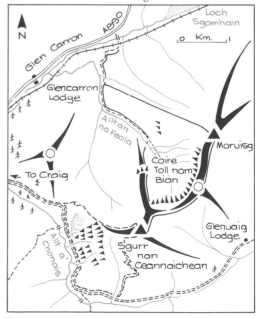

Maoile Lunndaidh from the east end of Loch Monar   D.J. Bennet

Maoile Lunndaidh; 1007m; (OS Sheet 25; 135458); M122; *bare hill of the wet place*

Another very remote Munro, Maoile Lunndaidh rises to the north of Loch Monar in the wild hinterland between Glen Carron, Glen Strathfarrar and Strathconon, and is roughly equidistant from starting points in these three glens. In appearance it is a flat-topped hill, almost Cairngorm-like in its character with a level plateau ending abruptly in deep corries. This appearance is particularly evident looking along Loch Monar from its east end. From Glen Carron the hill is invisible, and one has to go several kilometres up the Allt a'Chonais before seeing it and reaching the foot of its north face, cleft by the deep Fuar-tholl Mor.

Of the three approaches, the one from Craig in Glen Carron is the shortest (by a small margin) and has the advantage that one can cycle 9km to the foot of the hill. The Strathfarrar approach depends on being able to drive to Loch Monar (see page 185).

From Craig in Glen Carron take the track up the Allt a'Chonais to the watershed and continue for about 1km further to a small plantation before breaking off to the east across rough ground. Cross An Crom-allt and climb fairly steeply up the north-west flank of Carn nam Fiaclan (996m) close to the edge of the Fuar-tholl Mor. From this Top continue ESE then NE along the almost level ridge between the indentations of the Fuar-tholl Mor and the Toll a'Choin to reach Maoile Lunndaidh. (From Craig, 13km; 980m; 4h 40min).

The descent may be varied by going N down to a col at 750m, then turning W to descend across the foot of Fuar-tholl Mor and, still heading W, return to the track near the small plantation.

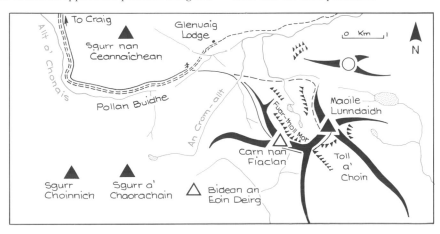

Liathach from Beinn Eighe   *G.F. Brunton*

SECTION 13

Coulin and Torridon

Maol Chean-dearg from the north   *K.M. Andrew*

Maol Chean-dearg; 933m; (OS Sheet 25; 924498); M241; *bald red head*

Maol Chean-dearg is one of three Munros on the north-west side of Glen Carron. It can be seen from the glen near Coulags, from where it is frequently climbed, partly hidden behind the nearer and lower Meall nan Ceapairean. It is rather an isolated mountain whose summit is a great dome of bare rock and sandstone boulders, making its name, bald red head, particularly apt.

From the A890 road bridge just west of Coulags follow the right of way up the east side of the Fionn-abhainn, crossing a bridge to the west bank after 2½km. Continue past Coire Fionnaraich bothy to the Clach nan Con-fionn, the stone to which the legend-

ary Fionn tethered his hunting dogs. In a further ½km take the path which bears off W and climbs more steeply to the col at about 590m between Maol Chean-dearg and Meall nan Ceapairean.

From the col climb NW up a rather indistinct path in the quartzite screes to reach a level shoulder. Continue along it and climb the final dome of Maol Chean-dearg, which is composed of sandstone boulders. The summit is a little plateau, with the large cairn near its north-west edge. (7½km; 900m; 3h 10min). From a point a few metres beyond the cairn there is a spectacular view down the steep north face to Loch an Eoin.

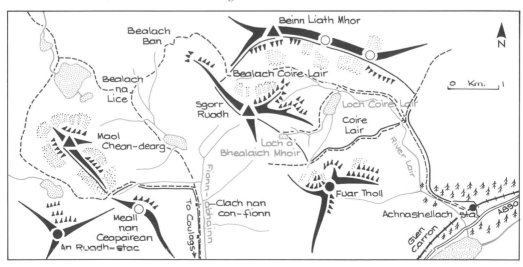

Sgorr Ruadh from Coire Lair   *A. Tibbs*

Beinn Liath Mhor; 925m; (OS Sheet 25; 964519); M258; *big grey hill*
Sgorr Ruadh; c.960m; (OS Sheet 25; 959504); M191; *red peak*

The mountainous country between Glen Torridon and Glen Carron tends to be neglected, perhaps because it is overshadowed by the Torridonian mountains to the north. This is a pity, for the peaks are full of interest with many fine rock features, splendid corries and a network of good stalker's paths.

Coire Lair above Achnashellach is an impressive place surrounded by three mountains of character: Fuar Tholl (907m) is very much a rock climbers' peak with its great Mainreachan Buttress; Sgorr Ruadh is the shapely highest summit of the group with big sandstone cliffs towering above Loch Coire Lair, and what Beinn Liath Mhor lacks in height it makes up for in the length of its summit ridge on the north side of Coire Lair. The white quartzite screes of this mountain are in striking contrast with the dark sandstone cliffs of the other two peaks on the opposite side of the corrie. The traverse of these three mountains round the rim of Coire Lair is an excellent hillwalk.

Park at the side of the A890 road near the end of the private road leading to Achnashellach station. Walk up to the station, cross the line and go about 100 metres along a forest road to a junction. There turn left and go about 400 metres until a path through the rhododendrons on the left leads to the main path up Coire Lair. This path continues through the forest and onto the more open hillside where scattered pines cling to the steep sides of the ravine through which the River Lair plunges. At a height of 370m, with Coire Lair opening out ahead, there is a junction of paths. If the river is in spate, it is worth going along the left-hand one for a short distance to inspect the crossing which may have to be made at the end of the day. There are no better crossing places lower down.

Continue along the right-hand path which climbs NNE on its way to Loch Coulin. In ½km the summit of this path is reached. The hardest part of the day's climbing comes next: the long, steep and rough slope of heather and boulders leading to the 876m east top of Beinn Liath Mhor. From there traverse 2km WNW along the undulating ridge of quartzite scree and moss to the main summit. (7km; 1030m; 3h 20min).

Some care is needed on the descent to the Bealach Coire Lair. Go WSW down the ridge and in ½km turn SSW. The rock changes from white quartzite to red sandstone, with big steps and some crags to bypass. There is a knoll to cross and the two lochans, one before it and the other beyond it at the bealach, are useful landmarks in thick weather.

From the Bealach Coire Lair (c.650m) climb SW to the tiny lochan on the north-west ridge of Sgorr Ruadh, and follow this ridge over scree to the summit. (9½km; 1380m; 4h 30min). The descent goes SE down an open slope of grass and boulders and leads to the broad col where there are several lochans, Loch a'Bhealaich Mhoir being the largest one. Continue SSE beyond this loch past a few smaller ones to reach a stalker's path. It would be quite possible to climb Fuar Tholl from there by its west ridge, thereby completing the traverse of the Coire Lair peaks.

The return to Achnashellach, however, goes E down the stalker's path below the imposing crags of Fuar Tholl to the crossing of the River Lair. If previous inspection has shown this crossing to be difficult or dangerous, then descend E down the stream flowing from Loch a'Bhealaich Mhoir, go round the west side of Loch Coire Lair, and rejoin the Coire Lair path at the north end of the loch. Map on page 193.

Beinn Alligin across Loch Torridon   D. Scott

Beinn Alligin; 985m; (OS Sheets 19 and 24; 866613); M160; *possibly jewelled hill*

The Torridonian tryptych of Beinn Alligin, Liathach and Beinn Eighe is rightly regarded as one of the finest mountain groups in Scotland. They rise in castellated tiers and battlements of red Torridonian sandstone, in places crowned with white quartzite. Their long narrow ridges give serious expeditions with some difficult scrambling. Of the three, Beinn Alligin is the least complex, and is possibly the one which should be tackled first by visiting climbers.

The narrow road from the head of Loch Torridon to Inveralligin passes below Beinn Alligin, and the most convenient starting point is at the car park on the west side of the bridge over the Abhainn Coire Mhic Nobuil. Climb NNW across the rising moor to the foot of Coir'nan Laogh, and continue NW then N up to the head of the corrie to reach Tom na Gruagaich (922m). This is a fine peak with a tremendously steep north-east face plunging into Toll a'Mhadaidh Mor. Descend N down a rocky ridge to the col at 766m, beyond which the crest becomes broader, though still precipitous on its east side. Climb NNE over a knoll (858m) and then NE to Sgurr Mhor, the summit of Beinn Alligin. Just below the top the ridge is interrupted in startling fashion by the Eag Dhubh, *the black cleft,* a sheer-sided gash in the steep hillside. (5km; 1130m; 3h).

The quickest and easiest return is by the route of ascent, and the best escape route in bad conditions is W down to An Reidh-choire followed by a long walk round the west side of the mountain. However, the great pleasure of the Torridonian mountains is to traverse their narrow castellated ridges, and on Beinn Alligin this means the crossing of Na Rathanan, the Horns of Alligin.

Descend from the summit steeply ENE then E down a narrow ridge to the col at 757m, and traverse the three Horns. There is a well marked path over these rocky tops, giving some exposed but (in summer at least) perfectly easy scrambling. From the third top continue the descent SE down the crest of the ridge to the moor below, where a stalker's path is joined and followed down Coire Mhic Nobuil to the road.

No restriction on climbing in the stalking season.

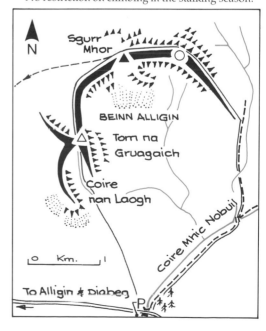

Spidean a'Choire Leith from the east   *J.E.S. Bennet*

Spidean a'Choire Leith; 1054m; (OS Sheet 25; 929580); M72; *peak of the grey corrie*
Mullach an Rathain; 1023m; (OS Sheet 25; 912577); M105; *summit of the row of pinnacles*

The central, highest and most awesome of the Torridonian tryptych is Liathach, the grey one. Its great terraced wall rising above Glen Torridon is unique among Scottish mountains in conveying the impression of impregnability, an impression which is quite correct for there are few chinks in Liathach's armour. The mountain is a huge 7km-long ridge with two principal summits, both Munros: Spidean a' Choire Leith near the eastern end and Mullach an Rathain towards the west. The ridge between these summits is narrow, and for almost half its length it is riven into a succession of pinnacles, Am Fasarinen.

The traverse of this pinnacled ridge is an exposed and in places difficult scramble, particularly in wet weather, so the complete traverse of Liathach, one of the great mountaineering expeditions in Scotland, is reserved for those with experience of scrambling and a good head for heights. In winter conditions the traverse is a major undertaking calling for a high level of mountaineering ability. However, the two main summits can each be climbed more easily by routes which are described below, but even they are likely to be serious climbs in winter, requiring skill and proper equipment.

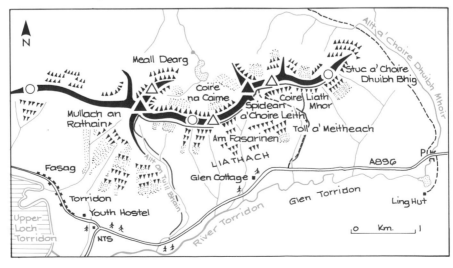

Looking west along the ridge of Liathach to Mullach an Rathain   R. Robb

The route to Spidean a'Choire Leith starts from the A896 road in Glen Torridon about ¾km east of Glen Cottage. The path begins about 50 metres west of the Allt an Doire Ghairbh, crosses this stream and climbs steeply up its east bank into the Toll a'Meitheach. Heather, steep grass and rocky steps are all encountered. High up at about 550m the stream forks and straight ahead are the dark cliffs at the head of Coire Liath Mhor. One route bears right (NE) up steep ground, still following a tenuous path, to reach the col on the main ridge at 833m. From this col a short diversion leads to Stuc a'Choire Dhuibh Bhig (913m), the easternmost peak of Liathach and a fine viewpoint.

Returning to the 833m col, the ascent to Spidean a'Choire Leith follows the main ridge along quite a well-defined path on quartzite screes and rock, NW at first, then W over the two tops of Bidein Toll a'Mhuic (983m) to the final bouldery summit cone of Spidean a'Choire Leith. (3km; 1120m; 3h).

An alternative and more direct route from Toll a'Meitheach bears left from the stream junction on a rising traverse NW. There a several small sandstone cliffs which can be avoided with the exception of one which requires a short scramble. Above it a steep scree slope leads to the col between Bidein Toll a'Mhuic and Spidean a'Choire Leith.

The descent is best made by the route of ascent, as otherwise one may unexpectedly encounter some vertical drops, invisible from above; such is the nature of Liathach's terraced sides.

Mullach an Rathain is also best climbed from Glen Torridon, leaving the road near the small pinewoods 1km east of the National Trust for Scotland's Informa-

tion Centre at the Torridon road junction. Head NNE across the rough rising hillside over many slabby sandstone terraces towards the mouth of the Toll Ban, at first on the west side of the Allt an Tuill Bhain, then on the east side. Higher up the slopes become grassier and much steeper as the head of the corrie is approached, but there are traces of a path. To avoid the steep headwall of the corrie bear left (W) onto the crest of the SSW ridge of Mullach an Rathain and climb this easily to the summit. (3km; 1000m; 2h 30min). Return to Glen Torridon by the same way.

The hillside to the west of Mullach an Rathain overlooking Torridon village is steep, craggy and has two or three big scree gullies. They are not recommended either as routes of ascent or descent, for their combination of scree, boulders, little crags and heather makes for purgatorial progress.

The ridge between the two main summits of Liathach is easy in its western half from Mullach an Rathain down to the col. From there the traverse of Am Fasarinen is exposed, but there is good scrambling on the crest with a steep pitch near the east end of the pinnacles. The alternative is to follow a narrow path on the south side of the ridge below the crest. This path avoids the pinnacles, but it also is exposed, slippery in wet weather and at the places where it crosses the several steep gullies it is dangerously eroded. It should not be regarded as an easy route. In winter this path may be a long traverse across steeply banked snow. At the east end of the pinnacles a broad slope of quartzite boulders leads up to Spidean a'Choire Leith.

No restrictions on climbing in the stalking season.

Looking west along the main ridge of Liathach to Am Fasarinen and Mullach an Rathain   M. Moran

Looking east along the main ridge of Liathach to Spidean a'Choire Leith   C. Simpson

The west end of the ridge from Am Fasarinen
towards Mullach an Rathain   J F S Bennet

The traverse path along the south side of Am
Fasarinon   H M Brown

Beinn Eighe from Loch Coulin   *D.J. Bennet*

Beinn Eighe (Ruadh-stac Mor); 1010m; (OS Sheets 19 and 25; 951611); M117; *file hill (big red peak)*

Beinn Eighe is the easternmost of the Torridonian mountains, and unlike its two neighbours it is characterised by the pale quartzite screes and rock of the long ridge which links its several Tops on the north side of Glen Torridon. The great corries of Beinn Eighe all face north into country that is totally desolate and seldom penetrated by hillwalkers, while the long scree flanks facing Glen Torridon give the mountain a disheartening appearance, possibly suggesting a giant treadmill.

The finest feature of the mountain is Coire Mhic Fhearchair, with its dark loch mirroring the Triple

Buttress that forms the headwall of the corrie. Any ascent of Beinn Eighe should include a visit to this corrie, one of the finest in Scotland, and from it the highest of the mountain's seven tops, Ruadh-stac Mor, can readily be climbed as it lies on a spur directly overlooking the corrie.

The starting point in Glen Torridon is at the car park on the A896 road just west of the Allt a'Choire Dhuibh Mhoir. Follow the footpath up the Coire Dubh Mor round the east end of Liathach to the watershed. At this point, near a small elongated lochan, take a branch path N round Sail Mhor, whose

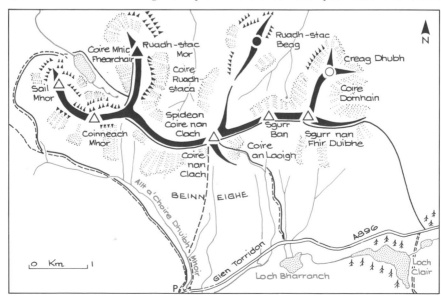

Sgurr Ban and Sgurr nan Fhir Dhuibh from the west   D.J. Broadhead

northern prow is split by a great gully, and reach Loch Coire Mhic Fhearchair at about 580m. Cross the outflow and go round the east side of the loch. The corrie floor is rough, and great curtains of scree pour down the flanks of Ruadh-stac Mor from crags high above. Continue upwards towards the south-east corner of the corrie by the pools that drain into the loch and gain the col at about 860m that separates Ruadh-stac Mor from the main ridge of Beinn Eighe. Finally go 1km N along a broadening ridge to the summit. (9km; 930m; 3h 40min).

The return may be made by the same route, but it is better to traverse one or two more of Beinn Eighe's Tops before descending. From the 860m col climb a short distance SW to the cairn at the east end of the flat mossy summit of Coinneach Mhor. Turn SE to follow the main ridge down to the next col (821m) and climb 1km E to Spidean Coire nan Clach (972m), *peak of the stony corrie.*

To return to Glen Torridon from this Top, descend a spur SSE off the main ridge for a short distance and turn E down into Coire an Laoigh. Follow the burn for 1km to reach a stalker's path which leads to the A896 road 2km east of the starting point. A more direct descent from Spidean Coire nan Clach can be made by turning W off the spur into the top of Coire nan Clach. Continue S down this corrie on the west side of the stream by mainly grassy and heathery slopes to the road near the car park.

The traverse of Beinn Eighe can be continued east from Spidean Coire nan Clach along the main ridge to Sgurr Ban (971m), *white peak,* and Sgurr nan Fhir Dhuibh (963m), *peak of the dark men.* The ridge is well-defined and stony all the way. From the latter Top the easiest descent to Glen Torridon is SE for ⅓km down a steep slope, then easily along the east ridge for 1km until scree-free slopes

lead S down to the glen.

No restriction on climbing the south-west side of Beinn Eighe in the stalking season. See OS map for boundary of NTS property.

Beinn Eighe from Liathach   M. Moran

Slioch from Loch Maree   *C. Pashley*

SECTION 14

Loch Maree to Loch Broom

On the ridge from Slioch to Sgurr an Tuill Bhain   *D.J. Bennet*

Slioch; 980m; (OS Sheet 19; 005688); M169; *from Gaelic sleagh, a spear*

The south-eastern end of Loch Maree is dominated by Slioch, a magnificent Torridonian sandstone mountain rising like a huge castle above its foundation of Lewisian gneiss. It is one of the great sights of the Northern Highlands, well seen from the opposite side of the loch, and its summit commands fine views of the surrounding mountains, some of them in the wildest part of Scotland. Around three quarters of its perimeter Slioch is defended by towering sandstone buttresses and steep crags and scree. Only on its south-east side, above Gleann Bianasdail, are there any easy routes to the summit.

Start from Incheril, a group of cottages and crofts 1km east of Kinlochewe, where cars can be parked at the roadside. Take the road, degenerating to a track and then a footpath, which goes NW through some fields and then along the beautifully wooded bank on the north-east side of the Kinlochewe River. This path reaches the shore of Loch Maree, and 1km further crosses the Abhainn an Fhasaigh by a footbridge. Once across the bridge turn NE up the path which leads through Gleann Bianasdail to Lochan Fada.

In less than 1km (before reaching the steepening of the path at a rocky bluff) bear due N, following a less distinct path to the col between the rocky point of Sgurr Dubh and the knoll of Meall Each. Continue up Coire na Sleaghaich on the south side of the stream for almost 1km and then climb a short steep grassy slope to reach a tiny lochan nestling on the south-east ridge of Slioch. Climb this ridge over a false summit and across a wide col to the true summit. (10km; 940m; 3h 50min). The north top at (004691) is the same height, but is a much finer viewpoint, being perched at the top of the great north-west buttresses of the mountain.

To make a traverse of the mountain, go E along a narrowing ridge to Sgurr an Tuill Bhain (933m). From there a descent due S leads down across Coire na Sleaghaich to the col between Sgurr Dubh and Meall Each where the uphill route is rejoined.

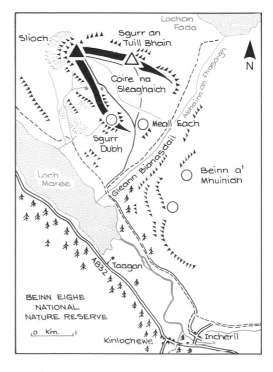

North of Slioch and Loch Maree the Letterewe and Fisherfield forests are a wild and uninhabited tract of mountainous country with no road access. The six Munros in this area are collectively the remotest in Scotland, only Seana Bhraigh and Lurg Mhor can rival them for inaccessibility. The routes to these mountains from points on the perimeter of this great wilderness area are very long, and hillwalkers have to be fit to walk in, climb their peaks and walk out again in a single day. The three points of access are Kinlochewe in the south-east, Poolewe in the west and Corrie Hallie near Dundonnell in the north, and routes from these places are described below.

The alternative approach to these mountains involves either camping or bivouacing in the interior of the area, or staying in bothies, of which there are two. Shenavall in Strath na Sealga is a good bothy from which all six Munros are accessible and can in fact be climbed in a single day by fit climbers. However, it is popular and often uncomfortably crowded. The stable at Carnmore is in a ruined state and does not provide comfortable shelter; enquiries about its use should be made from the estate factor or the keeper at Kernsary.

There is a good network of well-engineered stalker's paths throughout the area, but also an absence of footbridges at several crucial river crossings, so during and after heavy rain some of these crossings may be impossible. The old Ordnance Survey 'One Inch to the Mile' map is very inadequate in this area, lacking detail of the great cliffs and seriously inaccurate in its showing of contour lines and heights. The Letterewe and Fisherfield forests are jealously guarded deer-stalking country, and should not be visited by hillwalkers during the stalking season without prior consultation with the local stalkers.

Slioch from Fionn Bheinn   A. O'Brien

Looking west from A'Mhaighdean across Fionn Loch and the wilderness of Letterewe   *I. Brown*

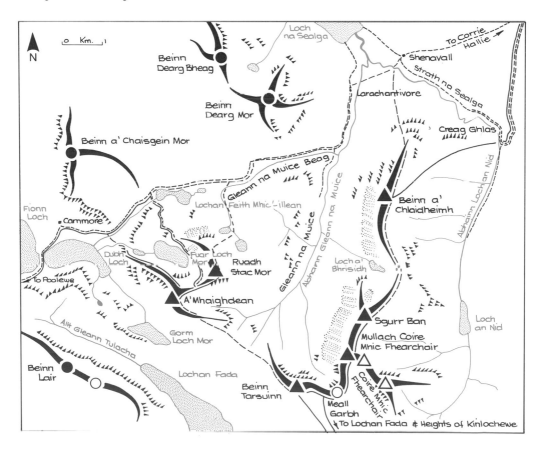

A'Mhaighdean; 967m; (OS Sheet 19; 008749); M184; *the maiden*
Ruadh Stac Mor; 918m; (OS Sheet 19; 018756); M267; *big red peak*

A'Mhaighdean and Ruadh Stac Mor stand in the centre of the Letterewe wilderness, the former a cliff-girt bastion which is one of the most spectacular viewpoints in Britain. These two are among the most highly prized Munros for hillwalkers by virtue of their remoteness and the beauty of their setting. It is worth saving them for a fine day. The approach from Poolewe is described.

With permission a car can be taken from Poolewe for about 3km up the east side of the River Ewe to Inveran, a small but possibly important help at the beginning (and end) of a very long day. Continue 2½km along the road to the stalker's house at Kernsary, and then E and SE through the forest to gain the path on the north bank of the Allt na Creige. This path peters out, but after descending below the steep north face of Beinn Airigh Charr to pass Loch an Doire Chrionaich it becomes clear again. It makes a short diversion south to cross Srathan Buidhe, and then descends gradually to the south-east end of the Fionn Loch.

Now the heart of the wilderness is reached, and A'Mhaighdean soars up beyond the Dubh Loch. Cross the causeway between these two lochs and continue along the good stalker's path towards Carnmore, then E, climbing into the valley of the Allt Bruthach an Easain. Cross this stream and traverse SE across the hillside to the little stream flowing out of the Fuar Loch Beag, and reach the long stepped crest of A'Mhaighdean's north-west ridge. This has plenty of crags, but any difficulties can be avoided, and the scenery is impressive. The ridge ends on a domed plateau with the summit perched above the cliffs at its south edge. (19km; 1090m; 6h 10m).

Descend NE from A'Mhaighdean by easy, mainly grassy slopes to the col at about 750m, where there is a good bivouac in a cave under a large boulder. From there Ruadh Stac Mor seems well defended by a ring of sandstone crags, but there is a faint path which zigzags up the steep hillside and leads without difficulty to the trig point of this mountain. (20½km; 1260m; 6h 50min).

Return by the route of ascent to the col and take the stalker's path (not completely shown on the OS map) which starts there and makes a descending traverse between the crags and screes of Ruadh Stac Mor above and the dark waters of Fuar Loch Mor below to reach the outflow of Lochan Feith Mhic'-illean. Go SW along the path which leads down the Allt Bruthach an Easain to Carnmore and the long return journey towards the sunset and Poolewe. The total distance for the day is about 40km.

Map on page 205.

Ruadh Stac Mor and A'Mhaighdean from the west across Fionn Loch   *D.J. Bennet*

Beinn a'Chlaidheimh, Sgurr Ban and Mullach Coire Mhic Fhearchair from Beinn Tarsuinn   H.M. Brown

Beinn Tarsuinn; 936m; (OS Sheet 19; 039727), M234; *transverse hill*
Mullach Coire Mhic Fhearchair; 1019m; (OS Sheet 19; 052735); M109; *summit of the corrie of Farquhar's son*
Sgurr Ban; 989m; (OS Sheet 19; 055745); M153; *white peak*

This is another hard to reach group, but while A'Mhaighdean is a peak that collects superlatives, the Mullach and its neighbours fail to inspire such enthusiasm. The scenery is less majestic, the quartzite capping gives some tedious walking and the paths all end many rough, boggy kilometres from the summits. However, the traverse of these Munros gives a long, hard day of considerable character. The approach from Kinlochewe is described, although it is also possible to reach these peaks from the east by way of Loch a'Bhraoin.

From Incheril, 1km east of Kinlochewe, there are two possible approaches to the south-east end of Lochan Fada, where the actual climbing begins. The first is the same as the route described to Slioch, continuing up Gleann Bianasdail along a fine path high above the deep gorge of the glen and then dropping down to the outflow of Lochan Fada. The crossing of this stream may be impossible in bad weather, in which case the alternative route from Incheril by the private road to the Heights of Kinlochewe and up Gleann na Muice is advised. The latter way is slightly longer and less fine scenically, but a bicycle can be used along it for several kilometres.

From the south-east end of Lochan Fada the going is rough and boggy at first, but improves as height is gained. Head N until the craggy hillside at about 500m is passed, then bear NW towards the summit of Beinn Tarsuinn along a gently rising ridge, then a steeper slope of stepped sandstone. (14km; 910m; 4h 40min). Beinn Tarsuinn has a narrow crest running in the direction of A'Mhaighdean, and fills the head of Gleann na Muice as a grand bastion.

Descend ESE to the col (c.730m) below Meall Garbh and follow a well-worn deer track across the north-west face of this little peak to the next col (c.760m) below Mullach Coire Mhic Fhearchair. The final climb to the summit of this mountain goes up shattered quartzite boulders. (16km; 1200m; 5h 40min).

Sgurr Ban lies about 1½km NNE across a col at about 820m. As the name hints, it is a quartzite peak, and while the traverse presents no technical difficulty, the unstable rocks and boulders give rough walking and require care when wet. The summit is well to the north-east on the flat quartzite plateau. (17½km; 1390m; 6h 20min).

The return from Sgurr Ban to Kinlochewe is very long and tedious. The most direct route is probably back over Mullach Coire Mhic Fhearchair to the col between Meall Garbh and Beinn Tarsuinn, and then S to retrace the ascent route. The descent east from Sgurr Ban leads down huge areas of bare quartzite slabs towards the head of Loch an Nid and a long re-ascent over the Bealach na Croise. It cannot be recommended as a better alternative.

Map on page 205.

Beinn a'Chlaidheimh from the north; Sgurr Ban to the left, Ruadh Stac Mor to the right   *P. Hodgkiss*

Beinn a'Chlaidheimh; 914m; (OS Sheet 19; 061775); M277; *hill of the sword*

This mountain, which just reaches Munro height and no more, lies 3km north of Sgurr Ban and is the northern outlier of the group just described. It overlooks the beautiful Strath na Sealga, and is most easily climbed from Dundonnell. Beinn a'Chlaidheimh is much more a sandstone mountain than its southern neighbours, and shows the characteristic terracing of this rock. The summit ridge is quite narrow, and the western slopes drop very steeply into Gleann na Muice.

Start from the A832 road in the strath of the Dundonnell River 3½ km above the head of Little Loch Broom where there is a roadside car park at Corrie Hallie. Take the track south up the beautifully wooded Gleann Chaorachain, and follow it over the featureless pass to Strath na Sealga. The crossing of the Abhainn Loch an Nid may present a problem if it is in spate, for there is no bridge between Loch an Nid and Loch na Sealga. In such conditions it would be better not to attempt Beinn a'Chlaidheimh.

Once across the river, climb SW up fairly rough ground, getting steeper as the rocky upper slopes are reached. The final climb is up the ridge just east of the summit. (11km;1130m;4h 20min). Return by the same way, with 270m more climbing up the track from Strath na Sealga over to Corrie Hallie.

The complete traverse of the 'Big Six' Fisherfield and Letterewe Munros is a magnificent expedition, quite possible for fit hillwalkers in a single day, particularly if Shenavall is used as the base for the trip. This is a justifiably popular bothy, but it should not be visited in the stalking season. The earlier remarks about river crossings are particularly apt. The Abhainn Srath na Sealga has to be crossed both at the beginning and the end of the day, and it is a sizeable river in normal conditions; in spate it is quite impassible.

From Shenavall cross this river and climb directly up the north-west shoulder of Beinn a'Chlaidheimh, a steep ascent with rough heather and minor crags, most of which can be avoided. At the top a fine narrow ridge leads to the summit. Continue S over a knoll, then SSE to the col (c.600m) east of Loch a' Bhrisidh. At that point the quartzite slopes of Sgurr Ban are reached, and a long climb leads SW to its summit. Continue to Mullach Coire Mhic Fhearchair and Beinn Tarsuinn as already described.

From Beinn Tarsuinn descend the fine narrow ridge W then NW, and drop down W to the low boggy col at about 520m between Gleann na Muice and Lochan Fada. The long ascent to A'Mhaighdean is up a broad grassy ridge, and the route continues to Ruadh Stac Mor as already described.

The most direct return to Shenavall goes along the north-west ridge of Ruadh Stac Mor for almost ½km, then NE down quite easy slopes towards Lochan a'Bhraghad. From there go N along the stream flowing from the lochan to reach the stalker's path at the head of Gleann na Muice Beag. This path leads down to Gleann na Muice 1½km upstream from Larachantivore. The bridge shown on the map near there is in total disrepair and unsafe, so wade across the Abhainn Gleann na Muice and finally cross the level boggy Strath na Sealga to wade its river opposite Shenavall.

Map on page 205.

Corrag Bhuidhe and Sgurr Fiona from Loch Toll an Lochain   D.N. Williams

Bidein a'Ghlas Thuill: 1062m; (OS Sheet 19; 069844); M69; *peak of the greenish-grey hollow*
Sgurr Fiona; 1059m; (OS Sheet 19; 064837); M70; *light coloured peak, or perhaps peak of wine*

An Teallach, *the forge*, is deservedly regarded as one of the finest of Scottish mountains. Forming a high massif between the heads of Little Loch Broom and Loch na Sealga, it is seen to best advantage from the A832 road crossing the divide from Braemore to Dundonnell. This aspect is dominated by three eastward projecting ridges, Glas Mheall Mor, Glas Mheall Liath and Sail Liath, and the two great corries which they enclose, Glas Tholl and Toll an Lochain. The highest summit lies at the head of the central ridge, and the other Munro, Sgurr Fiona, is at the upper end of the pinnacled crest which curves round the southern corrie to end at Sail Liath. An Teallach is largely of dark red Torridonian sandstone, but its dramatic rocky outline is enhanced by the Cambrian quartzites which cap its eastern spurs and form distinctive light grey screes.

Two routes of ascent are widely used. The shorter one starts near Dundonnell Hotel, but it hardly does justice to the mountain; it does, however, avoid all difficulties. Leave the A832 road ½km SE of the hotel and follow a path zigzagging up the steep and in places rocky shoulder of Meall Garbh until the angle falls back. After the path ends at about 750m follow the broad, stony ridge S over a knoll to a second knoll from where a short ascent ESE leads to a top (not named on the OS 1:50,000 map) at the edge of Glas Tholl, the northern corrie. Descend S to a col

and climb the imposing but easy ridge to the summit of Bidein a'Ghlas Thuill. (6km; 1120m; 3h 20min). Sgurr Fiona lies 1km south-west and is reached by descending easily to a col and climbing the steep and in places rocky ridge for 140m. (7km; 1260m; 3h 50min).

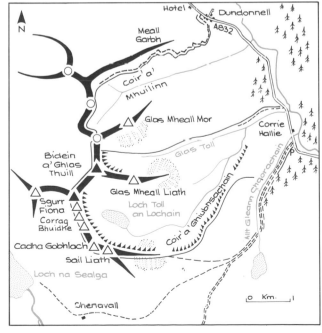

The pinnacled crest of Corrag Bhuidhe and Sgurr Fiona   D. Rubens

An Teallach from Beinn Dearg Mor across   H.M. Brown
Strath na Sealga

A much more interesting route begins at the Corrie Hallie car park on the A832 road at (114850). Follow the track SSW through the birches of Gleann Chaorachain for lkm, then cross the stream and climb SW up grass and heather to reach the crest of the ridge overlooking Coir a'Ghiubhsachain. This ridge forms a prominent quartzite escarpment, and provides a splendid highway to the foot of Sail Liath, curving high above the slabby sandstone pavements below the Toll an Lochain. Alternatively, the track may be followed for 3km to the point where the Shenavall path strikes off WSW, and from there a rough walk of 1½km west leads to the lochan at the foot of Sail Liath.

Climb W from this lochan, at first up grassy slopes, then over quartzite boulders and scree to Sail Liath (954m), the first peak on the ridge. Continue across a dip and cross a rocky knob before dropping to the Cadha Gobhlach, *forked pass*. From there a small peak is traversed to the foot of the Corrag Bhuidhe Buttress. The imposing terraced nose which rises ahead and the continuation to the first tower of the Corrag Bhuidhe is the steepest part of the An Teallach traverse; the direct line is clearly worn and includes a steep 10m pitch high up. The crest of Corrag Bhuidhe (1020m) gives excellent scrambling over four airy rock towers, followed by the leaning spire of Lord Berkeley's Seat. However, all difficulties on Corrag Bhuidhe can be avoided by traversing along narrow paths on the south-west side of the ridge below the crest, but much of the excitement of the climb is lost by going this way. The spectacular part

The crest of the Corrag Bhuidhe ridge   D.J. Bennet

of the ridge ends with a climb up to the shapely peak of Sgurr Fiona. (7½km; 1300m; 3h 50min).

The descent NNE to the col is steep and rocky, but there is no difficulty, and the last 140m pull up to Bidein a'Ghlas Thuill crowns one of the best days to be had in the Highlands. (8½ km; 1440m; 4h 20min).

The return to Dundonnell can be made by the first route described above. To return to Corrie Hallie go down to the col ½km north of Bidein and descend E into the Glas Tholl by a steep slope, taking special care if there is any snow. Continue directly down the corrie on the north side of the stream; there is a faint path across the heather-clad slopes and sandstone slabs to the Garbh Allt waterfalls where a better path is joined. This leads down the north-west bank of the stream to a pine wood where the path disappears into overgrown thickets of rhododendron. It is probably advisable to cross to the opposite side of the stream where there is a better path leading to the road ¾km from the Corrie Hallie car park.

Looking south-east from Sgurr Fiona to Corrag Bhuidhe and Sail Liath   W.D. Brooker

On the ridge from Beinn Liath Mhor Fannaich towards Sgurr Mor   *W.D. Brooker*

This range of mountains, nine Munros in all, lies between Loch Fannich and the A835 road from Garve to Ullapool. Seven of the Munros form a fairly continuous chain, with short side ridges. The last two are western outliers, separated from the rest by a low bealach at about 550m height.

The northern side of the Fannaichs, between the A835 road and the main mountain massif, has a lot of very rough ground — vast expanses of tussocky heather, rough grass, peat and boulders, which make for tiring walking if paths are not followed. By contrast, the upper parts of the mountains are much less rough, and most of the peaks give good easy going along broad smooth ridges of moss and short grass.

On the south side of the main ridge the approaches from Loch Fannich are shorter and easier, but the loch can only be approached along a private road, not accessible to cars. It might be possible to cycle from the A832 road at Grudie Power Station to Fannich Lodge; the distance is 12km.

Beinn Liath Mhor Fannaich; 954m; (OS Sheet 20; 219724); M204; *big grey hill of Fannich*
Sgurr Mor; 1110m; (OS Sheet 20; 203718); M41; *big peak*
Meall Gorm; 949m; (OS Sheet 20; 221696); M210; *blue hill*
An Coileachan; 923m; (OS Sheet 20; 241680); M261; *the little cock*

Three of these hills lie on the main ridge of the Fannaichs which extends north-west from the east end of Loch Fannich to terminate at Meall a'Chrasgaidh; the fourth, Beinn Liath Mhor Fannaich, is on a spur projecting NE from Sgurr Mor. The main ridge has a number of small corries scooped out of its north-east side; most are rocky and contain little lochans, and all but those of An Coileachan drain toward the A835 by two long shallow valleys. The route described below allows all four peaks to be climbed in a long horseshoe traverse, approaching along one of these valleys.

Start at the bridge over the Abhainn an Torrain Duibh just west of Loch Glascarnoch and follow the river upstream by a rough path on its west side. After crossing the Allt an Loch Sgeirich, leave the main river and follow this stream W trending gradually up the slope leading to Creag Dhubh Fannaich. Cross the top of this minor summit to the col beyond and climb Beinn Liath Mhor Fannaich by the easy slope of its south-east ridge. (8½km; 710m; 3h 10min).

Sgurr Mor lies 2km SW around the upper bowl of Coir a'Mhadaidh. Reach the connecting ridge by descending steeply for 100m to the col. The ridge is sharply defined on its north-west side by the edge of the corrie, and dips more gradually on the other side, and there is a stalker's path along it which further on diverges across the south-east face of Sgurr Mor. The last part of the climb is up a steep grassy slope eroded into big steps, and leads to the summit cairn of Sgurr Mor, which is perched close to the brink of the north cliff. (10½km; 990m; 4h).

Return down the SSE ridge over the flat rock slabs of Meall nam Peithirean (974m) and continue along the broad crest as it turns ESE round the corrie of the

Fuar Tholl Mor to join the stalker's path which comes up from Fannich Lodge. This path leads to the flat bouldery summit of Meall Gorm. (13km; 1130m; 4h 50min).

A few hundred metres east of the summit, where the path leaves the ridge to descend S, there is a small stalker's shelter made of rock slabs. The wide ridge continues E then SE, increasingly stony, but still easy walking ground. It descends to the Bealach Ban (775m) and then rises up broad, boulder- patched and grass-banded slopes to the top of An Coileachan, which is a conspicuous little crag. (15½km; 1300m; 5h 40min).

It is best to return towards the Bealach Ban and descend N, taking a line which keeps slightly E to gain the saddle below Meallan Buidhe. From there pass above the outlet of Loch Gorm and descend the gentle slope to the Abhainn a'Ghiubhais Li. Follow this stream by one of the rough paths which appear on both sides further downstream, and eventually return to the day's starting point.

The other access route from the A835 road into the Fannaichs is from the dam at the west end of Loch Droma. Follow the pipe road W to the Allt a'Mhadaidh, and continue along the path up this stream to the outflow from Loch a'Mhadaidh. Go W onto the north-east ridge of Meall a'Chrasgaidh to join a stalker's path which leads across the east face of this hill to the col ½km south-east of its summit. From there Meall a'Chrasgaidh is a short distance north-west.

Carn na Criche is reached by going SE then E from the col, and beyond it a steep bouldery ridge leads to Sgurr Mor. A good circuit can be completed by traversing to Beinn Liath Mhor Fannaich. From there descend NE down a grassy corrie and head for the north-west end of Loch Sgeireach, from where an easy descent N leads to the bridge over the Allt a'Mhadaidh.

From Fannich Lodge the ascent of these hills is greatly simplified by the splendid stalker's path from the lodge up the south ridge of Meall Gorm which gives quick access to the main Fannaich ridge on both sides of this peak. Sgurr Mor and An Coileachan are both within easy reach, and even Beinn Liath Mhor Fannaich is not beyond the range of a reasonably fit walker.

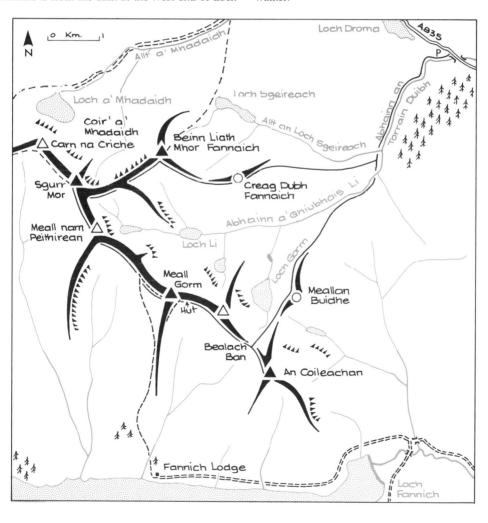

Sgurr nan Clach Geala and Sgurr Mor from Meall Gorm   R. Robb

Meall a'Chrasgaidh; 934m; (OS Sheet 20; 184733); M239; *hill of the crossing*
Sgurr nan Clach Geala; 1093m; (OS Sheet 20; 184715); M51; *peak of the white stones*
Sgurr nan Each; 923m; (OS Sheet 20; 184697); M262; *peak of the horses*

These three central peaks of the Fannaichs lie just east of the path which crosses the pass from Loch a'Bhraoin to the head of Loch Fannich. They are on a ridge extending from Sgurr nan Each in the south, over Sgurr nan Clach Geala to Meall a'Chrasgaidh which also lies at the north-west end of the main Fannaich ridge. Sgurr nan Clach Geala may well be considered to be the finest of the Fannaichs, its tapering buttresses, soaring ridges and high hanging corrie combining in classic mountain architecture.

Two starting points are possible for the traverse of these three peaks: either the west end of Loch Droma as described on the previous page, or the A832 road near Loch a'Bhraoin at the north-west corner of the Fannaichs. The latter gives the shorter approach and will be described.

Start from the A832 road at (162761) several kilometres south-west of Braemore Junction and walk along the private road to Loch a'Bhraoin to cross its outlet by a footbridge. Go S on the stalker's path which crosses the Allt Breabaig at a rocky linn, or a ford some 200 metres upstream. Continue along the path for ½km as it climbs the hillside on the east of the stream, then strike due E uphill, easily selecting a way through steep mossy grass, heather and boulders. Higher up trend left towards the north-west ridge of Meall a'Chrasgaidh until the slope lessens and leads to the top over patches of grass and weathered rock. (6km; 690m; 2h 30min).

From the summit a smooth slope dips SE to a wide mossy saddle at 819m, from which it is easy to traverse in the same direction to the foot of the north-east ridge of Sgurr nan Clach Geala. However, the Top of Carn na Criche (961m) lies barely 1km to the east and is worth including en route. From it the shapely cones of Beinn Liath Mhor Fannaich and Sgurr Mor can be seen to advantage, as can the Coire Mhoir face of Sgurr nan Clach Geala. The impressive profiles of its fine buttresses of mica-schist indicate the main climbing ground of the Fannaichs, at its best under winter conditions.

Descend SW from Carn na Criche to the wide col whose lush grass in summer provides ample feeding for the deer, hence the name Am Biachdaich, *the place of fattening.* A lochan lies on this col at the start of the ridge which sweeps above the great cliffs to the trig point on Sgurr nan Clach Geala. It rises in two sections, the upper one being narrow but offering an easy and enjoyable passage along the brink of the crags which plunge into the corrie below. The summit is an excellent viewpoint from which to appreciate the layout and character of the Fannaichs, all but one of which can be seen from there in clear conditions. (9km; 1080m; 3h 50min).

There is an easy descent south by grass slopes to the 807m col of the Cadha na Guite. The ridge crest beyond rises gently to the summit of Sgurr nan Each in an elegant asymmetric double curve with steep crags falling into Coire Mhoir on the east. (11km; 1200m; 4h 30min).

The approach to the Fannaichs from Loch a'Bhraoin, looking south to Sgurr nan Clach Geala   *D.J. Bennet*

Return N along the ridge to the Cadha na Guite and descend W down grassy slopes to the pass at the head of the Allt Breabaig. From there follow the stalker's path N back to the east end of Loch a'Bhraoin to rejoin the road leading to the day's starting point.

Map on page 216.

Sgurr nan Each from Sgurr nan Clach Geala   *D.J. Broadhead*

Sgurr Breac; 1000m; (OS Sheet 20; 158711); M135; *speckled peak*
A'Chailleach; 999m; (OS Sheets 19 and 20; 136714); M137; *the old woman*

These two peaks are the most westerly of the Fannaichs, and lie south of the A832 road from Braemore Junction to Dundonnell. They are connected to the main group by a narrow col at the head of the Allt Breabaig at a height of 550m from which a ridge extends west over Sgurr Breac and the Top of Toman Coinich to A'Chailleach. Northward from this summit ridge the two spurs of Sron na Goibhre and Druim Reidh enfold the corrie of Toll an Lochain. There are no recognised climbing crags on these hills, but they have a generally steep and rocky northern aspect.

From the A832 road at (162761), several kilometres south-west of Braemore Junction, walk along the private road to Loch a'Bhraoin and cross its outlet by a footbridge. Go S on the stalker's path which crosses the Allt Breabaig at the rocky linn or the ford some 200 metres upstream. Take care if the burn is in spate. The path continues higher on the east side of the glen until it reaches the pass leading over to Loch Fannich. From the pass climb the east ridge of Sgurr Breac,

quite steeply through little rock outcrops at first, then up an easy-angled ridge, (9km; 750m; 3h 20min).

Continue by traversing Toman Coinich (937m), or skirting its summit on the south side, and descending to the bealach at 810m. Ascend the ridge along the rim of the Toll an Lochain to its junction with the Sron na Goibhre spur, then bear SW along the gently rising crest to the summit of A'Chailleach. (11km; 1020m; 4h 10min).

Return NE to the junction of ridges above the Toll an Lochain and descend, steeply at first, the spur of Sron na Goibhre, well marked by fence posts. Avoid the rock outcrops at the north end of this ridge by descending E towards the stream in the Toll an Lochain down steep and boulder-strewn grassy slopes. Follow this stream for some distance along its west bank, then cross to the east side and go diagonally down the grassy hillside NE towards Loch a'Bhraoin to regain the private road back to the day's starting point.

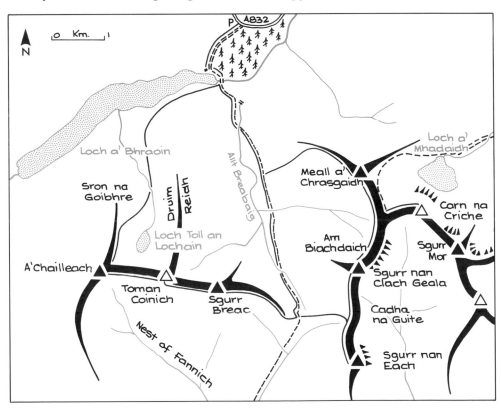

On the summit ridge of Fionn Bheinn   *H.M. Brown*

Fionn Bheinn; 933m; (OS Sheets 20 and 25; 147621); M240; *pale-coloured hill*

The only Munro of the Fannaichs to lie south of Loch Fannich, Fionn Bheinn rises directly on the north side of the A832 road at Achnasheen. With its smooth grassy slopes and subdued contours, it presents an undistinguished appearance to the south and keeps its more interesting north side concealed from most visitors.

The easiest approach is directly from Achnasheen, by following the Allt Achadh na Sine, keeping on its north-east side and gaining the nose of Creagan nan Laogh *(crag of the calf)*. From there ascend NW by gentle slopes of mossy grass to reach the summit in just over 1km. (5km; 780m; 2h 30min).

A different descent route which adds variety and allows the mountain to be traversed is as follows:- Go E, skirting the edge of the steep slabby face which plunges into the Toll Mor and follow the ridge E, then SE down a steeper slope close to the rim of another slabby corrie, the Toll Beag. Where the slope levels out, a prominent drystone wall leads E and can be followed, with a few gaps, until it intersects an old grass-grown path crossing the hill from north to south. Turn right down this path until it approaches a plantation, diverge to the right to avoid this obstacle and descend to Achnasheen. If the streams are in spate, it is better to diverge left from the path and go round the east side of the plantation to reach the road 1km east of Achnasheen.

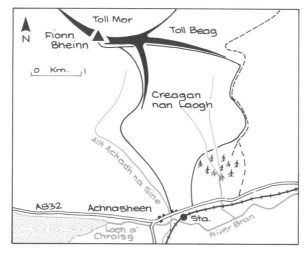

Looking south-west from Ben Wyvis to the mountains of Torridon   A. O'Brien

SECTIONS 15 and 16

Ben Wyvis to Ben Hope

Ben Wyvis from the Glascarnoch River   *H.M. Brown*

Ben Wyvis, Glas Leathad Mor; 1046m; (OS Sheet 20; 463684), M83, *Ben Wyvis is from the Gaelic fuathas, meaning perhaps awesome hill. Glas Leathad Mor means big greenish-grey slope.*

Ben Wyvis (the name applies to the whole range) is a solitary hulk of a mountain shipwrecked far to the east of other northern hills. The highest summit, Glas Leathad Mor, is a high level ridge with two impressive corries on its eastern face, and long uniform grass slopes sweeping up from the dark forests on the west. Its isolated position makes it a good viewpoint. Despite the vast plantings of the Garbat Forest, the approach from the west is still the one most used, as any route from the south or east is much longer.

Park off the A835 road from Garve to Ullapool opposite Garbat and walk S along the road for ½km to the bridge over the Allt a'Bhealaich Mhoir. Follow the footpath on the north bank of that stream up the forested hillside through a gap between trees and burn. There are additional plantings above the forest not shown on the OS 1:50,000 map. Cross the fence above them by a stile and turn NE to ascend steeply to An Cabar (946m), the end prow of the Wyvis ridge. The summit lies 2km north-east along a mossy ridge which gives delightful walking. (6½km; 920m; 3h).

The quickest descent is to return by the route of ascent. Alternatively, a traverse of the mountain can be made by continuing down the NNE ridge and climbing Tom a'Choinnich (955m). Descend its grassy WSW ridge to the Allt a'Gharbh Bhaid and follow this stream downhill to the point where it flows into the Garbat Forest. Go S along the fence for about ½km to a gate, then descend W down a break in the trees to a track leading to Garbat.

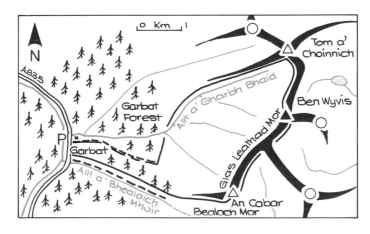

Am Faochagach; 954m; (OS Sheet 20, 304794); M206; *the place of the shells*

The great range of rounded hills which forms the heart of the Strathvaich Forest between Loch Glascarnoch and Strath Vaich culminates in Am Faochagach. Like its lower outliers, it is a massive rounded hill, well seen from the north-west end of Loch Glascarnoch, from which it lies 6km to the north.

The road up Strath Vaich is private, and the shortest approach to the hill is from the A835 road at the north-west end of Loch Glascarnoch, starting at the bridge over the Abhainn an Torrain Duibh. From this point the route to Am Faochagach is trackless, and the first 1½km across the level strath is over rough boggy ground normally very wet underfoot, and includes the crossing of the Abhainn a'Gharbhrain. In normal conditions this crossing will entail wet feet; in wet conditions (which some might regard as normal) the crossing may well be impossible, and a diversion upriver to try a higher crossing may be no more successful. Am Faochagach is, therefore, a mountain for dry conditions, or a hard winter's day when frost grips the ground.

Apart from these obstacles, the ascent is straightforward. A course NNE from the road across the bog leads to the river crossing, then bear NE, keeping on the side of the Allt na h-Uidhe. The going becomes easier as bog and tussocky heather give way higher up to smoother grassy slopes, and the col on the main spine of the range 3km south of Am Faochagach is reached. From there the going is very easy along the broad grassy ridge, over barely perceptible rises, past a few cairns until the final steeper slope, where the effects of solifluction are evident, leads to the flat summit of Am Faochagach crowned by two cairns a few metres apart. (7km; 690m; 2h 50min).

It is possible to combine the ascent of Am Faochagach with Cona'Mheall, described below. Descend NW from Am Faochagach down a broad grassy ridge over the slight rise of Meallan Ban to reach the outflow of Loch Prille. This loch is in a fine remote setting, with the stream cascading from it down to Coire Lair, and the east ridge of Cona'Mheall rising directly from it to the summit of that peak.

Cona'Mheall; 980m; (OS Sheet 20, 275816); M170; *hill of the dog or hill of the meeting*

This mountain is one of the Beinn Dearg group, and although it can be climbed from the north-west with the others of the group (see page 222), the character of Cona'Mheall can best be appreciated if it is climbed from the south, and the extra effort needed for this rather rugged approach is well worthwhile. The finest

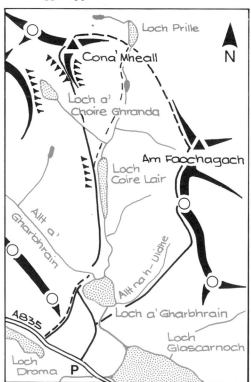

feature of Cona'Mheall is its narrow south-east ridge, on both sides of which the mountain drops precipitously. Coire Ghranda on the west side is the finest corrie of the Dearg group, a remote and impressive sanctuary; on the east side of the ridge the slopes of Cona'Mheall above Coire Lair are extraordinarily wild and rocky.

The approach from the south has very much the same character as the mountain itself, rough and wild. A path leaves the A835 road 9km north-west of Aultguish Inn near the south-east end of Loch Droma, climbs slightly to the NE and continues N, descending to the ruins of an old shieling at the north-west corner of Loch a'Gharbhrain. Cross the Allt a'Gharbhrain, notoriously difficult or even impossible in spate, and continue N over trackless peat and heather towards Loch Coire Lair. Half way along the loch start climbing towards the lip of Coire Ghranda where the stream comes down over bare slabs; a very faint path helps in places, but the climb is steep, traversing grass ledges across and up the steep slabby hillside.

Coire Ghranda is in a superb setting with the cliffs of Beinn Dearg across the loch. Climb directly towards the south end of Cona'Mheall's south-east ridge, scrambling steeply up grass and easy rocks to reach the more level upper ridge. This is narrow, but quite easy with two short descents and occasional scrambling, and the ridge becomes broader as it leads up to the bouldery summit. (8km; 800m; 3h 40min).

The descent may be made by the same route, but great care is needed on the lower part of the south-east ridge. A very interesting alternative is the east ridge which drops steeply a few metres north-east of the cairn. The route leads down by a series of wide ledges and shelves, but care must be taken, particularly in misty weather, as these shelves, formed by the strata of the rock, tend to lead too far south onto steep ground. It is necessary to check the correct route

The approach to Beinn Dearg and Cona'Mheall from the south-east   *J. Renny*

towards the outflow of Loch Prille.

From there the descent south down the Allt Lair is steep at first, and lower down the corrie the uphill route is rejoined on the west side of Loch Coire Lair.

Alternatively, continue the traverse to Am Faochagach by reversing the route described on the opposite page.

Beinn Dearg and Cona'Mheall from Am Faochagach   *A. O'Brien*

Beinn Dearg from Coire Ghranda   *A. O'Brien*

Beinn Dearg; 1084m; (OS Sheet 20; 259812); M55; *red hill*
Meall nan Ceapraichean; 977m; (OS Sheet 20; 257826); M172; *perhaps from ceap, meaning a back or hilltop*
Eididh nan Clach Geala; 928m; (OS Sheet 20; 258842); M249; *web of the white stones*

These mountains, known collectively as the Deargs, lie to the south-east of Loch Broom. From Ullapool, Beinn Dearg itself appears as a great high dome rising above its neighbours. From elsewhere, distant views of this group show it as an undulating plateau rather than separate mountains, and its many superb corries are hardly seen. Only by penetrating into its heart can the true character of this group of mountains be appreciated.

The best approach is from the A835 road at the head of Loch Broom where, a few hundred metres north of Inverlael House, a private road leads for 3km through the Lael Forest into the lower part of Gleann na Sguaib. Beyond the forest follow a stalker's path up this glen on the north-east side of the River Lael past some fine falls and a beautiful little lochan nestling below the cliffs of Beinn Dearg to the col at the head of the glen. There another lochan lies in a desolate stony landscape.

To climb Beinn Dearg first, go S to reach a dry stone dyke of massive proportions and climb the slope of stones and boulders on its west side. Towards the top, where the dyke turns W, go through a gap in it and bear SSW for a few hundred metres across the flat dome of Beinn Dearg to its summit. (10km; 1070m; 4h).

Return to the col by the same route and climb the easy-angled ridge of Meall nan Ceapraichean. (12km; 1190m; 4h 40min). Continue N then NE along a broad stony ridge to Ceann Garbh (967m). Descend NE, easily at first, but lower down small crags and rock bands have to be circumvented and the next col is reached at (265838). From there an easy grass slope leads to Eididh nan Clach Geala where there are two cairns, the north-west one being the summit. (14½km; 1370m; 5h 30min). Just below the cairn, on the north-west side, are the white quartzite boulders which may well give the mountain its name.

Descend W down a grassy slope for ½km, then turn SW into the corrie west of Lochan na Chnapaich where a good stalker's path is joined and followed downhill to the main path in Gleann na Sguaib.

Several other routes are possible in these mountains. It is easy to climb Cona'Mheall from the col at the head of Gleann na Sguaib, and its inclusion with the three mountains described above adds little more than an hour to their traverse.

Beinn Dearg can be climbed from the south. Start from Loch Droma and take the path to the head of Loch a'Gharbhrain (as for Cona'Mheall), then continue up the Allt a'Gharbhrain for 2km, cross this stream and climb N towards Loch nan Eilean. Before reaching this loch bear left onto the south ridge of Beinn Dearg and climb it along the edge of the very steep cliffs above Coire Ghranda. (8km; 870m; 3h 20min). The continuation to Cona'Mheall and the descent of its south-east ridge makes a very fine circular traverse.

Cona'Mheall from Beinn Dearg   A. O'Brien

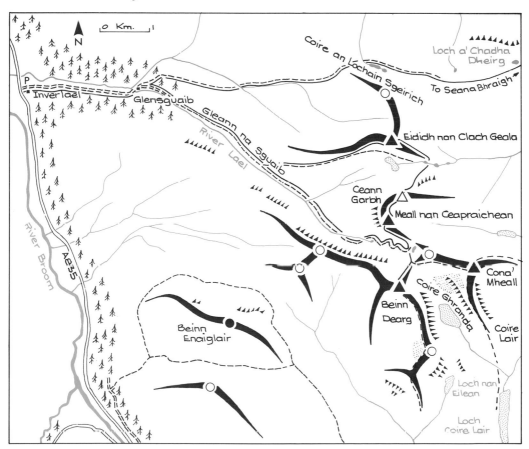

The approach to Seana Bhraigh up the Corriemulzie River   *D.J. Bennet*

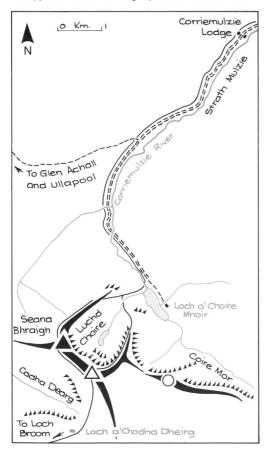

Seana Bhraigh; 927m; (OS Sheet 20; 281879); M254; *old upper part*

Seana Bhraigh, which occupies a remote situation in true wilderness country in the heart of Ross-shire, competes with A'Mhaighdean and Lurg Mhor for the title of most distant Munro. It is the eastern outlier of the Beinn Dearg group, a high plateau bounded on its north by the Luchd Choire, the most impressive corrie in this group of mountains.

No matter which way one takes to reach Seana Bhraigh, the approach from the nearest public road is long. The two most practicable routes are from Inverlael at the head of Loch Broom, and up Strath Mulzie from Oykell Bridge in Strath Oykell. The latter route involves a long approach up a private road; it may be possible to get permission to drive much of the way, and it is also possible to cycle a long way up this strath, almost to the foot of the mountain. The Strath Mulzie route has the advantage of showing the finest side of the mountain, its great corries at the head of the strath and the fine ridge which rises from Loch a'Choire Mhoir to Creag an Duine, the eastern promontory of the Seana Bhraigh plateau.

The approach from the west starts from the A835 road to Ullapool at Inverlael and the first few kilometres are the same as for Beinn Dearg. Walk through the Lael Forest as far as Glensguaib, then take the stalker's path out of the forest onto the Druim na Saobhaidhe ridge, crossing the wide upper corrie of Gleann a'Mhadaidh and rounding a spur of the hill above to continue up Coire an Lochain Sgeirich which has a peculiar succession of lochans in it. ·

The path vanishes in a boggy wilderness at about 750m, and in poor visibility very careful navigation is required for the continuation to Seana Bhraigh across

Looking across Luchd Choire to the summit of Seana Bhraigh   D.J. Bennet

rough terrain. There are crags above the south bank of the burn flowing into Loch a' Chadha Dheirg, and peat hags and minor bumps abound. In bad visibility one way is to find the lochan at (271856) near the end of the path, navigate to Loch a'Chadha Dheirg and the tiny lochan at (288860) from where a course due N leads up easy slopes to the 906m dome. Follow the cliff-edge of Luchd Choire NW to Seana Bhraigh, whose cairn stands right on the edge of the corrie. (13½km; 1100m; 4h 50min). Return by the same way.

The Strath Mulzie route may be considered to start at Duag Bridge, although it is possible to cycle some distance further. There is a good track up the strath which leads to the outflow of Loch a'Choire Mhoir, but the crossing of the river 1½km lower down may be a problem. From the loch climb SW beside the stream flowing from the Luchd Choire to the mouth of the corrie. From there the easiest route is up the ridge on the west side of the corrie. It leads past a tiny lochan direct to the summit. (From Duag Bridge: 13km; 830m; 4h 20min).

A much finer route is up the ridge on the east side of the corrie. It is steep and involves some scrambling, but leads splendidly to the little pointed peak of An Sgurr from where a short awkward descent and reascent bring one to the edge of the plateau at Creag an Duine. From there a lofty walk past the 906m dome ends at the summit of Seana Bhraigh. The ridge on the west side of the corrie gives the best descent route.

Creag an Duine from the summit of Seana Bhraigh   H.M. Brown

Ben More Assynt from Conival   *D.J. Bennet*

Conival; 987m; (OS Sheet 15; 303199); M154; *hill of the dog or hill of the meeting*
Ben More Assynt; 998m; (OS Sheet 15; 318201); M140; *the big hill of Assynt (Norse: ass, a rocky ridge)*

These two mountains are the highest peaks of wild Assynt, but they have a hidden, secretive character compared to their lower but bolder neighbours like Suilven or Quinag. They are rough, rocky peaks at the heart of an unusually rough part of the harsh, empty northlands. Inchnadamph is the usual starting point, and the hotel there is a favourite with hillwalkers, fishermen, botanists, cavers and scientists who all delight in this geologically interesting region.

Leave the A837 road just north of Inchnadamph Hotel by a farm track on the north bank of the River Traligill. Beyond Glenbain cottage a good track continues to a small plantation. Just beyond this point the main path crosses the river to reach the Traligill Caves. The route to Conival, however, continues on the north side of the glen with a rising traverse up the south-west face of Beinn an Fhurain. Progress is easy over grassy, heathery slopes with occasional animal

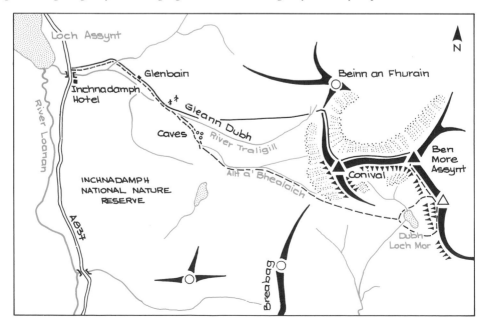

tracks; aim fairly high up, but keep below the line of crags to reach the high grassy alp below the Beinn an Fhurain — Conival col at 750m. From the col the final ascent of Conival is up rough quartzite scree, followed by a fairly level ridge to the large summit cairn. (7km; 920m; 3h 10min).

Ben More Assynt lies 1½km east along a dipping crest of the same rough, demanding terrain: a mixture of scree and crag, narrow in places, steep flanked and exposed to all the storms that blow. In poor visibility it may be difficult to decide which of two shattered bumps is the summit of Ben More; it is the northern one. (8½km; 1050m; 3h 40min).

The simplest return is by the same route. A more interesting continuation, however, is to go out along the south-east ridge for 1km to the South Top of Ben More

Beinn an Fhurain from the north ridge of Conival   *D.J. Bennet*

Assynt (960m). This traverse involves a narrow, rocky section of ridge sometimes compared with the Aonach Eagach; however its 'bad steps' are no more than exposed slabs and there are no difficulties of any consequence.

The descent from the South Top, however, may cause some problems as the south-west face of this peak above the Dubh Loch Mor is steep and craggy, and unless one returns along the ridges one has to descend to this loch. One possibility is to return a short distance NW along the ridge and descend towards the north end of Dubh Loch Mor. Another possibility is to go south down the ridge towards Carn nan Conbhairean and descend towards the south end

of the loch. If in doubt, continue southwards until the slope on the west side of the ridge becomes easy. This may well be the best course if visibility is bad or the craggy hillside is wet. A direct descent from the South Top to the loch is not advised.

From the north end of Dubh Loch Mor go W, climbing a little to reach the deeply cut pass between Conival and Breabag Tarsuinn.

Once through this pass, continue along the south side of the Allt a'Bhealaich on a path which leads to the caves near the Traligill River. These are worth a visit (with a torch) before continuing down Gleann Dubh to Inchnadamph.

The South Top of Ben More Assynt above Dubh Loch Mor   *D.J. Bennet*

Ben Klibreck from Vagastie   *H.M. Brown*

Ben Klibreck; 261m; (OS Sheet 16; 585299); M190; *hill of the speckled cliff*

This great isolated mountain rises above the desolate moorland of central Sutherland. The extraordinarily vast and featureless character of the landscape in this part of Scotland gives to Ben Klibreck an equal impression of remoteness, although in fact its summit is only 4km from the A836 road between Lairg and Tongue.

The spine of the mountain is a long curving ridge between Loch Naver and Loch Coire, and the summit, Meall nan Con, is the highest of several tops along this ridge. The north-west side of the mountain facing Altnaharra is quite steep, and on the west side, some distance below the summit, there is a steep prow of broken crags. By contrast, the south-east side is carved into wide grassy corries above Loch a' Bhealaich and Loch Coire.

The inns at Crask and Altnaharra are possible starting points for the ascent, but the shortest and easiest route starts from the A836 road through Strath Vagastie near (545303) where there is a roadside parking place. Cross the river and continue E across the moorland to the south end of Loch na Glas-choille. From there the route continues ESE, following the line of a fence, to reach the outflow of Loch nan Uan. If the river in Strath Vagastie is in spate, start at a footbridge at (537289) near Vagastie, and from there cross the moor directly past Loch Bad an Loch towards the south end of Loch nan Uan.

The face of Ben Klibreck immediately above the loch is very steep, with crags to the north-east under Meall nan Con. The easiest ascent goes E from the loch to climb steep grassy slopes to the main ridge at its lowest point 1km south-west of the summit. Finally an easy walk along the smooth grassy ridge and a short pull up a bouldery slope lead to the cairn. (5km; 790m; 2h 30min).

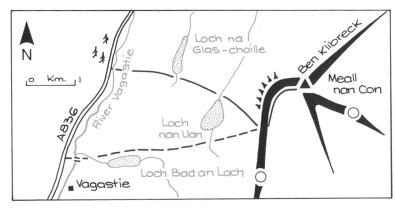

Ben Hope from the north-east across the expanse of the Moine   H.M. Brown

Ben Hope; 927/m; (OS Sheet 9; 477502), M253; *hill of the bay*

Ben Hope, with its Viking name and splendid isolation, is a worthy peak for the most northerly Munro. Its long west flank above Strath More and Loch Hope is double-tiered and has plenty of crags, but the ascent up this side is not unduly difficult. The easy southern and eastern slopes can only be reached by long approaches, so are seldom used. It would not be difficult to climb both Ben Hope and Ben Klibreck in a single day, with a short drive by car between them.

To reach the mountain, branch west at the crossroads north of the hamlet of Altnaharra on the A836 road from Lairg to Tongue and follow the narrow road westwards over the moors to descend into Strath More. After several kilometres the interesting broch of Dun Dornaigil is reached, then the farm of Alltnacaillich. About 2km north of Alltnacaillich park near the stream which flows down from the Dubh-loch na Beinne terrace on the west flank of Ben Hope.

Climb up a path beside the stream for ¾km NE and continue up the east tributary which comes down from the vast bowl of the mountain's southern slopes. This leads through a break in the line of cliffs which is clearly seen on the OS map, and the path then leads up the broad grassy ridge, not far from the western cliffs, to the little summit plateau, where the trig point is near the north-east edge. The setting is spacious and majestic. The best viewpoint is slightly to the north, but this does not lead to a descent route. (3½km; 920m; 2h 20min).

Return by the route of ascent, or by the Alltnacaillich variation. This slightly longer alternative starts at Alltnacaillich farm and takes the path up the south bank of the Allt na Caillich *(the old woman's burn)*. After crossing the stream above a fine waterfall, the ridge of Leitir Mhuiseil is followed N along the edge of its western escarpment to join the route described above.

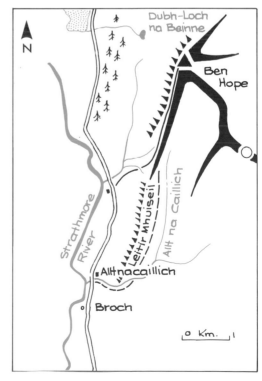

The Black Cuillin: The Inaccessible Pinnacle and Sgurr na Banachdich　　　　　*J.E.S. Bennet*

SECTION 17

The Islands of Mull and Skye

Ben More from A'Chioch   *I. Brown*

Ben More; 966m; (OS Sheet 48; 526331); M185; *big hill*

The only island Munro outside Skye, Ben More dominates the western group of hills on Mull and gives them their impressive form, especially when seen from the south. Splendid views of the Ben More group are also obtained from the B8035 road along which the climber comes from Salen to reach Loch na Keal and the foot of the mountain. Ben More itself is a fine isolated peak, its summit at the apex of three ridges. Of these the finest is the north-east which leads to A'Chioch, a sharp subsidiary top, and the traverse of this ridge is the best route to Ben More.

Start from the shore of Loch na Keal at the foot of the Abhainn na h-Uamha and follow paths and sheep tracks along this stream past many attractive pools and waterfalls up the grassy Gleann na Beinne Fada to reach the bealach between Beinn Fhada and A'Chioch. Turn south and climb towards A'Chioch; as height is gained the ridge becomes steeper and rockier, and gives a delightful scramble up a rocky staircase without any difficulty.

The continuation to Ben More maintains the interest, and the connecting ridge can look impressive when framed by cumulus clouds or sharpened by snow on the north face of Ben More. On the final ascent from the col the climb is reminiscent of the Aonach Eagach or Liathach, but there are no comparable difficulties, just the same exhilaration and unforgettable views from the summit if the day is clear. (6km; 1060m; 3h 10min).

The quickest descent route is down the broad north-west ridge, following a path down screes marked by many little cairns. This path continues down the grassy slope on the south-west side of the Abhainn Dhiseig to the roadside near the farm at Dhiseig, 1½km from the starting point at the foot of the Abhainn na h-Uamha. A more direct descent to this point can be made by leaving the path about 1½km from the summit of Ben More and bearing north across the Abhainn Dhiseig and down the grassy lower slopes of An Gearna to the lochside.

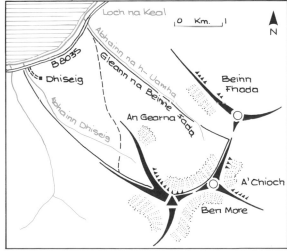

The Cuillin Ridge in winter; a view south-west from Am Basteir   *R. Robb*

The Cuillin are the most challenging mountains in Scotland, with airy crests, girt with precipices, and with only a few walking routes to their tops. Climbing these mountains is very different from the perfectly simple hillwalking which is involved in the ascent of all but three or four of the mainland Munros, Most of the Cuillin require some scrambling to reach their summits, and one — The Inaccessible Pinnacle — calls for rock-climbing. Much of the scrambling is fairly easy, but there are places where, for a few metres, the difficulties are more akin to easy rock-climbing. There are also many places where the narrowness of the ridges and their exposure are such that a slip might have serious results. In such situations surefootedness and a good head for heights are essential.

In spite of the fact that the Cuillin are composed of gabbro, one of the finest of climbing rocks, there is a great deal of loose rock, and care should be taken at all times. There have been many accidents over the years due to loose rock in otherwise straightforward situations.

There are a number of places on the Main Ridge and close to it where the compass is unreliable due to local magnetic anomalies. Thus in mist one should at all times retain a firm sense of one's whereabouts. These anomalies do not occur on lower ground. The OS 1:50,000 map is not really adequate for navigation except on the lower ground and in the corries. The Ordnance Survey produces an excellent 1:25,000 map of the Cuillin (back-to-back with a map of the Torridon mountains), and the Scottish Mountaineering Trust publishes a double-sided map of the Cuillin: on one side a 1:15,000 chart with paths marked, and on the other side a relief map of the range of scale 1:12,500.

All the routes described (except that for Bla Bheinn) are on the Sligachan and Glen Brittle side of the Main Ridge. These two places provide the easiest access to the mountains and most of the accommodation for climbers in hotels, hut, hostel, campsites etc. Consequently most of the normal hillwalkers' routes on the Cuillin start from them. Loch Coruisk, on the other hand is much more remote, and for that reason if no other routes on that side of the Cuillin tend to be more serious. The peaks and corries are steeper and wilder on that side, and the ways less well marked by footpaths.

Sgurr nan Gillean; 965m; (OS Sheet 32; 472253); M187; *peak of the young men*

Sgurr nan Gillean is a superb mountain from all aspects, offering from its summit on a clear day one of the world's great mountain views. Even by the easiest route the final ridge is an airy scramble. It is well seen from the roadside at Sligachan, and its conical tip is visible from the slipway at Kyle of Lochalsh as one crosses to Skye.

Because of the featureless nature of the lower ground and the precipitous terrain higher up, route finding may prove to be difficult in poor visibility.

Start 200 metres south-west of Sligachan Inn at a car park. Opposite, on the south side of the road, a faint path leads in 200 metres to, and then crosses, the Allt Dearg Mor. Thereafter it meanders SSW amongst peat hags, endeavouring without much success to avoid the boggiest terrain until in 1½km it reaches the Allt Dearg Beag. The path, now much improved, follows the west bank for ½km to a bridge, where it divides. Ignore the branch which continues up the burn, but cross the bridge and follow the path which

Sgurr nan Gillean from the north   *A. O'Brien*

heads S and climbs slightly. By now the crags of Nead na h-Iolaire are slightly to the left (E) with a plateau visible beyond. At about the 300m contour the path crosses an oval area of small stones 15 metres in diameter. Ignore the faint path to the right and continue S, dropping slightly as one enters Coire Riabhach, and pass some 200 metres west of a lochan over the side of some rocky hummocks.

Ahead may be seen a band of rocks broken by a scree-filled gully. The route, well worn and clearly visible, ascends this scree. Above the steep section, on easier terrain, the well-cairned path leads up to the south-east ridge of Sgurr nan Gillean at 750m. This ridge, which is not visible from Sligachan, is at first broad and rises to the NW. Higher up it narrows, and care is required for the final scramble to the summit. (6km; 950m; 3h). Return by the same route.

Map on page 234.

The Pinnacle Ridge of Sgurr nan Gillean from the Basteir Gorge   *A. O'Brien*

Am Basteir, with Sgurr nan Gillean beyond, from Sgurr a'Fionn Choire   H.M. Brown

Am Basteir; 935m; (OS Sheet 32; 465253); M236; *meaning obscure, but probably not, as is commonly supposed, the executioner*

A blade of rock, vertically sided to the north and very steep on the south, Am Basteir may nevertheless be ascended relatively easily by its east ridge. However, it is no place for those without a good head for heights, and no place to have a slip. The setting is dramatic, and much to be recommended.

From Sligachan follow the route for Sgurr nan Gillean as far as the oval area of stones at 300m where the Sgurr nan Gillean path continues south. Branch rightwards on a faintly discernible but adequately cairned path which climbs SW towards the broad rocky spur that falls from the north side of Sgurr nan Gillean. This spur is obvious even when seen from Sligachan.

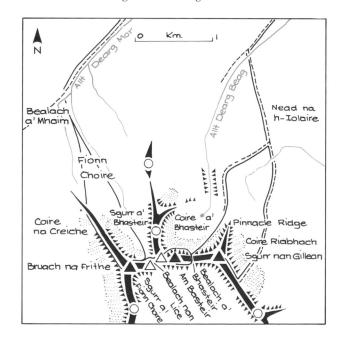

From the crest of this spur impressive cliffs fall away on the right to the Basteir Gorge, but the path keeps well away from the edge. The spur flattens out a little below the level of the lip of Coire a'Bhasteir from which a delightful tumbling burn emerges.

Beyond the flattening the spur steepens towards the lowest rocks of the Pinnacle Ridge. Climb towards the rocks until a rather faint path leads rightwards on a traverse well below the rocks of Pinnacle Ridge and above the screes of Coire a'Bhasteir. The traverse leads across screes, grass and some easy-angled slabs towards the head of the corrie where a steeper climb up screes and boulders leads towards the foot of the steep rocks of Am Basteir. Keep slightly to the left to reach the Bealach a'Bhasteir (833m). Am Basteir and its steeply-sided east ridge now lie immediately to the west.

From the bealach the route to Am Basteir goes directly up its east ridge, easy at first, but becoming narrower and more exposed higher up, and giving a good scramble with one place of slight difficulty near mid-point where an awkward descent of a few steps has to be made. (5½km; 930m; 2h 50min).

The summit of Am Basteir is a spectacular place with vertical drops to the north and west. For the walker the only route of descent is back down the east ridge to the Bealach a'Bhasteir. From the bealach, if returning to Sligachan by the ascent route, beware of dropping too low into Coire a'Bhasteir, for there may be difficulty in regaining the crest of the spur that leads back to Sligachan.

Alternatively, the continuation west along the Main Ridge from the bealach goes a short distance down on the Coire a'Bhasteir side of Am Basteir, following a path in the screes below its north face. This path leads back up to the ridge just west of the Basteir Tooth at the Bealach na Lice. From there one may either continue along the ridge to Bruach na Frithe, traversing the little peak of Sgurr a'Fionn Choire (930m), or return to Sligachan more directly by descending NW into the Fionn Choire, as described on the next page.

Am Basteir from the east   H.M. Brown

Bruach na Frithe from the east   *H.M. Brown*

Bruach na Frithe; 958m; (OS Sheet 32; 461252); M198; *slope of the deer forest*

A fine viewpoint and a peak whose outline would excite attention in any other less imposing environment, Bruach na Frithe is the only one of the Cuillin which is not defended by cliffs. It is not seen in the view from Sligachan, but from a short distance westwards along the road to Dunvegan it appears behind the nearer but lower peak of Sgurr a'Bhasteir.

From a point ⅔km west of Sligachan take the private road towards Alltdearg House. Pass to the north of the house and follow the path leading SW along the north-west bank of the Allt Dearg Mor towards the Bealach a'Mhaim and Glen Brittle. At about 280m above sea level the path bears SSW as the top of the pass is approached.

To the south-east lies a smooth grassy corrie known as the Fionn Choire. The terrain is quite featureless and in misty conditions can be very confusing. At a height of about 300m, 1km before reaching the pass, bear south up the corrie, where smooth grassy slopes and patches of stones alternate.

In good visibility there is no problem in finding an easy way south onto the crest of the north-west ridge of Bruach na Frithe where it is broad and easy-angled. Continue up the ridge, which becomes narrower and rocky. A good path goes up the west flank of the ridge, joining the crest higher up near the summit.

There is, however, no undue difficulty in scrambling along the crest all the way to the summit. (7km; 940m; 3h 10min).

Bruach na Frithe may also be ascended by way of the Fionn Choire, and in bad visibility this may be the better route. Leave the Allt Dearg Mor path 1km before reaching the Bealach a'Mhaim and bear SSE up the corrie to the Bealach nan Lice. The going is easy and there is a spring high up towards the Main Ridge. Impressive views may be had from the col down into Lota Corrie on the south and up to the overhanging blade of rock forming the Basteir Tooth. From the col head W over Sgurr a'Fionn Choire (935m) to reach Bruach na Frithe without difficulty up its east ridge. (8km; 970m; 3h 30min).

Either of the above routes may be used for the descent. However, it must be stressed that in bad visibility very careful navigation is required until one is below the cloud base. In such conditions the easiest descent is to go down the east ridge for about 200 metres to the col before Sgurr a'Fionn Choire, then descend due N into the head of the Fionn Choire. Once below the rocks and screes bear NNW down the corrie for 2km until the path leading across the Bealach a'Mhaim is reached.

Map on page 234.

Sgurr na Banachdich from Sgurr Alasdair   G. Blyth

Sgurr na Banachdich; 965m; (OS Sheet 32; 440225); M186; *meaning obscure, according to Forbes it may be smallpox peak from the pitted appearance of some of its rocks, or perhaps from banachdag, a milkmaid*

This fine peak of three summits, of which the northern one is the highest, fills the head of Coire na Banachdich, and it is by this corrie that the ascent from Glen Brittle is usually made. The Bealach Coire na Banachdich is one of the few easy passes over the Main Ridge, and the path to it is well marked.

Starting near the Glen Brittle Memorial Hut, take the path on the north side of the Allt Coire na Banachdich and in ¾km cross this stream just above the Eas Mor waterfall. Leave the obvious Coire Lagan path and follow another one on the south side of the Allt Coire na Banachdich to pass below the prominent Window Buttress and reach the wild and rocky inner corrie.

In front great slabby walls bar progress directly upwards, and the path, now only a faint trail but well cairned, bears right beside the southernmost tributary stream. Aim to the right (S) of the slabby cliffs where an open gully filled with scree and boulders provides the way, still well cairned. Above the gully bear left (NE) on a rising traverse above the slabby cliffs and finally go directly up scree to the Bealach Coire na Banachdich.

From the pass climb directly along the south ridge of Sgurr na Banachdich over its two subsidiary tops, either scrambling along the crest which is narrow and shattered in places, or traversing easy ledges on the west flank just below the crest. (4½km; 950m; 2h 40min).

On the descent from the Bealach Coire na Banachdich to Glen Brittle, do not go straight down, but after the first 100m traverse left (SW) where cairns indicate a slightly rising passage before the path leads down towards the boulder-filled gully.

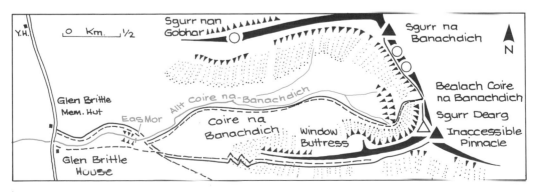

Sgurr a'Ghreadaidh and Sgurr a'Mhadaidh   *I. Brown*

Sgurr a'Mhadaidh; 918m; (OS Sheet 32; 446235); M266; *peak of the fox*
Sgurr a'Ghreadaidh; 973m; (OS Sheet 32; 445232); M181; *peak of torment, anxiety*

The central part of the Cuillin Main Ridge is dominated by Sgurr a'Ghreadaidh, a great twin-topped peak which on its Coruisk-facing buttresses has the longest rock-climbs in Skye. Just to its north Sgurr a'Mhadaidh shows an elegant outline of four peaks, but only the south-west one reaches Munro height. These two mountains are central in the view up Loch Coruisk towards the Cuillin.

On the Glen Brittle side Sgurr a'Ghreadaidh and the highest top of Mhadaidh overlook Coire a'Ghreadaidh, and it is by the northern arm of this corrie, the Coire an Dorus, that the ascent of both is most easily made. In the north-east corner of Coire an Dorus an easy scree gully leads up to An Dorus *(the door)*, the col between the two peaks, and it gives the easiest route to both. However, a more interesting though more difficult route is described below which gives a fine traverse of them.

From the Youth Hostel follow the path up Coire a'Ghreadaidh on the south side of the stream for about 2½km. Cross to the north side and beyond a grassy alp follow the tributary stream which comes down from the innermost north-east corner of Coire an Dorus. When the last grassy patches are reached below An Dorus bear N and climb scree towards the col between Sgurr a'Mhadaidh and Sgurr Thuilm. Some broken rocks and slabs just below the col are climbed by fairly obvious ledges.

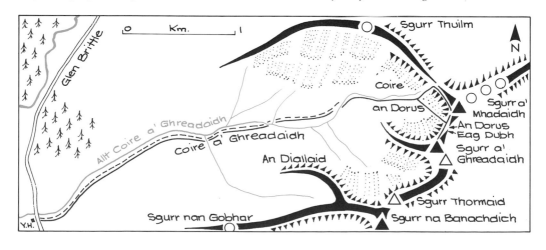

At the summit of Sgurr a'Mhadaidh, looking towards Sgurr a'Ghreadaidh   *D. Rubens*

From the col traverse a narrow horizontal ridge SE to the foot of a steep buttress bounded on both sides by dark gullies. The ascent of this buttress is a very fine but in places difficult scramble, with considerable exposure. After about 80m the angle relents and easier scrambling leads up to a cairn from which a scree-covered ledge goes right and diagonally up to the summit of Sgurr a'Mhadaidh. (4km; 900m; 2h 30min).

Descend easily down broken rocks to the An Dorus col. The last few metres of the descent are steep and awkward, as are the first few metres of the ascent of Sgurr a'Ghreadaidh on the opposite side of this narrow gap. Continue up the crest of the ridge, soon bearing over to the left side to cross, with hardly any drop, the top of the Eag Dubh *(the black notch)*, from which steep gullies fall on both sides. Continue along the crest towards an impressive looking tower which appears to block the ridge. It is something of an imposter, however, as a broad easy scree ledge leads round its west side and a short distance higher the summit of Sgurr a'Ghreadaidh is reached. (5km; 1030m; 3h).

The lower South Peak (969m) is a hundred metres away, but the connecting ridge is narrow and exposed, and the continuation of the Main Ridge southwards gives no easy descent to Glen Brittle for a long way. Unless one wants to embark on a long traverse, one should return to An Dorus and descend its screes and boulders to Coire an Dorus where the uphill route is rejoined.

Sgurr a'Mhadaidh and Sgurr a'Ghreadaidh above Coire an Dorus   *H.M. Brown*

Sgurr Dearg and the Inaccessible Pinnacle   R. Robb

Sgurr Dearg; The Inaccessible Pinnacle;
986m; (OS Sheet 32, 444215); M159; *red peak*

The most notorious peak in Skye, the Inaccessible Pinnacle is a vertical blade of rock which just overtops the nearby cairn of Sgurr Dearg. It is the only Munro that calls for rock-climbing ability, and most Munro-baggers have to call for help from their rock-climbing friends to get to the top of this one.

The ascent of the Pinnacle should not be attempted without at least one experienced climber in the party, a rope and some previous practice in the art of abseiling, and it should probably be avoided on a wet and windy day when the ascent of the Pinnacle's narrow and exposed edge might be distinctly unnerving.

Follow the path from the Glen Brittle Memorial Hut towards Coire Lagan to a point a short distance south of the Eas Mor waterfall. The main path to Coire Lagain heads ESE across the moor towards Loch an Fhir-bhallaich, however follow another path E up the rising hillside towards the great boulder-strewn west shoulder of Sgurr Dearg. Above the lower grassy slope the path zigzags more steeply up screes and past little crags.

The Inaccessible Pinnacle, looking up the east ridge
D.J. Bennet

Climbers on the east ridge of the Inaccessible Pinnacle   D.J. Bennet

Higher up the ridge narrows and there is some exposure as one scrambles along the crest over some minor bumps to reach the cairn on the scree-covered dome of Sgurr Dearg. (3½km; 970m; 2h 30min).

A short distance to the east is the imposing, possibly even intimidating obelisk of The Inaccessible Pinnacle, showing no easy way to its top. Technically the easiest route is the east ridge, whose foot is reached by cautiously descending scree and slabs below the south face.

Though only Moderate in standard (in rock-climbing terms), and fairly easy-angled, the east ridge is narrow and remarkably exposed, with vertical drops on both sides and a disconcerting lack of really reassuring handholds. There is a stance and belay about halfway up which should be used.

On the descent it is usual to abseil down the short west side, and it may be desirable to have a spare safety rope for the reassurance of those members of the party who are unfamiliar with the technique or overawed by the exposure on this, the most spectacular of Munros.

Map on page 237.

Abseiling down the west face of The Inaccessible Pinnacle   G.F. Brunton

Sgurr Mhic Choinnich and Sgurr Alasdair above Coire Lagan   R. Robb

Sgurr Alasdair; 993m; (OS Sheet 32; 449208); M147; *Alexander's peak, named after Sheriff Alexander Nicolson who made the first recorded ascent in 1873*
Sgurr Mhic Choinnich; 948m; (OS Sheet 32; 450210); M211; *MacKenzie's peak, named after the well known Cuillin guide, John MacKenzie.*

By common consent Coire Lagan is the grandest of all the Cuillin corries, and the peaks which enclose it — Sgurr Dearg, Sgurr Mhic Choinnich and Sgurr Alasdair — are a superb trio. All three are guarded by steep buttresses and gullies, and the screes of An Stac and the Great Stone Shoot are the most notorious in Skye. High above, the crest of Coire Lagan is one of the most dramatic sections of the Main Ridge, both in appearance and in the quality of its climbing.

Sgurr Alasdair, the highest of the Cuillin, is a sharp-pointed peak commanding an unexcelled view over its neighbouring mountains to the islands on one hand and the mainland on the other. Sgurr Mhic Choinnich, though much lower, is an impressive wedge of rock with steep cliffs falling from its narrow summit ridge into the depths of Coire Lagan, and it is one of the more difficult peaks of the Cuillin from the hillwalkers' point of view.

Both peaks share the same approach walk from Glen Brittle into the heart of Coire Lagan, where the ascent routes diverge. Starting either at the Glen Brittle Memorial Hut or at the camp site, take one of the many worn paths eastwards over rising moorland past Loch an Fhir-bhallaich and below the cliffs of Sron na Ciche to reach Loch Coire Lagan, set amid huge glaciated slabs. Ahead, great curtains of scree and rock drop from the rocky crest above to the depths of the corrie. Walk round the north side of the loch and beyond it reach the innermost recess of Coire Lagan.

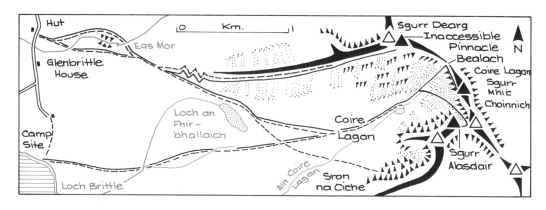

Mhic Choinnich, Thearlaich and Alasdair above the clouds at the head of Coire Lagan   *D. Rubens*

The route to Sgurr Alasdair goes up the big stony gully, the Great Stone Shoot, that rises in the south-east corner of the corrie between steep walls to reach the high col between the peak and its neighbouring Top, Sgurr Thearlaich (984m). Once a highly mobile scree, now nearly all the small stones have been shifted to the foot of the slope by thousands of scree-runners, and the upper part of the gully consists of medium-sized boulders and big lumps of rock in a fairly stable state. A worn path zig-zags up the gully and gives a tiring and tedious ascent which is hardly worthy of the Cuillin's highest peak. From the col at the top of the Stone Shoot a short easy scramble leads W to the summit of Sgurr Alasdair. (5km; 1000m; 2h 50min).

Going to Sgurr Mhic Choinnich from Coire Lagan, bear NE from the loch to the foot of the huge scree slope which plunges down from the Bealach Coire Lagan, the col between Sgurr Dearg and Sgurr Mhic Choinnich. This slope is ascended with considerable effort, trying to find the most stable stones and boulders up which to make progress; very much a case of two steps up and one step down. Do not aim for the gap about 120 metres south-east of the true bealach as it involves rock climbing. Once on the col turn SE and ascend the north-west ridge of Sgurr Mhic Choinnich, which is airy and exposed and involves some difficult scrambling in places. (5km; 950m; 2h 50min).

Sgurr Mhic Choinnich from the south   *D.N. Williams*

Sgurr Dubh Mor, Sgurr Dubh an Da Bheinn, Gars-bheinn and Sgurr nan Eag from Sgurr Alasdair   G. Blyth

Sgurr Dubh Mor; 944m; (OS Sheet 32; 457205); M222; *big black peak*
Sgurr nan Eag; 924m; (OS Sheet 32; 457195); M259; *peak of the notches*

Sgurr Dubh Mor is a fine sharp-topped peak lying to the east of the Main Ridge on a long subsidiary ridge which rises from the edge of Loch Coruisk. The lower part of this ridge above the loch is formed by a huge expanse of bare gabbro slabs which sweep up to Sgurr Dubh Beag, from where a narrow crest continues to Sgurr Dubh Mor and on to join the Main Ridge at Sgurr Dubh an Da Bheinn (938m). The ascent of this, the Dubhs Ridge, is one of the great Cuillin scrambles, (it is hardly a rock climb in the accepted sense, although a rope should be taken for one short abseil), and it is without doubt the finest route up Sgurr Dubh Mor. For the climber based in Glen Brittle, however, the approach to this peak by Coir' a'Ghrunnda is much shorter and easier.

Sgurr nan Eag, the southernmost Munro on the Main Ridge, is not a particularly distinguished peak by Cuillin standards, although it does have some steep crags overlooking An Garbh-choire. It too is most easily climbed from Coir'a'Ghrunnda.

From the Glen Brittle campsite take the well-worn route to Coire Lagan for lkm and diverge ESE across the moor towards the lower end of Sron na Ciche. If coming from Glenbrittle House, follow the Coire Lagan path to Loch an Fhir-bhallaich and strike SE across the Allt Coire Lagan along quite a good path to join the former route. Continue contouring SE below Sron na Ciche, and reach the foot of Coir'a'Ghrunnda. Climb into the corrie by a well-cairned path on the west side of the burn and reach

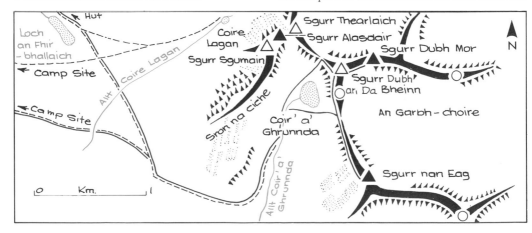

Sgurr Dubh Mor and Sgurr Dubh an Da Bheinn   R. Robb

Loch Coir'a'Ghrunnda. Go round its north-west side and climb easy slopes to the col on the Main Ridge ¼km north-west of Sgurr Dubh an Da Bheinn. Climb this peak easily and descend E along the ridge to Sgurr Dubh Mor, whose ascent requires some scrambling. (6½km; 990m; 3h 10min).

Return to Sgurr Dubh an Da Bheinn and descend S along the Main Ridge. The col between Coir'a'Ghrunnda and An Garbh-choire has a prominent gabbro castle astride it, the Caisteal a'Garbh choire. Do not attempt to climb over the castle, but traverse below it on either the east or west side where there are ledges. Continue S then SW along the Main Ridge, which at this point is quite straightforward with some easy scrambling, to reach Sgurr nan Eag. (8km; 1170m; 3h 50min).

Return down the ridge as far as the south end of Caisteal a'Garbh-choire, then descend W round the south side of Loch Coir'a'Ghrunnda to rejoin the uphill route.

The southern Cuillin from the path along Loch Scavaig   P. Hodgkiss

Bla Bheinn from Torrin   *C.A. Simpson*

Bla Bheinn (Blaven); 928m; (OS Sheet 32; 530217); M251; *perhaps blue hill from Old Norse bla (blue), and Gaelic bheinn (hill)*

Bla Bheinn is a magnificent isolated mountain, capturing the heart of the lover of mountain scenery. Girt with precipices and rising directly from sea-level at the head of Loch Slapin, it gives the impression of a hill far higher than it actually is. Though of gabbro rock like the main range of the Cuillin, it stands apart and so offers a superb perspective of the Main Ridge.

Take the road from Broadford to Elgol. As the village of Torrin is approached, the great massif of Bla Bheinn fills the western view on the opposite side of Loch Slapin. Continue round the head of the loch and start the climb at the Allt na Dunaiche, 1km south of the head of the loch on its west side. Follow the path along the north bank of this stream, first past a beautiful wooded gorge and then up the moor toward the foot of Coire Uaigneich.

Cross to the south side of the Allt na Dunaiche and follow the path which climbs more steeply on the north-west side of the burn tumbling out of Coire Uaigneich, first on heather and then grass to reach a delightful little grassy alp at 400m. At this point two great slabby buttresses rise to the right (NW), and between them are steep grass and rocks bounded on the left (S) by a vertically walled gully.

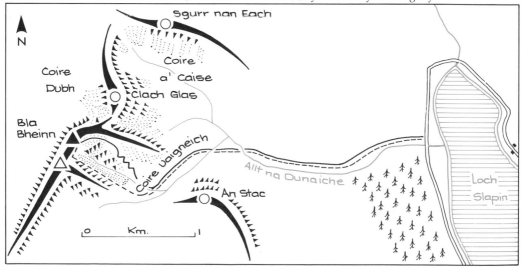

Bla Bheinn and Clach Glas from the Allt na Dunaiche   *I. Brown*

The path zigzags up the slope to the right of the gully. At about 600m the grass gives way to scree, and the path, now well cairned and clearly visible, continues to a shoulder at 780m. This shoulder is followed WSW on rocks with occasional scrambling to reach the main ridge of Bla Bheinn and gain the summit dome. (4km; 930m; 2h 30min)

The return may be made by the same route. Alternatively, a rapid descent goes S from the summit for 150 metres to the col between the north and south tops. From there plunge down the gully to the east to regain eventually the grassy alp of the upward route.

Bla Bheinn and Clach Glas across Loch Slapin   *D.J. Bennet*

INDEX